Praise for *From Stuckness to Growth*

"The beauty of this new Enneagram and ~~Coaching book is~~ ... have created a non-pathologizing methodology that recognizes both our humanness and our spiritual core. They continuously draw on the wisdom of all three Centers in their process for helping clients become unstuck. They also clearly emphasize the more life-embracing sides of type, and include type-specific guided meditations and practices that are grounded in presence and self-awareness. We highly admire the spirit and depth of their approach to coaching with the Enneagram."

—**Don Riso and Russ Hudson,** best-selling authors of *Personality Types* and *The Wisdom of the Enneagram*

"Coaches can never have too many tools in their kit—and *From Stuckness to Growth* is a grounded, practical, yet robust addition. Study it for a deeper understanding of how personality types affect our pursuit of core needs, resulting in different detours or even dead ends in the journey toward meaning and purpose. Use it to ponder the patterns in how you might misinterpret clients because of type differences and then tailor your coaching moves in ways that will resonate with each individual. Keep it nearby as a handy reference for insights into changing your style to meet their needs."

—**Jane Kise, Ph.D.,** executive coach and author of *Differentiated Coaching,* past president Association for Psychological Type International
www.edcoaching.com

"*From Stuckness to Growth* is an exceptionally well written book that makes it easy for coaches to learn helpful ways of using the Enneagram as a tool for change with their clients".

—**Katherine Chernick Fauvre and David W. Fauvre, MA,** Founders of Enneagram Explorations & Fauvre Research

"*From Stuckness to Growth* by Yechezkel and Ruth Madanes is quite possibly the best coaching book I have read. Their "seven reasons why the Enneagram works as a coaching tool" helps to frame the way a coaching session might evolve. The Madanes' have outlined coaching strategies for each type in a rich, deep and meaningful way. Finally, I thoroughly agree with the "coaching protocols" that they suggest for each type. I consider this book a must read for anyone doing coaching, therapy or spiritual direction."

—**Deborah Ooten, Ph.D.,** past president International Enneagram Association and CEO, Conscious Dynamics LLC

"This book fills a niche in both Enneagram and coaching literature. It provides thorough background information on Human Needs Psychology, explains exactly how our mindsets develop a rigid worldview and how we can become "unstuck". Part Three offers practical and immediately accessible advice for coaches using the Enneagram in their practice. Authors, husband and wife team, Yechezkel and Ruth Madanes, have spent many years perfecting this methodology. Their book is a practical guide that will be invaluable to all coaches, and anyone interested in helping others understand themselves."

—**Janet Levine**, Enneagram author and expert on Enneagram applications to education and parenting

"In *From Stuckness to Growth*, authors Yechezkel and Ruth Madanes offer an excellent resource for anyone utilizing the Enneagram to support change and personal growth. This well written and organized book explores how type may be influenced by Jungian preferences and Covey's principles as well as the authors original framework for recognizing motivational patterns. Best of all the authors scrupulously avoid the limits of pathology and overgeneralization."

—**Carolyn Bartlett, LCSW,** author of *The Enneagram Field Guide: Notes on Using the Enneagram in Counseling, Therapy and Personal Growth*

FROM
STUCKNESS
TO
GROWTH

ENNEAGRAM COACHING
ENNEAGRAM, MBTI & ANTHONY ROBBINS-CLOE MADANES HNP

HOW TO READ YOUR COACHEES
AND TRANSFORM THEIR LIVES

Our gift to you

2 video-modules, totally for free, of the acclaimed Certificate in Enneagram Coaching.

Contact info@madanesschool.com
to claim your free gift.

To learn more about our Enneagram programs
please visit **www.madanesschool.com**

Copyright © 2011 by Yechezkel and Ruth Madanes. All rights reserved.
ISBN 978-1466496842

No part of this publication may be reproduced, stored in a retrieval system, or transmitted in any form or by any means, electronic, mechanical, photocopying, recording, scanning or otherwise, without the prior written permission of the authors.

The Myers-Briggs Type Indicator ® and MBTI are registered trademarks of Consulting Psychologists Press, Inc.

Limit of Liability/Disclaimer of Warranty: While the publisher and authors have used their best efforts in preparing this book, they make no representations or warranties with respect to the accuracy or completeness of the contents of this book and specifically disclaim any implied warranties of merchantability or fitness for a particular purpose. No warranty may be created or extended by sales representatives or written sales materials. The advice and strategies contained herein may not be suitable for your situation. You should consult with a professional where appropriate. Neither the publisher nor authors shall be liable for any damage, loss of profit or any other damages, including but not limited to special, incidental, or consequential. This book is intended for educational purposes only and the information in it is not intended to substitute for expert medical advice or treatment; it is designed to help you make informed choices.

Readers should be aware that Internet Web sites offered as citations and/or sources for further information may have changed or disappeared between the time this was written and when it is read.

CONTENTS

DISCOVER YOUR ENNEAGRAM TYPE – TEST.................................. IV
FOREWORD BY DR. CLOE MADANES... VII
ACKNOWLEDGMENTS...…............... IX
INTRODUCTION BY YECHEZKEL & RUTH MADANES.................. XI

PART I. THE ENNEAGRAM, THE JUNGIAN PREFERENCES AND HUMAN NEEDS PSYCHOLOGY

The Enneagram... 3
The Jungian Preferences (MBTI).. 12
Robbins-Madanes' Human Needs Psychology.. 21

PART II. FROM STUCKNESS TO GROWTH: THE MODEL

The Stuckness Zone... 28
The Ways Out of the Stuckness Zone.. 30
Breathing as a Bridge to Our Soul.. 31
Interrupting the Patterns... 34

PART III. COACHING THE NINE PERSONALITY TYPES

Coaching Protocol for Type One - The REFORMER 49
Coaching Protocol for Type Two – The HELPER 65
Coaching Protocol for Type Three – The ACHIEVER 79
Coaching Protocol for Type Four. - The INDIVIDUALIST............................... 95
Coaching Protocol for Type Five – The INVESTIGATOR............................... 113
Coaching Protocol for Type Six. - The LOYALIST... 131
Coaching Protocol for Type Seven – The ENTHUSIAST................................ 149
Coaching Protocol for Type Eight - The CHALLENGER 167
Coaching Protocol for Type Nine – The PEACEMAKER................................ 183

BIBLIOGRAPHY... 199
RECOMMENDED RESOURCES.. 206
ABOUT THE AUTHORS... 209
COACHING SESSIONS & SEMINARS WITH THE AUTHORS OF THIS BOOK............ 209

ENNEAGRAM PERSONALITY TEST

Discover Your Enneagram Type

Instructions for Completing the Test

The Enneagram describes nine personality types.
In the following pages, you'll find a set of questions for each of the nine types.

For each type:

1. Put a check by each statement that "sounds true" to you and that describes your personality.
2. Count the number of checked statements that you got for each type and write it down at the bottom of each page.
3. Compare the scores that you got in each type: the type with the highest number of checked statements is likely to be your Enneagram type.

Total scores for each of the nine types:

Type	Score
Type One: The Reformer	
Type Two: The Helper	
Type Three: The Achiever	
Type Four: The Individualist	
Type Five: The Investigator	
Type Six: The Loyalist	
Type Seven: The Enthusiast	
Type Eight: The Challenger	
Type Nine: The Peacemaker	

The type names employed are property of The Enneagram Institute. © The Enneagram Institute, 2014. Used with permission.

Type One: The Reformer

1. I am a serious and formal person: I dutifully do my job and work hard.
2. I am responsible and hold standards and values higher than most people. Principles, ethics, and morality are central issues in my life.
3. People say I am strict and very critical—that I never let go of even the slightest detail.
4. I believe that people do things either right, or wrong. No grays in the middle.
5. I lose my patience and get irritated easily.
6. Things that are done in a sloppy manner can really annoy me.
7. I can't stand mistakes. I don't tolerate them well in myself or in other people.
8. It's hard for me to recognize an error. I can't imagine admitting that I did something "incorrectly."
9. Sometimes I can be extremely harsh and punitive with myself for not having met my own ideals of perfection.

My Score: ____

Type Two: The Helper

1. I have a special gift for detecting what other people need.
2. I know how to open my heart and give all my best: I can go to great lengths in order to help somebody.
3. It's easy for me to connect with people.
4. People say that I am a good person.
5. Sometimes in trying to help others, I overextend myself and end up exhausted and with my own needs unattended to.
6. The world's problems are to be solved with more love, not with more thinking.
7. I've been told that I am intrusive, but I think that what actually happens is that many times I know better than the other person what she or he really needs . . . and I can't help but intervene.
8. I feel hurt when others don't appreciate all I've done for them, or when they take me for granted.
9. It's hard for me to request help from other people: for some reason, I am always the one who is doing the helping.

My Score: ____

Type Three: The Achiever

1. I am a very confident person.
2. I am efficient, fast, and always super-focused on my goals.
3. It's critical to project the correct image, at the right time.
4. I am a workaholic: it doesn't matter if that makes me grab hours away from sleep or family.
5. When I set a goal, I will achieve it, no matter what.
6. To achieve success, one must put feelings aside and do whatever needs to be done to move forward.
7. I am very competitive: I believe competition brings out the best in oneself.
8. I am very impatient with people who can't follow my pace.
9. I am very professional: I take special care of my image, my clothes, my body, and the way I express myself.

My Score: _____

Type Four: The Individualist

1. I am a very sensitive person.
2. Sometimes I feel as if I don't belong in this world, that I am different from everybody else.
3. It's hard for me to adapt to a routine; I can't understand how others live this way.
4. I am often invaded by a deep state of melancholy.
5. I live in a constant state of dissatisfaction.
6. I am very imaginative and creative. I feel attracted to art, beauty, and aesthetics.
7. I am a romantic and my feelings are deeper than most people's.
8. I often feel misunderstood.
9. When I don't have something I want, I long for it. But when I finally have it, I lose interest in it.

My Score: ____

Type Five: The Investigator

1. People say I am very distant and cold. The truth is that it's important for me to have space and keep people at arm's length.
2. I feel drained by people and their emotions.
3. I am not very sociable, and whenever possible, I tend to avoid gatherings at which I'll be forced to interact socially.
4. Sometimes a good book is my best company.
5. I like to approach any issue in an objective, analytic, and systematic fashion.
6. It's important to conserve resources: I don't like other people to take control of my time, energy, and money, and I tend to easily feel intruded upon.
7. To "recharge the batteries," I go alone into my "cave" so nobody can bother me.
8. My head produces lots of ideas, but I often find myself unable to take action and put them into practice.
9. I think that most people do what "the masses" do, without much reflection and independent thinking, and this is a very non-intelligent way to be.

My Score: _____

Type Six: The Loyalist

1. I am a very loyal, trustworthy, and friendly person.
2. I am very anxious: I am always anticipating the things that could go wrong.
3. It's hard for me to trust others: I am quite skeptical of others and tend to look for hidden intentions.
4. I tend to be ambivalent, and it's not easy for me to make decisions. I consult with my friends and, if possible, with experts, to get their advice on what should I do.
5. I am very cautious. I think you must tread carefully in life.
6. I tend to catastrophize: I may react disproportionately to minor inconveniences.
7. I complain a lot. I often feel that if I don't complain, my efforts are not recognized.
8. I sometimes play "devil's advocate": I can defend an idea and simultaneously the opposite posture. I do that to test ideas.
9. I respect authority, and when I am loyal and obedient I feel safe and protected. But if I perceive injustice from authority, I may end up rebelling.

My Score: ____

Type Seven: The Enthusiast

1. I consider myself an optimistic and positive person.
2. I love life and all the opportunities that it offers.
3. I got bored easily, so I try to keep myself stimulated.
4. I am curious; I have the ability to learn fast and can speak on just about any subject.
5. I feel suffocated under a fixed routine: I prefer to leave things open and be spontaneous.
6. I tend to spend more money than I have.
7. I don't have strong discipline: although I do a lot of things and projects, I many times get bored after the initial excitement, and then it's hard for me to bring them to completion.
8. People say my enthusiasm and sense of humor are contagious.
9. I can't say "no" to myself: it's hard for me to put limits on myself, and once I want something, I don't stop until I get it.

My Score: _____

Type Eight: The Challenger

1. I am a natural leader, strong and dominant.
2. Power is not something you request or have granted to you. Power is something you *take*.
3. I am very direct and say things without dancing around, "in your face."
4. I tend to challenge others—I like to see where they stand.
5. Things are done my way. Whoever doesn't like it, there is the door.
6. I get angry easily and have no problem in manifesting it.
7. I can be protective and take care of the people in my intimate circle—or whoever I see is being treated unfairly.
8. In life you must be strong—otherwise, people will take advantage of you.
9. I don't let go of offenses against me. I wouldn't call it vengeance; I'd call it justice. I always "settle the accounts."

My Score: _____

Type Nine: The Peacemaker

1. I am a friendly person, easygoing and stable.
2. I try to flow with others and not cause conflicts.
3. I am diplomatic, and at the time of conflict I know how to put myself in other people's shoes to understand their point of view.
4. I often don't know what I want and end up following other people's agendas.
5. If I get pressured, I can become obstinate and stubborn.
6. Many times I've paid a big price for having avoided a conflict at all costs.
7. I often tend to think that problems will take care of themselves—and this causes me to not take appropriate action.
8. I tend to lose sight of my real priorities and get busy on inessentials while leaving aside the important and urgent.
9. I often say *yes* when I actually mean *no*.

My Score: _____

FOREWORD BY CLOE MADANES

All my life I have been fascinated by why people behave like they do and by the challenge of how to help people to change. Early in my career I rejected the psychoanalytic view with its deterministic theory that a person's life is dependent on early childhood experiences and that change is a long, difficult process. I believed in the humanistic view that we are in charge of our destiny and that there is always a choice to be made. I realized that our current relationships are more important than our past relationships in terms of shaping our behavior and I became immersed in systems thinking and communication theory. I was fascinated with Milton Erickson because of how he communicated at a different level than what I had known and because of how he could bring rapid change. Together with Jay Haley, we developed the school of Strategic Family Therapy and trained thousands of psychotherapists all over the world. Our mission was to help families to have harmonious, happy lives.

As I was developing always in a humanistic, family oriented direction, the field was becoming more and more entrenched in a medical model that was deterministic and oppressive. Then, in 2001, I met Anthony Robbins and observed some of his interventions with members of the audience at his events. Here was someone whose work stemmed directly from the work of Milton Erickson and who, like Erickson, had an uncanny ability to understand and to communicate at a different level. I saw how quickly and permanently he brought about change. We decided to partner and, together with Mark Peysha, we created the Robbins-Madanes Center for Strategic Intervention and, more recently, the online Robbins-Madanes Training program that integrates our approaches.

I met Yechezkel Madanes when he wrote to me from Israel about his interest in my work. It was wonderful to discover a relative that I had never met who was a kindred spirit. He was devoted to stopping violent communication in schools in several countries, he had published a best selling book on the subject and was a well-known lecturer. The prevention of violence was a major part of my mission so we had a great deal in common. I never met Ruth, Yechezkel's wife, in person but we have corresponded and I know that she is a kindred spirit as well. Yechezkel and Ruth became interested in our work and they now represent Robbins-Madanes Training in Israel.

Yechezkel was well versed in the Enneagram and in Jungian psychology and had used these methods in his work for the prevention of violent communication. Now, Yechezkel and Ruth have integrated this approach with the Robbins-Madanes methodology in ways that will prove invaluable to coaches and to all the helping professions. These powerful models will accelerate the coaching process by revealing a person's perceptual/distorting filters, underlying motivations, human needs, fears, and habitual patterns of thinking, feeling and behaving.

Identifying a client's personality style in the Enneagram will help coaches to understand their model of the world and how this model shapes their every decision. This unique insight will greatly advance the coaching process. Discovering one's type allows us to break free of the limitations of personality and unlock our unique gifts and potential. It allows us to become aware of our natural resources and strengths and also our unique challenges. Yechezkel and Ruth describe the negative cycles that each personality type is unconsciously stuck in, and the ways to break through and be fully present in life.

What is best about this book is its practical emphasis. *From Stuckness to Growth* is full of empowering strategies that can be applied right away with your clients.

Every coach, therapist, and everyone in the helping professions needs to read this book. You will not only get your clients unstuck and growing but you will get unstuck and grow yourself.

May we all contribute to a more harmonious world,

Cloé Madanes
La Jolla, California
November, 2011

ACKNOWLEDGMENTS

We own a deep debt of gratitude to Anthony Robbins and Cloé Madanes. Tony and Cloé, your teachings are with us every single day in our personal and professional lives. The worlds of coaching and psychotherapy are blessed for having you as leading authorities and as role models. You have created the best coach training program in the world, and we were truly blessed by the privilege of being able to study with you and work as your representatives in our country. You have empowered us and influenced our lives in so many positive ways!

To R. Daniel Oppenheimer, who has been a source of inspiration for us throughout the last decade and for teaching us what "walking the talk" is.

To the Sutton family, especially to David and Berta, for their wise advice and support throughout the years.

To Dr. Brian Gerrard, Associate Professor at the Counseling Psychology department at the University of San Francisco, for his kindness and for having been a major influence to us in using Myers-Briggs in our work.

Our appreciation also goes to the following dear people: Mark Peysha, CEO of the Robbins-Madanes Coach Training Program; Claudio Iedwab Sensei, founder of the Gorindo School of Martial Art in Ottawa, and to our lifelong friend Fernando Scopp.

To Lynn Cross—it's hard to find an editor of her stature; her work has been invaluable to us.

To the Enneagram teachers and researchers whose work has inspired us throughout our careers, and especially: Don Riso and Russ Hudson, Helen Palmer, David Daniels, Thomas Condon, Janet Levine, Gabriel Mayer and Osnat Yadgar, the pioneer of the Enneagram system in Israel.

To our students and coachees—we thank you for constantly inspiring us with your courage and honesty.

To our parents and children—your love have always been a source of encouragement for both of us. Thank you to each one of you, for the patience, tolerance, and compassion you show towards us when we get into our Stuckness Zones!

To G-d—for surrounding us with incredible human beings and helping us realize our dream of working in the profession we love.

INTRODUCTION

She was ten minutes late to our first coaching meeting. Judging by the puff of smoke that came into the room with her, I guessed that Linda had been smoking up until the very second that she opened the door. Five minutes later, she said, "There is something important I want to share with you: I've done therapy for three years, and my therapist said I have a 'major depressive disorder'. She prescribed antidepressants, and I took them for a while. The results were horrible. I felt a lot worse after taking them. Deep inside, I knew something was not right. A friend handed me a book about the Enneagram and I became fascinated with the subject. I finished it in a weekend. I discovered I am a Type Four. The descriptions were so accurate that I felt the book's author, without even meeting me, understood me better than my therapist whom I have had for years. To me, it was a relief to discover that my tendency to melancholy and mood swings was a normal, expected mechanism of my personality type. It was not something 'wrong', something that needed to be 'cured' or 'fixed'."

We have been working with the Enneagram system for almost a decade, and we, like Linda, have found ourselves fascinated by the accuracy of the descriptions of our own types. We wouldn't be exaggerating if we said that without this incredible map our personal and professional lives would look quite different today. If you are familiar with the system, you probably know the feeling. Our fascination with the power of this system was such that we reconfigured all our life and executive coaching practices to have the Enneagram as their base. We have applied the Enneagram in our programs with thousands of students, teachers, and parents in elementary and high schools in several countries. Over the years, we have also been experimenting with the cross-fertilization of the Enneagram with other important systems and have lately dedicated most of our research in that direction. This book is the fruit of all these years of research.

In an era of constant change and tremendous personal and professional stress, we believe it is critical for coaches to be equipped with the best human development tools available in order to help their clients reach their personal goals and dreams. Throughout this book, we will be presenting our innovative model that uses the Enneagram system as a basis for transformational coaching. Our election of the Enneagram system as a key instrument in our practice has its roots in an evolving cluster of dynamics:

First, there are the phenomena taking place in the psychiatric/psychological fields that are creating the need for more empowering solutions to the stresses of daily life.

From the 1950s on, the advent of humanistic psychology has brought hope that the mental health field, for the first time, was beginning to look beyond the then dominant disease-centered model. New therapeutic models challenged the concept of diagnosis and its associated problematisation of individuals. These revolutionary approaches warned of the risks of seeing people as a "label", instead of being able to see them as human beings. The humanistic movement acknowledged human choice and the possibility of self-actualization (Frankl, 1992.) Sadly, in spite of the great progress that was achieved, in the last decade there has been a strong backward movement in this respect and we are witnessing a return to the medical, pre-Freud model in which all causation is exclusively biological (Sharfstein 2005.) We are witnessing a dramatic increase in the prescription of psychoactive medications, not only to adults, but now massively even to children (Weiss, 2008.) When facing children they feel they can't manage, parents and teachers are sometimes tempted to use drugs as a substitute for dedication and patience—as a substitute for real education. While downplaying the potentially toxic chemical effects of psychoactive drugs, these policies have led to the socialization of millions of people worldwide into the belief that quick fixes and miraculous "cures" through magical pills are indeed possible (Moynihan and Cassels, 2005.)

Second, there are the phenomena taking place in the coaching field. The explosive growth of the coaching industry has brought hope to millions of people searching for ways to take charge and improve their own lives. In recent decades coaching has seen a tremendous expansion throughout the world and has gained recognition as an effective tool for the attainment of personal goals. However, this fast growth has also had some negative consequences, among them the proliferation of simplistic, "one-size-fits-all" approaches to coaching. Many coaching schools around the world keep repeating the mantra of "results," reducing coaching to a sort of efficient run towards a goal while removing any obstacles on the way. Being practical and concrete is usually overemphasized. The problem with such coaching approaches is that, although they project a pragmatic, bottom-line, committed-to-results image, they ironically ignore the inner configurations of people and the mechanisms that are the very key to producing lasting, meaningful results.

How can Enneagram coaching help in this difficult context? From point one discussed above emerges the need for non-pathologizing methodologies that can help people cope with the normal stresses of modern life. Here is where coaching with the Enneagram can be of help. This sophisticated personality types system provides us a detailed map that helps identify not only the main challenges each client has, but also the human potential that remains untapped in most people—their strengths. This is a great instrument for coaches and people in the helping professions that can help them inspire and empower people to shift from conformity to growth. Identifying people's potential encourages us to put forth our best energies and efforts and to take the time to get to know the human beings sitting with us, in order to help them unleash that very same potential. This is exactly the opposite of labeling. Under this particular mindset, the professional listens actively, in order to understand a client's needs and to be able to view the world from his or her perspective. Therapists equipped with the Enneagram are therefore more conscious that the abuse of awareness-numbing substances may interfere with a meaningful transformational process.

From point two above emerges the need for holistic, integrative, spiritual and non-judgmental approaches that won't look for merely surface behavioral changes. Here again is where the Enneagram is extremely relevant. The system allows for coaches and therapists to enter the world of diversity and spirituality, thus being able to understand the rich worlds of their clients. It enables them to tailor specific strategies and interventions to address each client's uniqueness, their personal differences and individual needs. This fosters a healthy curiosity and creativity. Professionals equipped with this tool are therefore less prone to use shortcut, quick-fix, one-size-fits-all simplistic approaches.

Outline and Aims of the Book

The goal of this book is to offer coaches, consultants, trainers, and therapists a comprehensive resource containing the necessary tools for successfully incorporating the Enneagram personality types system into their interventions.

The book is divided into three parts:

Part I provides the foundations of the Enneagram system and introduces the reader to the other systems that we use in our coaching model together with the Enneagram: the eight Jungian preferences and the Human Needs Psychology model of Anthony Robbins and Cloé Madanes. Synthesizing the Enneagram with these powerful methodologies provides for a much more complete vision of our clients' possibilities.

Part II provides complete coverage of the framework behind our interventions and gives a step-by-step explanation of the coaching model that we have developed.

Part III provides the coaching protocols that show you how to apply the model in a practical way and work with each of the nine Enneagram types. Each type has its own protocol that is packed with strategies you can put to use right away in your practice.

We have tried to make this book as practical and convenient as possible. We recommend that those who are new to the world of Enneagram read Part I first. Those who are already comfortable with the system can skip ahead to particular chapters of interest. The coaching protocols for each type have been written to be self-contained so the reader can jump to a particular type's protocol to get specific strategies and guidelines for that type. When writing this book we wanted to create a comprehensive source of information that could also be an accessible reference that will continue to be helpful throughout your personal and professional life.

It's our hope that this book will help you grow and sustain a creative coaching practice. We also hope you find coaching with the Enneagram as enjoyable and fulfilling as we do.

Yechezkel and Ruth Madanes

PART I

THE ENNEAGRAM, THE JUNGIAN PREFERENCES, & ROBBINS-MADANES' HUMAN NEEDS PSYCHOLOGY

THE ENNEAGRAM

The Enneagram is a system that studies the differences between people. It classifies human beings into nine personality types. These nine types are organized around a nine-point diagram. We all have the traits of the nine types, but in different proportions, and one type is usually dominant. This dominant type is our Enneagram personality style.

Figure 1-1. The Enneagram system of personality types.

Individuals in each of the nine types possess a unique set of psychological mechanisms and characteristics that *unconsciously* influences how they view the world, how they think, how they feel, and ultimately how they behave. The competitive behavior of Threes is derived from a set of beliefs pushing the Three to attain success and recognition at all costs. The cautious behavior of Sixes is derived from a set of beliefs that shapes their thinking, feeling, and acting in a world they perceive as dangerous. And so on: as a product of the filters of its type, each type arrives at a different subjective version of reality. (A full description of each type's psychological equipment is included in the protocols section in Part III.) Identifying these mechanisms, becoming aware of them, is thus fundamental if we want to produce change. A basic goal in every coaching process is to help the coachee to proactively take charge of his or her own life. Since each of the nine types has a unique set of mechanisms that shape their choices, we must help them uncover those mechanisms if they want to proactively pursue their dreams. In the words of Daniel Goleman (1985):

> The range of what we think and do is limited by what we fail to notice. And because we fail to notice that we fail to notice there is little we can do to change until we notice how failing to notice shapes our thoughts and deeds.

In order to begin to produce a lasting change in our lives, we must distinguish what is currently shaping our judging and our decisions. We must uncover our type's dynamics.

The Enneagram and Coaching

In contrast to many of the simplistic approaches to coaching that we see in the world today, the Enneagram provides us with a detailed map of our personality—our strengths, weaknesses, needs, fears, and potential. It also tells us a lot about how we tend to react in different areas of our lives. This can help coaches in a variety of ways. Why is it so important to discover our type and its autoexecuting dynamics?

Discovering our autopilot is key for living life from a place of true freedom. Being trapped in our compulsive mechanisms doesn't enable us to freely choose our actions and destiny. When we are not aware of our type's mechanisms, we cannot change them. We leave them unquestioned and unchallenged. We simply keep thinking, feeling, and acting out of these habitual patterns. In a sense, we are enslaved to them: they "dictate" and we automatically act. For this reason we use type as a tool with our clients, not to put a confining label on them, but precisely to help them identify and break free of their own restricting mechanisms.

Discovering our autopilot is key for uncovering the real reasons behind a coachee's lack of satisfaction and fulfillment. When we operate at surface levels, we address only the symptoms of our coachee's problems. Enneagram coaching is transformational, because it goes way beyond providing coping skills, and addresses the key beliefs, motivations, needs, and fears that propel the coachee's decisions. If we do not address them, they keep recurring automatically and hiddenly keep causing pain.

Discovering our autopilot is key for achieving lasting change. This follows from the previous point. Since Enneagram coaching is transformational, it produces lasting change. Coachees end the coaching process empowered with self-observation and transformation tools they can use for the rest of their lives.

Discovering our autopilot is the key to setting realistic expectations of the world, ourselves, and the people in our lives. Operating from the automaticity of our types causes us to set unrealistic, sometimes inhuman, expectations about ourselves, about how things should be, and about how other people should behave.

Discovering our autopilot is key for defining challenges in solvable ways. Without awareness of the coachee's type, we are not able to tailor-make our strategies to his or her needs. We may not even be able to put the challenges into solvable terms. Generic, one-size-fits-all strategies may reinforce the type's mechanisms, and therefore reinforce the troubles that caused the person to seek coaching in the first place.

Discovering our autopilot is key for both psychological and spiritual growth. The Enneagram provides a multilayered understanding of human nature. Without disidentifying from our personalities, it is difficult to attain spiritual growth.

Discovering our autopilot is key for attaining our potential, unleashing our true gifts, and making a contribution to the world. The Enneagram shows us the many growth possibilities that lie before us in a very accurate way. When we overcome our type's tendencies, our best qualities flourish, and there is always a positive contribution to the world in general and the people around us in particular.

Wings and Arrows

In the Enneagram diagram, each type is surrounded by another two types (wings). It is also connected to two other types via connecting lines (arrows). For instance, Type Six neighbors with Type Five and Type Seven. So a Six can have a Five wing, or a Seven wing, and in some cases, both. And Sixes are also connected to Types Nine and Three.

When in coaching we do an inventory of strengths and potential challenges with our coachees, the wings and arrows are a great tool, since each wing and connecting point shows potential and accessible strengths and desired qualities that could become a great resource to us, beyond the strengths and potential our type already has. In coaching we are interested in recruiting all those resources in order to produce lasting change. To continue with the example, a catastrophizing Six may use the resources available from wings and arrows in the following way: they can use the spontaneity and freshness of Sevens to compensate for their magnification filters; they can use their Five wing to bring objectivity; they can use their arrow to Nine to become grounded and calm; and they can use their arrow to Three to regain self-confidence and not become paralyzed by their fears.

The Triads

During the last centuries, intellectuals from different schools of thought have been debating regarding the supposed primacy of one part of the human being over another. In the eighteenth century, the thinkers of the Enlightenment, who blossomed after the age of Rationalism, emphasized the primacy of reason. It was a period of revolutionary scientific changes. In the late eighteenth and early nineteenth centuries, Romanticism emerged as a reaction to the Enlightenment. Romanticism emphasized the primacy of emotion, feeling, and imagination. The battle between the different schools of thought manifested itself in the artistic, literary, scientific, and intellectual fields.

So, what part of a human being is most important? In recent decades, this question has lost relevance and a new concept has emerged: there are *multiple* intelligences, and all of them are valid and valuable. These new approaches showed that there is no sense in keeping our perception limited by filtering the world through one specific intelligence. Since the research work of Howard Gardner in 1983, the subject has gained mainstream popularity. The world has begun to accept the existence of multiple intelligences and talents in people. *Emotional Intelligence*, the internationally best-selling book authored by Daniel Goleman in 1996, showed the world how EQ was as important as the traditional measure of IQ. It began to be clear for all that the development and the integration of the different parts of ourselves may help us develop and grow as human beings, instead of putting one part over another, or having them competing against each other. In the late twentieth century, we have witnessed the development of holistic thinking that has led to the development of more systemic approaches. According to those approaches, we are more than a collection of different parts. The system as a whole is a separate entity with dynamics of its own. The human entity cannot be simply explained by just one of its parts.

The Enneagram system covers the subject of multiple intelligences from a very interesting, holistic angle by describing three centers of intelligence. The nine Enneagram types can be grouped into three big groups, or Triads. Each Triad relates to a specific intelligence and contains three of the enneatypes, as follows:

The Heart Triad consists of Type 2, Type 3, and Type 4.
The Head Triad consists of Type 5, Type 6, and Type 7.
The Body or Gut Triad consists of Type 8, Type 9, and Type 1.

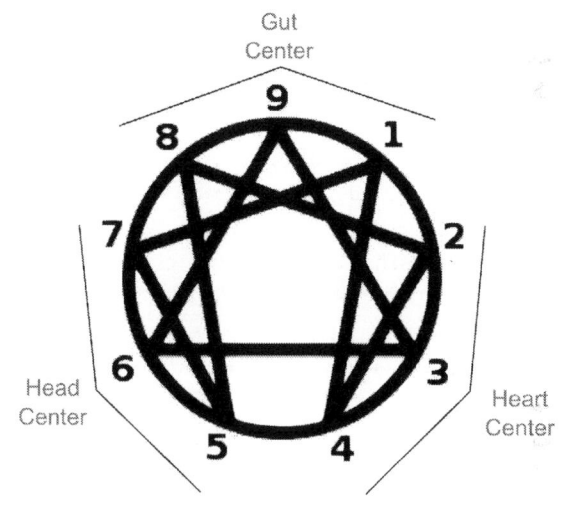

Figure 1-2. The centers of intelligence.

The Heart Triad (2,3,4)

People driven by their hearts tend to have underlying issues with the emotion of shame. Since they place much attention on relational issues, people in this Triad are more conscious of their image, of how they look to others and are perceived by them, than people on the other Triads. They speak the language of the heart: pay attention to their vocabulary, and you will have direct or indirect references to acceptance/rejection issues. Inside the Triad, however, there is much variance, and each of the types takes the issue of acceptance to a different place: Twos are concerned with being seen as good people, Threes want to impress others and be seen as successful, and Fours want to be perceived as unique and special. What they share is a need for the validation of others in order to maintain a sense of self-esteem.

The highest, healthy expression of this Triad brings empathy, compassion, the empowerment of others, the injection of hope in others, sensitivity and a sense of connection, and a healthy interdependence with other people. The overuse of the Heart energy leads to imbalances typical in these types: from taking things too personally to the development of hypersensitivity to criticism, fears of rejection and identity problems.

The Head Triad (5,6,7)

People driven by their heads tend to have underlying issues with the emotion of fear, which is mainly an emotion originating in the forecasts of the mind that is busy with events that haven't happened yet. All three types in the Head Triad share this issue, but manifest it in different ways. Fives tend to react to their fear by putting distance between themselves and others, disconnecting themselves, and going to live in their heads. Sixes alternate between phobic and counterphobic reactions to their fears. Sevens try to deal with or directly escape from their fears by keeping themselves busy with a myriad of activities, jumping from one distraction to the next. It is very common to see coachees with a dominant Head center engaging in extensive analytic activity. For these people, a lot of activity takes place in their heads, usually at high speed and with intense inner chatter, activity that cannot always be perceived by an external observer.

The highest, healthiest expression of this Triad brings objectivity, rational decision making, problem-solving abilities, inventiveness, idea generation and brainstorming. The overuse of the Head energy leads to imbalances typical in these types: overanalysis, getting lost in data and complications in decision making, difficulty in taking action, overwhelming fears, being perceived as cold and impersonal by others.

The Body/Gut Triad (8,9,1)

People driven by this Triad tend to have underlying issues with the emotion of anger, which is mainly an emotion that metaphorically and sometimes literally manifests as if powerfully coming from the belly. The instincts are also referred as to coming from that area of the body. All the three types in the Gut Triad share this issue, but manifest it in different ways. Eights tend to express their anger "as is," spontaneously and unfiltered, in a direct way. Nines tend to be unconscious of their own anger, so they are usually untrained in expressing it. Ones try to repress their anger, and when they do express it, they feel guilt about it. People in this Triad usually have a certain quality of sensitivity on their bodies, recognizable through their non-verbal language. (The bodies of Eights and Ones quickly show visible reactions to the stimuli around them; Nines are usually in the opposite pole.)

The highest, healthiest expression of this Triad brings intuition, the ability to *know* and decide on a best course of action without the need to reflect much on it. It also brings all the benefits of anchoring awareness to the "here and now": presence, mindfulness, groundedness, stability, centeredness, equanimity, honesty, patience, and flow. The overuse of the Gut energy leads to imbalances typical in these types: tension, anger (especially in Eights and Ones), reactivity, the inability to give adequate forethought to one's actions, usually related to the inability to connect deeply with one's heart and head centers.

The Triads as a Coaching Tool

We all have the intelligence of the heart, the intelligence of the head, and the instinctual, gut intelligence of the body. But people differ in their *dominant* mode: they perceive the world *mainly* from a particular intelligence. Although we all have all three centers, there is a certain order in which they get activated.

The Triads are a great coaching tool that can help us approach many challenges. Heavy triadic imbalances are easily recognizable.

Example: an unemotional Five coachee may come to coaching with relationship issues. The first thing you can do is check if there are imbalances in the Triads. Is the Five coachee living "in his head"? How often does he access his Heart Triad? You can check, for instance, how frequently in his personal life he is demonstrative with love gestures.

Permission to Fall and the Art of Restoring Equilibrium

The art of living is *not*, to a large extent, the complete avoidance of falling or making mistakes—that's impossible. Humans fail and fall. They don't operate out of their true nature, out of their souls, 100 percent of the time. Many times a day we act automatically, on autopilot, reacting to life from our ego, our personality.

So the art of living begins with the art of knowing ourselves: Why do we do the things we do? What are our automatic reactions? It's by knowing our automatic reactions, by becoming aware of them, that we can stop and choose a better, more appropriate response to every situation (or at least delay or flexibilize our reactions, if we are not yet able to replace them with better chosen responses).

So if we, as humans, tend to inevitably and automatically react to the events around us, and even to ourselves, according to specific patterns, we need to become good at **the art of restoring equilibrium.** Stephen Covey (1999) teaches this principle with the following metaphor: airplanes always have a road map, a plan by which they will fly from city A to city B. But throughout the flight, the plane is *out* of the plan 99 percent of the flight time. What, then, is the mission of the pilot? To permanently correct the small or big deviations from the plan. That's what pilots do. That's also what we do in our lives, every single day. Every day we face an infinite number of situations that require our decisions. We can *react* from our egos, or we can *respond* from our real, healthy selves, using our free will instead of acting on automatic. But our ego inevitably gets involved and we find ourselves paying the consequences. That's part of being human. We, however, can learn, as the pilots, to get up, to adjust, fine tune, and restore the equilibrium.

> "Master, it's incredible, you never lose your equilibrium, how do you do that?" "Son, I am always losing my equilibrium. All I tried to learn throughout my life is how to become good at recovering it." (*Dialog attributed to Aikido founder Morihei Ueshiba and a student*)

The Enneagram is a fantastic tool to help us in this regard. Our type protects us in many ways. It gives us an identity. But it also challenges us. It challenges us to grow. It maintains a constant tension with our real self, so we can overcome this tension and grow.

"I Want a Shortcut"

R. Daniel Oppenheimer in his parenting book writes: "The purpose of this work is not to present a compilation of solutions that—with just reading them—will solve every circumstance. It's not the recipes book (if they are "magic recipes," even better) that some believe they could use in moments of difficulty. There is no such a book." In today's world we see a myriad of approaches promising this kind of magical recipe. Applying manipulative techniques that address the challenges at surface level can produce only short-lived results. No magic pill can teach a One to think in non-dichotomous ways. Or a Three to drop the mask and connect with his or her true self. A pill can't teach active, empathic listening to Eights, or make Twos become aware of their own needs.

To the contrary, Enneagram coaching is about growing. It's a *transformational* process. And here comes the paradox: Enneagram coaching is faster than any other methodology, since it enables the acceleration of the coaching process in many ways. It enables the coach to quickly establish rapport, to support and empower the coachee the way he or she needs and wants to be supported and empowered. It enables the coach to become aware of his or her own type and pay attention to the advantages and challenges it has for the coaching session. Equipped with a detailed map of the coachee's psychological characteristics, the coach knows the coachee's strengths, talents, and potential as well as challenges, needs, fears and blind spots. If the coachee has identified correctly his or her type, the Enneagram coach has a monumental amount of knowledge regarding the coachee's perceiving, thinking, feeling, and acting patterns, right from the beginning.

Enneagram Coaching is not Theoretical

All of us operate from "mental models" (Kise, 2006), not just our coachees. In order to be effective in your coaching using the Enneagram, you must go through your own journey of self-knowledge, discovering your own type and uncovering your habitual patterns of thinking, feeling, and acting. You must go through your own personal growth processes. It's not possible to learn Enneagram coaching in a theoretical fashion. You cannot help others grow if you don't grow as well. It's not only understandings, it's action. Going through the awareness, pattern interruption, and re-wiring processes yourself. Self-experimenting with the materials. Falling. Regaining balance. Achieving. Falling again. By doing this you'll not only be most effective as a coach—you'll also lead others—and yourself—toward a more fulfilled life.

THE JUNGIAN PREFERENCES

In the first decades of the twentieth century, Carl Jung, the famous Swiss psychiatrist, began his research on psychological types. Considered one of the "fathers of psychology" together with Sigmund Freud and Alfred Adler, Jung devoted his life to discovering what is behind human behavior, what can explain it. He discovered that human behavior is not random, and can in great part be explained by certain opposing pairs of psychological attributes present in each person. For example, when looking at how we deal with our social life, we all have the ability to use the preference for Extraversion and Introversion. However, at a certain point in life, we unconsciously begin using one of them more than the other. That means that one of them becomes our preferred mode. We may, for instance, have Extraversion as our preferred strategy for dealing with our social life. This doesn't mean we cannot Introvert. What it does mean is that our *dominant* mode is Extraversion.

In order to achieve growth, in order to move out of our Stuckness Zones, Jung stressed the importance of *individuation*: the process of exploring and re-integrating those psychological functions into our human equipment. According to Jung, when we use mostly one attribute out of each pair, we are limited in our perception of reality and we cannot achieve our full potential as human beings. That's because we see the world through the lenses of our particular dominant preferences, thus missing other important aspects of reality.

Consequently, our self-realization will come when we are able to explore ourselves, to gain self-knowledge, to understand what functions in us are on autopilot, and to what degree. If, to the contrary, we allow the functions to remain undiscovered, it will bring much suffering to us. In Jungian terms, it will lead to the appearance of "neurotic symptoms."

Jung's findings were first published in his famous work of 1921, *Psychological Types*. The preferences for Extraversion/Introversion, Sensing/iNtuiting, and Thinking/Feeling were all described. In the 1940s, two American woman, Isabel Myers and Katharine Briggs, created a model using Jung's psychological functions. Their work has become the most widely used psychological assessment in the world: the MBTI (Myers Briggs Type Indicator™). To the three pairs of opposing preferences described by Jung, they added a fourth: Judging/Perceiving.

Extraversion (E) – Introversion (I)
Sensing (S) – iNtuiting (N)
Thinking (T) – Feeling (F)
Judging (J) – Perceiving (P)

The assessment measures the dominance of a particular function in each pair. This results in a four-letter code. For instance, a person who has a dominance of Introversion in the first pair gets the "I" letter in their four-letter code. If the person has a dominance of Sensing, the "S" will be the second letter. And so on, for the third and fourth letters. As a result, there are sixteen personality types according to the MBTI instrument. Figure 1.3 gives an example of an ENTJ coachee.

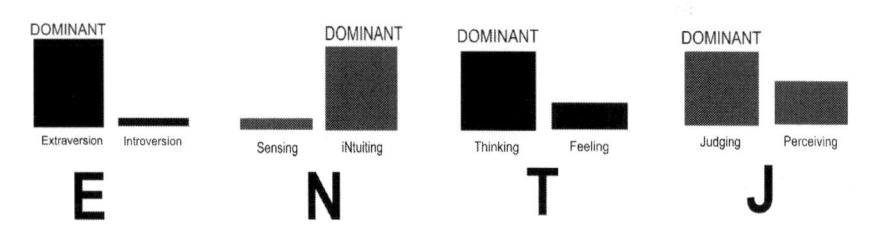

E   N   T   J

Figure 1-3. Determination of coachee's dominant Jungian functions. An example of an ENTJ type

In the following sections we describe the eight preferences in more detail.

First Realm: Social and Energization Preference

The first dimension of the personality identified by Jung was Extraversion/Introversion. What this dimension measures is our preference regarding social activity and the way we manage and restore our energy levels.

Extraversion ("E")

At their best. People who have a preference for Extraversion are externally oriented, sociable, and talkative, and recharge their energy levels through social and external activities. They are enthusiastic, active, animated, fast paced, and energetic. They are interactive, and they tend to exteriorize their thoughts in order to process them. Their conversational style often uses more words and a louder voice. They are more action oriented than Introverts and tend to act (and talk) more spontaneously. They interact well in groups and are good at generating ideas within them.

When communicating with them, respect their need for spontaneous expression. They prefer face-to-face encounters or speaking on the phone over written communication like e-mail. It's important to make eye contact. If you are an Introvert, understand and be patient with the way Extraverts externalize their thoughts (sometimes without much forethought).

Code words: *social, activity, encounter, meeting, group, enthusiasm, expression, face-to-face, talkative, assertive, quick, outward.*

In the Stuckness Zone. When overused, the Extraversion preference brings with it some costs. Their "act first-think later" approach may cause them to take action too quickly, sometimes regretting the consequences. In the Stuckness Zone, they may also talk excessively. Consequently, they become bad listeners. They interrupt. They keep talking without noticing if the other person is or isn't interested in what they say. They may also feel the need to fill the silences compulsively, especially when interacting with Introverts. Introverts may also resent them, and trust can be damaged, if they see the Extravert has difficulty guarding secrets and respecting privacy.

Introversion ("I")

At their best. People who have a preference for Introversion are internally oriented, reserved, and private, and recharge their energy levels by spending time alone. They are reflective and contemplative. They have a calm, controlled manner and a slower pace. Their speaking style is characterized by fewer words, pauses, and a quieter voice. They like having space, physical and in terms of time, to enjoy their solitary activities. They usually have only a few, close friends. Many of them like reading.

When communicating with them, respect their need for taking their time to think and process what is being said in the conversation. Listen actively and don't overwhelm them with too much talking. There may be little or no eye contact. Since they tend to think and reflect before acting, it usually takes them a little longer to act; don't rush them. They function well with written communication like e-mails, when they naturally have more time to give adequate forethought to their responses. In person, they prefer one-to-one interactions rather than group-based or social.

Code words: *reflection, insight, introspection, one-to-one, forethought, consideration, inward, listening, alone, space, low-key, intimate, private, contemplative, calm, "hard to know," slow.*

In the Stuckness Zone. When overused, the Introversion preference brings with it some costs. Their "think-act-think again" pattern may cause them to feel compelled to think too much before deciding and taking action, even when the situation may require otherwise. This causes them to be tense and over-prepare in advance of meetings.

Their preference for privacy may cause others to sometimes perceive the Introvert as arrogant or unfriendly. Under stress, they may also get hypersensitive to perceived invasion of their space, and get quickly annoyed by people and noise—all causing them to want to stay in the background even more privacy.

Second Realm: Information Precessing

Human beings are constantly exposed to a huge amount of external information and stimuli. But the ways that information is being perceived and processed are not the same for everyone. Different people tend to automatically perceive different aspects of reality. Jung distinguished two different, main ways that people usually use to take in and process external information. The first one is called Sensing, and the second Intuiting.

Sensing ("S")

At their best. People who have a preference for Sensing tend to perceive reality in a *down-to-earth* fashion. They are focused in the present. Their sight, hearing, smell, taste, and touch senses are quite awake most of the time, acting as receptors to the world around them. Their senses are their *preferred* tools to perceive reality in a reliable way.

Sensors have a strong need for clarity, and they are realistic and pragmatic. They are good at noticing the details in everything.

When problem-solving, they are interested in gathering uninterpreted, plain facts. They want to know if things work, and they trust proven solutions that have worked in the past. They also have the ability to convert ideas into practical applications.

When communicating with them, is important to be straightforward and clear. Don't overwhelm them with complex models and theories: present the facts, give examples, and be specific. Remain practical at all times. When describing something to them, be sequential, and show things in a step-by-step, clear fashion.

Code words: common sense, present, real, concrete, here and now, works, facts, functional, specific, details, guidelines, proven, experience, "tried and true," clarity, routine, procedure.

In the Stuckness Zone. When overused, the Sensing function brings with it some costs. If Sensors keep taking everything literally, they don't develop their imagination. They may not be able to think "outside the box" and imagine future possibilities, catch trends, or simply see beyond their sensory input. Their tendency to over-stick to proven ideas may inhibit their creativity. Also, paying too much attention to details may cause them to lose the big picture.

iNtuiting ("N")

At their best. People who have a preference for iNtuiting tend to perceive reality in an *inferential* fashion. Their attention tends to go to the "why" of things. They trust their hunches, their imaginations, over their senses. Since they focus on the big picture, they look at reality as if from an aerial view: this way, they perceive all the elements involved, the connections and the interrelationships among them. They are good at noticing concepts, possibilities, trends, patterns, implications. They have a deductive, connotative ability: how the present events are suggesting something in addition to what is explicit or directly expressed.

When problem-solving, they are good at brainstorming and the generation of ideas. They like experimentation and will deviate from past and proven solutions if necessary. They are interested in the possibilities: on one hand, they look for other ways to look at and solve a problem; on the other, they look at the latent, the potential: whatever is capable of being but is not yet in existence. They are also good at rearranging things in order to find meanings and relationships.

When communicating with them, it is important to be global before moving on to any detail. Don't overwhelm them with details and the specifics: be conceptual, present the general ideas and show the big picture, how things interconnect, and what are the implications. Remain close to the "why" of things. When describing something to them, use metaphors and associations.

Code words: *inspiration, insight, future, creativity, ideas, brainstorm, new, trends, patterns, possibilities, imagination, abstract, holistic, hunch, nuance, implicit, theory, model, subtleties, connotation, implication, rearrangement, meaning, integrative, novel.*

In the Stuckness Zone. When overused, the iNtuiting function brings with it some costs. If iNtuitives keep taking everything figuratively, they don't develop a good sense of the here and now. They may not be able to make decisions on the basis of factual information. Their tendency to over-stick to inspiration, creativity, and possibilities may inhibit the use of a practical approach when the situation requires it. Also, too much "reading between the lines" may cause them to get distracted with speculations while losing sight of the obvious.

Third Realm: Decision Making

As we have just seen in the previous pair of preferences, human beings are constantly exposed to and processing a huge amount of external information and stimuli. In *Psychological Types*, Jung explained that after judging what external events mean to us, we engage in a decision-making process. However, here too there are two different filters through which we can do this process: Thinking and Feeling.

These preferences are not mutually exclusive, and we all have them and use them both. But people do have a preference towards one or the other.

Thinking ("T")

At their best. People who have a preference for Thinking prefer to make decisions in a logical manner. They value objectivity. Before deciding, they weigh the costs against the benefits. They also pay attention to causality: how something will impact on something else, what is the expected consequence.

When communicating with them, it's important to be logical and objective. Don't overwhelm them with feelings: remain calm and objective at all times. When describing something to them, be clear and organized, and put an emphasis on explaining cause and effect.

Code words: *objective, analysis, detachment, logical, cause-effect, cost-benefit, criteria, evaluation, consequences, information, knowledge, weighing.*

In the Stuckness Zone. When overused, the Thinking preference brings with it some costs. They may over-stick to logic and rule out any other criteria for decision making, to the point of ignoring other types of intelligences, such as the intelligence of the Heart or the Gut. They may become too impersonal. People may perceive them as cold and uncaring. Also, their decision-making process may suffer when they over-think a situation and get trapped in "paralysis of analysis," postponing decisions and never taking action.

Feeling ("F")

At their best. People who have a preference for Feeling prefer to make decisions in a more personal and subjective manner. They want to make their decisions based on values and principles. Before deciding, they weigh how their decision will impact them and other human beings.

When communicating with them, it's important to listen actively. Speak from the heart and don't overwhelm them with logic: show that you care, and remain personal and receptive at all times. When describing something to them, show how values are playing a role in the issue at hand, and what impact there is (or will be) on people's feelings and well-being.

Code words: *sensitivity, personal, care, feelings, communication, human, appreciation, emotions, empathy, relationships, values, principles, compassion, expression, harmony, friendly, nurturing, support, interactions.*

In the Stuckness Zone. When overused, the Feeling preference brings with it some costs. They may over-stick to feelings and rule out any other criteria for decision making, to the point of ignoring other types of intelligences, such as logic (Head) or gut intelligence (Body center). They may become too personal and sensitive to criticism. People may perceive them as illogical. Also, their decision-making process may suffer when they act impulsively, without forethought, out of "what their heart dictates."

Fourth Realm: Life Structuring

In the 1940s, Katharine Briggs and Isabel Briggs Myers began working on the creation of a personality type assessment tool based on the theories of Carl Jung. In addition to the three pairs of preferences proposed by Jung (Extraversion/Introversion, Sensing/iNtuiting, Thinking/Feeling) they proposed a fourth: Judging/Perceiving. Thus, the MBTI instrument that later resulted from their research went on to include this dimension as well. What do these two added preferences measure? They measure some general preferences regarding *structure* and *closure*: Do we prefer a structured, organized, planned lifestyle or a more spontaneous one? And, do we like to keep our options open, or do we have a preference for things being closed and settled?

Judging ("J")

At their best. People who have a preference for Judging prefer to live life in a structured manner. They value order. They keep their schedules organized, are good at clarifying lists of tasks that need to be done, and like to bring all issues to completion. They like to close all their "open loops" and feel uncomfortable leaving issues unsettled. Punctuality and self-discipline are important for them, and they usually have well-organized routines.

When communicating with Judgers, it's important to be decisive. Don't overwhelm them with options: remain focused and "on target" at all times. Always be on time. When describing something to them, be short and organized, and put an emphasis on explaining how closure will be achieved.

Code words: *closure, organization, order, deadline, structure, determined, decided, settled, compliance, plan, control, task, schedule, timely, punctuality, discipline, productivity, perseverance, target, objectives, efficiency, prepared, ready, goal, timetable, "getting things done," focused, commitment.*

In the Stuckness Zone. When overused, the Judging preference brings with it some costs. Judgers may over-stick to order and control and rule out any other criteria for managing their lifestyle, to the point of trying to plan *all* aspects of their lives at all times. They may become too stressed. People may perceive them as critical, inflexible, and rigid.

Perceiving ("P")

At their best. People who have a preference for Perceiving prefer to live life in a less-structured, more flowing manner. They value spontaneity. They keep their schedules flexible and open, and they may adapt to events "on the go." They adapt quickly to changes and are able to shift course rapidly if the situation requires so. Their curiosity makes them good at exploring options and possibilities.

When communicating with Perceivers, it's important to be open. Don't overwhelm them with deadlines and don't rush them into deciding. Respect their need for some time to consider options before taking action. When the issue at hand is truly important and requires their immediate action, communicate with firmness but avoid preaching to them. When describing something to them, focus on *processes* and describe the many courses of action available.

Code words: flexibility, spontaneity, relax, curiosity, possibilities, latitude, openness, freedom, span, options, choices, "open-ended plans," easygoing, flow, process, eagerness, evaluation, consideration (of options), space, breadth, interest.

In the Stuckness Zone. When overused, the Perceiving preference brings with it some costs. Jumping to something else before finishing the issue at hand, considering too many options, shifting direction too often, and lack of order and organization may all result in poor performance and mediocre results. Perceivers' deficiencies in punctuality may cause other people to perceive see them as disrespectful or uncommitted.

HUMAN NEEDS PSYCHOLOGY

Human Needs Psychology is a new field created by Anthony Robbins and Cloé Madanes, and is a result of their joint research during the past decade. This powerful system works extremely well for Enneagram coaches because both systems stress the importance of finding the self-limiting patterns that remain largely out of awareness in most of us. Robbins and Madanes teach that in order to help produce change in our behavior, we must understand and manage our six human needs, which are powerful drivers behind human behavior. The model is explained in full detail in their 2010 book, *Relationship Breakthrough,* and here we will only cover some aspects of it that are relevant for our work with the Enneagram. The six human needs are:

The need for Certainty/Comfort. Every human being has a need for safety and has concerns regarding physical survival. We all need a sense of psychological security and stability in our own lives and in our relationships with others.

The need for Uncertainty/Variety. Every human being has a need for Variety. As a balance to the routine aspects of life, the challenges to and stimulation of our senses, minds, and bodies help us feel alive.

The need for Significance. This is the need to feel important. It's the normal human desire to be not only accepted but also valued by others. To obtain recognition. To feel special and unique. To be respected.

The need for Love and Connection. This is the need to love and be loved, to be cared for. This need is crucial for creating any emotionally significant relationship. This definition includes also the feelings of *connection* to others.

The need for Growth. This is the need to realize our own potential. To overcome our own challenges and grow, in order to bring out the best in us. We all want a sense of progress in the different areas of our lives. This makes us care and cultivate something in order to fill this need.

The need for Contribution. This is the need to give, to help others. To care about the interests of others and/or of society. To have an effect that can change a person or a group, to leave a legacy, a mark in the world. Contribution is the antidote to selfishness.

Working with the Enneagram and HNP

We all have all the human needs. All six. Among those six, two of them are usually *dominant*. Those needs act as strong drivers that give shape to the choices we make. When working with the Enneagram, it is extremely important to identify not only the coachee's Enneatype but also his or her dominant needs. As an Enneagram coach, do not automatically assume, for instance, that a Type Six will have a dominant need for Certainty. Although the pursuit of security is central to Sixes, there are other factors that may cause them to put an emphasis on a different need.

One of those factors are the Enneagram Instincts. (Those interested in what the Instincts are and how they work are encouraged to review the suggested bibliography at the end of this book.) To continue with the example, we may for instance have a coaching process with our Six coachee dealing with a Love/Connection issue.

Secondly, look at the ways your coachees are trying to meet their six human needs. The six human needs can be met in positive or negative ways. When in the Stuckness Zone, each type meets its needs in negative ways. For instance, a Type Four may get Significance by compulsively differentiating herself from others, as a way to feel special. When integrating healthily out of the Stuckness Zone, the same Four could use her empathic listening strengths, and positively obtain Significance by being able to understand not only her own but other people's inner life, needs, and suffering. She can offer compassionate and sensitive advice.

And thirdly, remember that **the integration out of the Stuckness Zone helps the coachee to simultaneously meet the needs of Growth and Contribution.** These two needs are the needs of the human spirit. That's why when every type in the Enneagram finds their healthy way out of the Stuckness Zone they feel fulfillment and plenitude, and a profound, spiritual sense of liberation. When each type goes through their point of courage, whenever they break free of the self-limiting habits of their personality, they grow. And when they grow, they always contribute to others. For instance, when Type Five integrates, they move from being intellectual recluses to putting their ideas into action. By doing so, not only do they grow, but they also give their gifts to the world. They become contributors. They take action and put their ideas and inventions out in the world, for society's good. When Type Ones integrate, they stop moralizing and become a guide by example, a true leader for others. When Type Threes integrate, they stop competing with others and become their motivators. And so on. That's the case with all the Enneagram types.

Later in the book, during the coaching protocol of each type, we will give you examples on how to specifically use the HN with each of them.

PART II

FROM STUCKNESS TO GROWTH
THE MODEL

In the following pages we describe the elements present in the theoretical framework that we developed for helping clients move from stuckness to growth. We begin by describing the key issue of distinguishing between reality and our interpretation of it.

Distinguishing Between Reality and Our Interpretation of Reality

Our mind is permanently trying to make sense of the external information it receives from the outside world. Like computers, we have "pre-installed" software to help us do the processing job that will help us make sense, that will help us discern, draw conclusions, and make decisions. According to the Enneagram, there are nine such software "packages" available to human beings. These software packages reside in the mind and help people process the information as it comes to them. The programs assign meanings to the events in our lives. They attach a mental commentary. An interpretation. Is this interpretation random? No. There is consistency. Each program package contains, built in, a specific model of the world, a map of reality. This model of the world causes us to focus on specific aspects of the world while ignoring others. It brings only *some* aspects of the world to our attention. Each of the nine personality types has a central theme, an area of reality that it tends to focus on and from which many of its preoccupations arise. As a result, the person's perception of reality is truncated and interpretations are biased accordingly. As Alford Korzybski would have said, this partial, subjective map is "not the territory." Due to its subjectivity, the program package creates an internal representation of reality that tends to differ from what actually happened. In other words, we may confuse our interpretation of what really happens around us with reality itself. As noted by Belgian artist Rene Magritte, "Perception always intercedes between reality and ourselves."

Reality = Our interpretation of reality	Reality ≠ Our interpretation of reality
AWARENESS	**AUTOPILOT**

Another important feature of these programs is their automaticity. They come with an autopilot mode. They are able to run in the background, out of sight, hiding in the unconscious, always ready to take over and quickly assign a meaning, even (or especially) without our instructing them to do so. To make things even more complex, these psychological mechanisms also have stealth, "radar-jamming" capabilities that prevent even their owners from detecting their activity.

Unaware of these interesting dynamics, we get used to living with the program's chatter in our heads and we fail to notice it. Since we don't notice it, we are not able to challenge it. We trust its logic as though it were true. Neurologically, these behaviors become habits. The more we fail to challenge these incessant mechanisms, the more they become wired in our brains and the more their reactions become habitual. As a result, we end up perceiving, evaluating, thinking, feeling, and acting based on these distorted patterns. We begin to notice that some areas of our life are not working. We don't feel fulfilled. Something is missing. We feel stuck.

The Stuckness Zone

The Stuckness Zone has the shape of an eight lying horizontally. It represents an endless, continuous loop in which we may become trapped. We adapted the idea from a teaching of Anthony Robbins and Cloé Madanes. In their model, which they call the "crazy eight," people alternate between two emotions when they try to meet their human needs (Figure 2-2.)

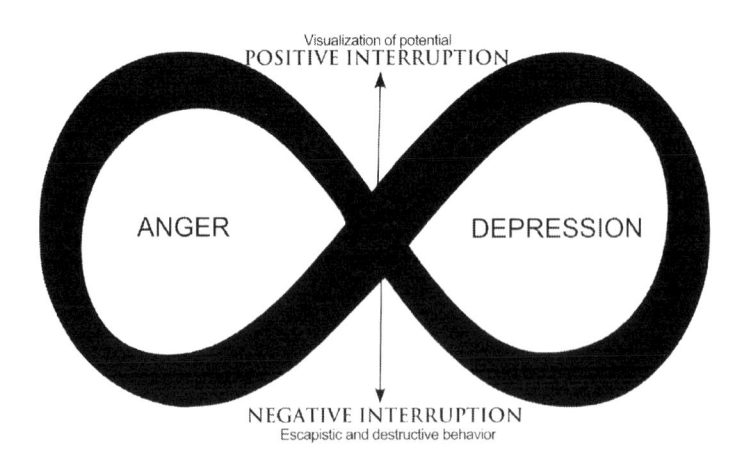

Figure 2-2. Robbins-Madanes "Crazy Eight" model. An example with the emotions of anger and depression.

When they get stuck in that loop, there is suffering, and this suffering causes people to try to escape from the loop they are in. There are two available exits, two ways out, represented by the two vertical arrows. The arrow pointing up represents a positive way out of the loop. The arrow pointing down represents a negative, usually escapist way out of the loop.

In our adaptation for the Enneagram (Figure 2-3), the looping includes all the automatic patterns of thinking, feeling, and acting of each personality type, to represent the range of possible Head, Heart, and Gut dynamics each type may be able to experience when stuck. It also includes typical attitudes that follow from the type's core beliefs.

Visualize potential
- responsible   • realistic
- productive   WHILE… • tolerant
- idealist   • having integrity
- hard-working   • guiding by example

POSITIVE INTERRUPTION

Critical of self and others
Judgmental
Stressed
Angry
Rigid
Impatient
"Can't see forest for the trees"
Point of Courage
Perfectionistic
Nitpicking Fault-finding
Intolerant Double-standards
Old resentments Tense
Reaction-formation Guilt
Moralizing

STUCKNESS ZONE

NEGATIVE INTERRUPTION
- Escapism
- Impact in physiology through food &/or substances
- Other unproductive or destructive behavior

Figure 2-3. Type One: Stuckness Zone and exit strategy

This doesn't mean that each type has *all* the patterns happening and looping at the same time. In reality, it may exhibit many patterns at the same time, or it may have just a few. What the model does reflect are most of the possible patterns that each type may find itself trapped in and among which it may find itself alternating. To continue with our example above, a Type One when stuck may, for instance, find itself alternating between a perfectionistic, fault-finding drive and the emotion of anger. Another Type One may find itself trapped and alternating between moralization, the constant criticism of others and strong feelings of resentment. And another may find itself alternating between sudden eruptions of anger and guilt. And so on.

The Stuckness Zone doesn't look the same for everyone. Each type has a particular, unique way of getting stuck. The coaching protocols in Part III explain each type's Stuckness Zone in detail.

The Ways Out of the Stuckness Zone

The costs associated with remaining stuck in the Stuckness Zone are high. When we keep reacting out of our type's autopilot program, we leave a trail behind us in many areas of our personal and professional lives. We suffer and cause others to suffer. We feel stuck and unfulfilled. We feel unhappy with ourselves and in our relationships. Facing these negative consequences, we begin to try to find ways to get out of this loop. We can liberate ourselves from this vicious circle in a positive way or in a negative way.

Negative Pattern Interruption

Caught in the Stuckness Zone, we may try to take ourselves out of the loop with a variety of escapist behaviors. One frequent example of this is altering our physiology, by means of food or any substance that temporarily promises to alleviate the symptoms of our suffering. But since the real causes are not addressed, the symptoms tend to come back. That's why no substance or medication can be a substitute for self-mastery and growth. Using substances while leaving our type's mechanisms unaddressed is similar to trying to fix a specific malfunctioning appliance by turning off the electricity in the whole house: the toxic side effects of the substances may reach many places in our life, even areas not related to the original problem. But perhaps their worst effect, their most debilitating impact, is our miseducation into believing that it is possible to achieve well-being without effort, without overcoming our psychological and spiritual challenges. That we are powerless and have no choices.

Positive Pattern Interruption

Weiji, the Chinese word for "crisis," is composed of two characters, one representing "danger" and the other "opportunity." Being in crisis in the Stuckness Zone presents us with not only the danger of going down into deeper suffering, through the Negative Interruption way out, but also with the opportunity of the Positive way out. Why is there an opportunity? Because we are in front of a key decision. This is a point at which we ask ourselves the following questions: Are we willing to attain our maximum potential in life? Do we want to continue living life this way? We called the exit point toward the positive way out the "point of courage." In order to pass through this point **we need to enroll the forces of our soul**. It requires our full engagement and determination, our resolution to take charge of our own lives and head towards our self-realization.

危机

DANGER   OPORTUNITY

Figure 2-4. The Chinese word for "crisis"

When a client comes to coaching, it's a moment of great opportunity. Good forces inside the person are shouting from the inside. They don't want to live life this way. They know, deep inside, that there must be a different way. **The role of the coach is to capitalize on that momentum, to help the client visualize his or her potential, and to produce leverage.** To show the costs and the impact that living this way is having. To encourage awareness. And to encourage the coachee to take charge of his life and live proactively.

Neshima: Breathing as a Bridge to Our Soul

In recent years, there has been extensive research in the scientific community, especially in the neuroscience field, on the benefits of meditation, helping to extend the traditional association of this subject beyond faith or religious practices. Mindfulness-Based Stress Reduction Therapy is one example of this trend.

In many ancient traditions, the act of breathing is seen as a bridge between our personality and our soul. For instance, the Hebrew word for soul, *neshama*, has the same letters as *neshima*, breathing, implying that by breathing we get access to the most transcendental part of our being, our soul. The Talmud explains that since our soul has a spark of the divine in it, every time we breathe we are able to experience our most profound connection to G-d and life. The key issue emphasized in almost all spiritual traditions is that we are more than our personalities. In the psychological field it was Carl Jung who was first to recognize that the positive psychological forces we can use to heal ourselves dwell inside of us *together*, side by side, with our ego structures. **If our personality acts as a distorting filter of reality, creating a misrepresentation of life and causing us to live "in a movie," then by breathing and connecting to our souls, we can temporarily detach from our personalities, disidentify from their content, and cultivate our Being.** Breathing can thus help us anchor our wandering minds to the present moment, setting up a meditative, contemplative state that is optimal for the activation of the Impartial Spectator.

נשמה   נשמה

BREATH   SOUL

Figure 2-5. The Hebrew words for "breath" and "soul"

The Impartial Spectator

The positive way out of our Stuckness Zone must begin with the development of awareness. Let's go back to the Daniel Goleman quote we brought in the beginning of the book:

> The range of what we think and do is limited by what we fail to notice. And because we fail to notice that we fail to notice there is little we can do to change until we notice how failing to notice shapes our thoughts and deeds.

In order to begin to produce a lasting change in our lives, we must identify what is currently shaping our judging and our decisions. We must uncover our type's dynamics. It is to this end that we begin developing the Impartial Spectator.

Our personality type is that part in us that subjectively processes reality. To compensate for the distortions and suffering it causes, we need to help our coachees develop a detached self-observing capability. We call this "bystander" the Impartial Spectator. Its function is to bring objectivity in a neutral, impartial way. According to Harvard professor Nava Ashraf, the term "Impartial Spectator" was coined by Scottish philosopher Adam Smith in the eighteenth century. Smith maintained that a person's impulsive, automatic behavior is moderated by a neutral inner voice that is able to detach and look at the situation from the perspective of an external witness (Cullen, 2006). In Enneagram Coaching, this allows us to watch our Head, Heart, and Body center activity without attaching a mental commentary to it. This way we are able to uncover our type every time it autoactivates, allowing us to decide whether or not to act on its premises, instead of automatically acting on them, without even being aware of it. In the Enneagram literature this external witness is referred to as the "Inner Observer" and is found in the pioneering works of Don Riso and Russ Hudson, and also Helen Palmer (Riso and Hudson, 1999; Palmer, 2009), who were the first to combine the Enneagram with contemplation and meditative practices. Thanks to the study of the meeting points between Eastern and Western psychologies in the last two decades, there is also a wide variety of psychotherapeutic approaches today that are consistent with mindfulness practices and are based on the development of an impartial witness (Didonna, 2010.)

According to Lutzl et al. (2008), there are two styles of meditation: Focused Attention (FA) and Open Monitoring (OM). The first type entails the "voluntary focusing of attention on a chosen object," while the second entails "non-reactive monitoring of the content of experience from moment to moment." In training the Impartial Spectator, we are mainly using the latter, which is also the approach of many Enneagram teachers (Riso and Hudson, 1999; Helen Palmer, 2009). As in mindfulness meditation, in order to train the Impartial Spectator we exercise the ability to acknowledge and develop awareness of the content of internal experience —all its divisions and constituents, what Palmer (2009) calls the "categories": our thoughts, our emotions, our sensations, and our past and future through memory and imagination. In order to do so, we need to ask the client to shift his or her attention from one category to another (Palmer, 2009; Forsyth, 2008; Robbins and Madanes, 2004). This is the approach that we will follow to train the Impartial Spectator in Part III's coaching protocols.

By training our Impartial Spectator, we are training our attentional aptitudes. Once we learn to identify our distorted patterns of thinking, we are able to stop being blindsided by them. By recognizing the filters that previously operated totally outside of our awareness, we are able for the very first time in our lives to relax our type's defenses and stop *automatically* filtering our experience through its limiting lenses.

Interrupting the Patterns

When our type autoactivates and produces a problematic interpretation of a situation, we tend to experience negative emotions. The distorting filters of our type cause us to have unrealistic expectations about ourselves, others, and the world. For instance, Ones in the Stuckness Zone have a constant chatter in their heads that permanently compares them and others to unattainable, unrealistic, almost inhuman ideals. They may feel both anger and guilt. Type One's autopilot has automatically taken over the interpretation of reality and has caused negative consequences.

To disrupt these patterns whenever you uncover your type autoactivating itself, you can follow the following sequence:

First, begin by inhaling and exhaling consciously. Follow the air in and out of your body. This helps create a meditative atmosphere conducive to contemplation.

Second, invoke your Impartial Spectator. Keep breathing slowly and gently detach from your personality, in order to be able to watch the situation from the perspective of an external witness.

Third, the Impartial Spectator begins to recognize how your type is acting in each Triad. First, the Head Triad: Acknowledge your thoughts. Ask: What am I thinking in this moment? Acknowledge the mental commentaries taking place right now. The key here is to remain non-judgmental. If your mind becomes judgmental, let the Impartial Spectator catch this new layer of thoughts and mindfully observe how it lies on top of the previous thoughts. You can gently do this whenever your mind begins to wander. Remember, there is nothing you need to *do* now besides letting the Impartial Spectator simply witness as a bystander. You can then shift your attention to your Heart. Acknowledge the emotional activity that is taking place right now. Ask: What am I feeling? Become aware of the emotions you are experiencing. Stay with your emotions for a moment, then shift your attention to your body sensations. Ask: What sensations am I having right now in my body? Where exactly?

At all times we keep breathing slowly and consciously. Following the path of the air in and out of the body. By breathing and connecting to our souls, we are able to *decenter*: I am more than my feelings, my thoughts and my sensations. I am not my feelings, thoughts and sensations. Yes, they are actually happening, but they are not *me* (Goldin, 2008.)

Fourth, begin to gently *reorient* your attention away from the misrepresentations of your type, and towards its true potential. Maintain a non-judgmental attitude and **bring a quality of compassion and gratitude in this important moment.** As Stanford University neuroscientist Philippe Goldin (2008) explains, "When the mind is distracted, and one becomes aware and brings it back, that's a key moment. That's actually when a lot of learning takes place."

Covey's Four Human Endowments

In his 1989 best-seller, *The Seven Habits of Highly Effective People*, Stephen R. Covey mentions the four endowments that are unique to human beings. These endowments play a crucial role in Enneagram Coaching, since they are crucial elements that affect our ability to exercise our choices. The endowments are:

- **Self-awareness:** Our ability to see ourselves from the perspective of an external, neutral witness. This is so far what we have been developing through the training of our Impartial Spectator. Developing a detached self-observing capability is critical for becoming aware of how our type's lenses are playing a role in our perception and decision-making process. It helps us understand that we are actually not predetermined by our type and that we do have choices.

- **Conscience**: Our capacity to distinguish between the positive and the negative, what is going to be constructive for us and others, and what is not. Each type has high values and traits they latently possess and which they can contribute to the world. Conscience is a key endowment that helps each type discern the constructive and the destructive. It is, thus, another key element behind choice.

- **Independent Will**: This is the human ability to think freely and not *automatically* accept others' ideas as a basis for our actions.

This is the ability to discern by ourselves free from external influences. It allows us to do what we believe is right and defy or swim against the trend whenever necessary.

- **Creative Imagination:** This is the ability to picture ourselves out of our present challenges. It's a key endowment for Enneagram Coaching, since it allows us to conceive and envision ourselves in the numerous growth possibilities available to us. This will become clear in the next section, when we begin with the issue of re-wiring.

To see why the four endowments are relevant in Enneagram Coaching, let's take, for instance, a Type Six client. Why is the endowment of self-awareness important? With low self-awareness, the client will be in reactivity most of the time, since he is not even aware of his type activity. Without developing this ability, it's impossible to break through the type's mechanisms and the client cannot take charge of his or her own life, a key challenge not only for Sixes but for all types. What happens if our Six client has low Conscience? They are unable to actively act according to positive principles. And what happens if our Six client lacks the endowment of Independent Will? The lack of Independent Will blocks our ability to decide what's best for us, and pushes us to automatically adopt other people's, a group's, or society's stance. This is a key issue for Sixes, that they tend to disempower themselves and favor others' thoughts over their own. This can also become a challenge with coachees of all Enneatypes who have a dominant Social Instinct. Last, the lack of the endowment of Creative Imagination will reinforce the "I can't" orientation of Sixes who tend to feel stuck and see no solutions to their problems.

Re-wiring After Pattern Interruptions

Until now our process took care of the "failing to notice that we fail to notice" problem. Having unlocked that via the awareness brought by the Impartial Spectator, we move on to help the client focus on achieving their coaching goals. In both Jungian and Enneagram literature, this process is called *Integration*, implying the incorporation of our less dominant aspects into our personality. In order to achieve this, we help the client to expand their frame of reference. This is often compared to developing the ability to write with both hands. Although we can all potentially write with both hands, one hand is our dominant one. However, with practice, it is possible to write with both. The same happens with our personality type. As Jung explains in *Psychological Types*, every person has all the psychological characteristics of all types, but some tend to be dominant and determine our basic type. The good news is that we can learn to use our untrained abilities. These resources are available to us at any moment, and we can access them by adopting another type's focus. The most readily accessible resources to our particular type are usually those of the wings and arrows over the Enneagram symbol.

In order to re-pattern, that is, to replace your old automatic patterns with new, healthier ones, you can follow the following sequence:

First, replace the unrealistic expectations and illusions of your type. This means simply becoming aware you are a human being. Each type, when in the Stuckness Zone, has an inhuman expectation of itself. Sixes, for instance, live under the illusion that it is possible to prepare oneself for all of life's problems. They expect themselves to attain a state of total security. Ones live as if what is expected from them is angel-like, completely error-free behavior. These inhuman expectations of themselves are the root cause underlying most of their troubles. Figure 2.6 shows common expectations each type holds when in the Stuckness Zone.

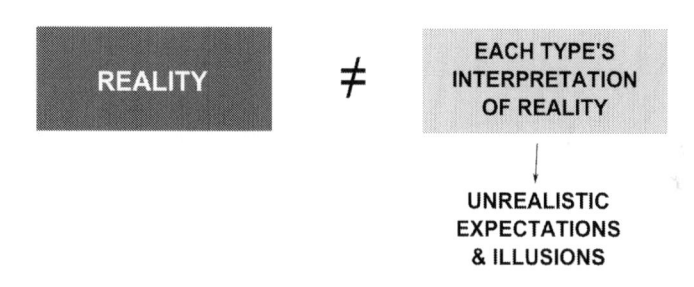

REALITY ≠ EACH TYPE'S INTERPRETATION OF REALITY
↓
UNREALISTIC EXPECTATIONS & ILLUSIONS

Ones: It is possible to achieve absolute perfection.
Twos: It is possible to be loved by everybody.
Threes: It is possible to be succesful in everything.
Fours: it is possible to be always unique and deep.
Fives: It is possible to attain total knowledge.
Sixes: It is possible to attain total security.
Sevens: It is possible to achieve absolute happiness.
Eights: It is possible to be strong and in control all the time.
Nines: It is possible to find absolute peace and calmness.

Second, become aware of your resources and the full range of choices that you actually have. **Contrary to the illusions and misrepresentations of reality that our type generates, we have a full range of choices that are indeed available to us.** The process here described gives us the ability to interrupt our type's automatic reactions and exercise our free will. One of Enneagram Coaching's basic tenets is that people can exercise their choice at any given moment. Instead of *reacting* to the events in our life, we can momentarily interrupt our automatic pattern and *choose* wisely. We can choose according to what is truly best for us. The exercise of these choices can help us fulfill our true life goals and is the key to our psychological and spiritual growth.

Our type's approach in the Stuckness Zone is very limiting, overusing some strategies as if there were no choices available. Every type has indeed a very wide range of resources and choices in their own equipment: the wings and their arrows. For instance, a Type Five has available a wide range of resources: the connection to the heart from the Four wing, the synergization of analytical abilities from the Six wing, assertiveness and practicality from the arrow to Eight, and lightness and a positive quality from their arrow to Seven. In Part III we show you how each type can capitalize on the many resources available to them.

Third, become aware of your coaching goals. Now that you are aware of your equipment and potential, how are you going to use them? Where do you want to get with them? What challenges do you want to solve? What dreams do you want to achieve? Clarifying your vision and goals before going out on the road is a vital step.

Fourth and last, shift your attention to adopting a necessary focus and taking action. Once you have become aware of your type and the mechanisms and challenges it poses, have recognized your psychological equipment and potential, and also have clarity regarding the goals you want to achieve, it's time to act! The repetitive and unaware autoexecutions of your type have conditioned you to react to situations in certain negative ways. Your brain got "wired" to produce those automatic reactions every single time you face specific trigger events. In order to achieve your life goals, you need to re-wire these habits by providing alternative new patterns to substitute for the old ones. Taking consistent action on these new integrating patterns helps in wiring them and fading out the old ones. The coaching protocols in Part III will provide a variety of tools that each type can use in the process here described.

Pattern Interruption Sequence -an example. It's part of the coaching process that we did with Clara, one of our coachees, a Type Two. In one session, she brought up her relationship with her nephew Enrique. The latter had moved from his hometown to a house that is a few blocks from Clara. Enrique was relocated by his company and Clara helped him and his wife find an apartment to move to. In doing so, she overextended herself beyond her resources, both physical and financial, taking care of all arrangements before the couple arrived. Her overextension caused her to miss an important deadline in her job. After a lengthy flight in which they lost their luggage, the exhausted couple finally arrived and got right into their hectic schedule. Although they made an effort to show their appreciation, Clara misinterpreted their chaotic first days in which the couple were running from one place to the other as rejection. She felt she had done so much, and the couple hasn't showed appropriate appreciation of her efforts.

We went through the pattern interruption sequence with her, step-by-step.

Reality vs. interpretation of reality. The plain facts were that the couple were exhausted from the physical and mental challenges resulting from their relocation. In contrast, Clara's interpretation of reality via her type's automatic reaction was that the couple were unappreciative of her efforts.

Unrealistic expectations and illusions. Her type's automatic reactions had conditioned Clara to have unrealistic expectations. She expected the fatigued couple to be demonstrative at an extremely stressful time.

Breathing and interruption of the sequence. In order to induce a meditative state, we began a breathing exercise. This sets the tone for beginning the work with the Impartial Spectator.

Acknowledging the three centers of intelligence activity with the Impartial Spectator.

> **Ruminating thoughts:** "I'd been working like hell for two weeks before they arrived. I took care of so many details in the house that went unnoticed. Why can't they show *more* appreciation for my efforts? I left *everything* to take care of them."
> **Feelings:** "I feel hurt. Resented. Disillusioned. Used. Rejected."
> **Bodily sensations:** "I feel exhausted. I sense a pain in my chest and in my legs."

Reorienting attention back to reality. We have done these exercises on a consistent basis and Clara has gained much awareness of her type with the passing of time. Although she was becoming more able to witness her type as it autoactivated, in this particular session, we kept doing breathing exercises and simply asked her to limit the Impartial Spectator to becoming mindful of her type reactions.

In following sessions we gradually moved to the Integration stage, while always practicing introspection through meditative breathing.

Realistic expectations and illusions. Clara understood that her "giving to get" pattern was causing her to neglect her own needs. She understood that she needed more human expectations of herself. It was inhuman to overextend to such lengths while neglecting her own needs. She also understood it was human for the couple to be exhausted in the first days and it was an inhuman expectation from them to wait for effusive gratefulness in such a stressful time.

Recognize full range of choices available. When on autopilot, it seemed to Clara that to act this way—that is, taking care of everything and overextending oneself with no limits—was the only option available. Brainstorming with her in the session, we arrived at a wide range of available options. She became aware of her type's wings and arrows. Using her arrow to Four she could have compensated her outward focus and look inside to see what her own needs were, first and foremost. Using her arrow to Eight, she could have asserted herself and requested some help from her daughters. Using her Three wing, she could have had a realistic and a bit more efficient look at her physical, emotional, and financial resources. Using her One wing she could have helped Enrique without neglecting her own job's obligations and commitments.

Goals and vision. We reminded Clara of the coaching goals that were originally determined in our first sessions, and helped her reconnect with them. They were: 1. To build self-esteem and self-worth independently from her deeds that help others and independent of external approval and validation.; 2. To recognize her own needs and take care of them in an orderly fashion.

Recognize strengths and potential. Borrowing from her past, we recreated moments in which she was able to let her altruistic and empathic nature become a gift for others, while maintaining healthy boundaries and asserting her own needs. Those memories were dated from long ago, from the days she was still living in Uruguay. This served as an empowering reminder of both her strengths and her potential.

From Stuckness to Growth

REALITY ≠ **OUR INTERPRETATION OF REALITY**

TYPE AUTOACTIVATES

When our type autoactivates and produces a problematic interpretation of a situation we tend to experience negative emotions.

UNREALISTIC EXPECTATIONS & ILLUSIONS

The distorting filters of the type caused us to have unrealistic expectations about ourselves, others and the world.

PATTERN INTERRUPTION SEQUENCE

BREATHING

① In order to induce a meditative state we begin breathing consciously.

Impartial Spectator

② In order to detach and bring objectivity we invoke our Impartial Spectator

THOUGHTS, FEELINGS & BODY SENSATIONS

③ The I.S. acknowledges the activity in all three centers, without commenting or judging.

REORIENT ATTENTION BACK TO REALITY

④ We gently reorient our attention back to the realm of REALITY: to human, realistic expectations and to our true strengths and potential.

REALISTIC, HUMAN EXPECTATIONS & ILLUSIONS

RECOGNIZE FULL RANGE OF CHOICES AVAILABLE

GOALS & VISION

RECONNECT TO STRENGTHS & POTENTIAL

ADOPT INTEGRATING FOCUS

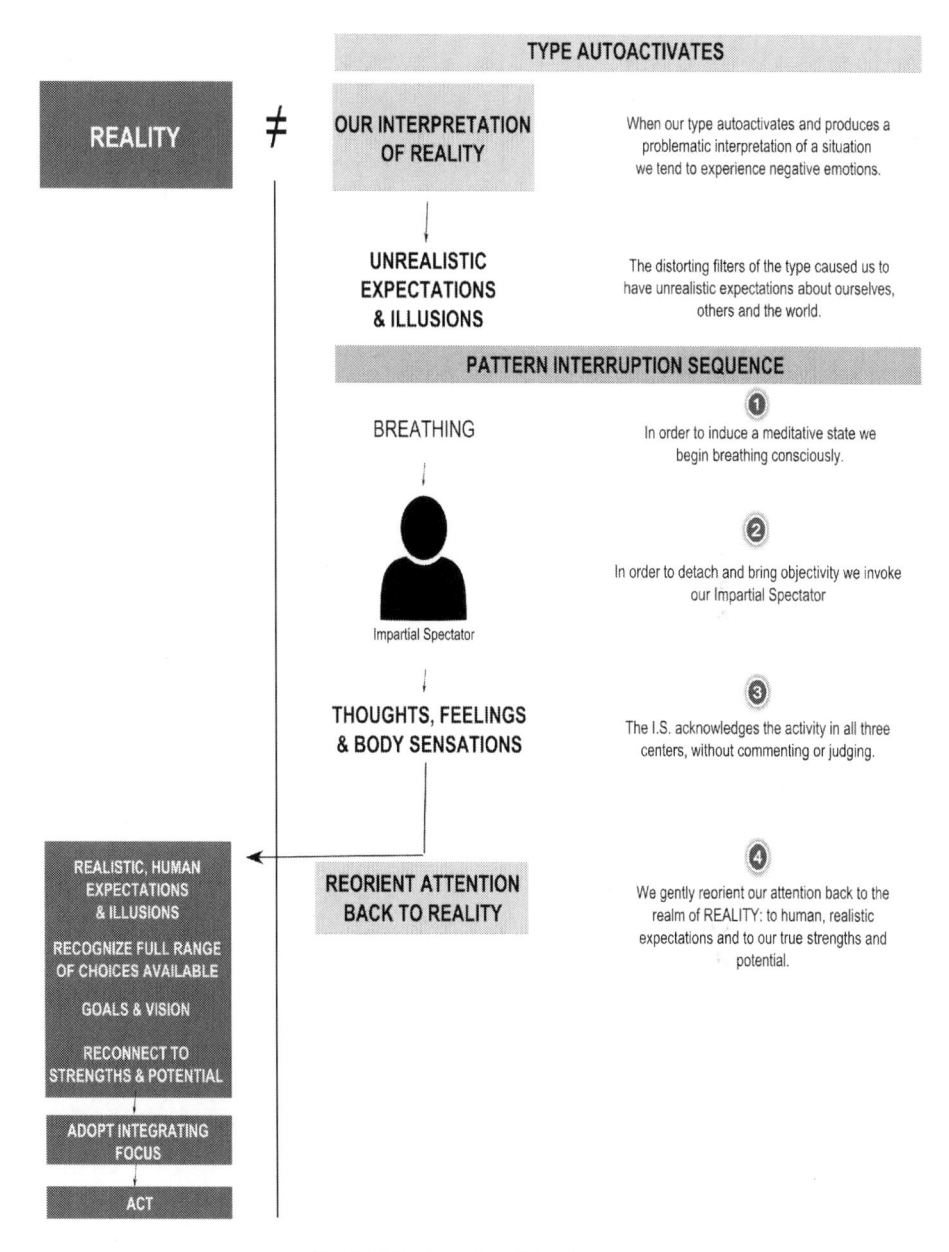

ACT

Figure 2-7. Pattern-Interruption and Integration processes.

41

Adopt integrating focus and act. In order to practice her arrow to Four, we gave the directive of finding a pleasurable activity for her to do by herself and for herself. Her disconnection to the Four energy was such that the first week she came back to the session, she didn't have a clue where to begin when doing this exercise. The next session we encouraged talking about activities she used to like. One such activity was buying used novels from a fancy bookstore in town and going to a quiet café to read. With the passing of the years the Two structure gained power and discouraged this kind of "selfish" activity. We asked her to begin by going once a week to a café she liked and reading a novel. Later, we developed a more complex strategy, in order to cover more aspects of her type's challenges: we asked her that in family gatherings (the whole family was meeting every Saturday since Enrique moved) every time she felt an urge to do something for others, including giving unrequested advice, she would have her novel at hand and find a space to go read by herself. This ritual was done as a means to re-condition her to think of her own needs.

Discovering Our Potential

In contrast to symptom-centered models, which have a "to-move-away-from" motivational approach, coaching with the Enneagram has a "towards" motivational approach.

When we relax our type's defenses, our gifts are able to come to the surface. For instance, when Ones relax their Stuckness Zone's criticizing habit, they discover their (until now) hidden leadership abilities. They are tolerant visionaries that lead others by example. All Ones have this potential. And it's critical for coaches to keep in mind at all times that the coachee moves along a continuum that includes this potential. To continue with the example: if our One coachee has a well-wired fault-finding habit, we must not be distracted by this and keep in mind what she *is* able to attain. We must see her potential as an integral part of personal identity.

The Enneagram shows us what's beyond the Point of Courage, waiting to emerge. It describes our latent strengths and talents. It shows us our unique path to growth. It shows us the unique treasures available to us and how we can contribute with those gifts to the world.

Integration: Growth and Contribution

As we move towards higher levels of awareness, we are able to know ourselves better. When we take the journey to pass through the point of courage, we recognize *all* aspects of ourselves, including the less positive ones. This requires honesty and strength. Sometimes, especially when under much stress, our type again takes over and leaves us with the consequences of badly made decisions. In this journey of growth, sometimes we even go down for the sake of going up. This process is an inevitable part of growing. But growing is what ultimately will bring us to our self-realization and fulfillment. And when we integrate our personality, when we grow, there is always a contribution to others. When people move into the Negative way out of the Stuckness Zone, they suffer and cause suffering to others. Symmetrically, when people pass through the point of courage into the Positive way out of the Stuckness Zone, they grow and contribute to others. (This is explained in more detail in Part I, and is illustrated in each type's protocol in Part III.)

In Part I we talked about an important principle: the art of living is, to a large extent, *not* to never fall or make mistakes—that's impossible. Humans fail and fall. We don't operate out of our true nature, out of our souls, 100 percent of the time. Many times a day we act automatically, on autopilot, reacting to life from our ego, our personality. So even when we become proficient with the Enneagram, and discover our nature and succeed in interrupting patterns, even then, since we are human, we are likely to continue, for the rest of our lives, with our type autoactivating.

Of course, with time, we become more and more aware, and are better able to uncover, question, delay, flex, interrupt and even replace our patterns. Remember the quote we gave you in Part I:

> "Master, it's incredible, you never lose your equilibrium, how do you do that?"
> "Son, I am always losing my equilibrium. All I tried to learn throughout my life is how to become good at recovering it." (Dialog attributed to Aikido founder Morihei Ueshiba and a student)

We can become good at the art of recovering our equilibrium. Since there are no shortcuts to human development, it takes time. Self-discovery can be the longest, yet most enjoyable, journey of our lives.

When you accept your humanity, you give yourself permission to fall and stop living according to unrealistic expectations. This attitude opens your heart and lets compassion, acceptance, and gratitude flow from it, towards yourself and other people. **Each time you gently, mindfully, and non-judgmentally redirect your attention away from your autopilot and towards your true nature, you become more mature and wise. That's why this work is the key to both your psychological and spiritual growth. And the key to lasting fulfillment.**

PART III

COACHING THE NINE PERSONALITY TYPES

In this section we present you with the coaching protocols for each of the nine personality types. The protocols were designed to equip you with a myriad of tools you can use when coaching each type. With these tools you can put each protocol to use right away in your practice. Always remember that coaching is an art: although the protocols are structured in a certain way, remain open-minded and creative, and use the strategies and tools that are best for your coachee at the present moment.

TYPE ONE
THE REFORMER

ONES

People see me as a very **responsible** person, sometimes a bit of a perfectionist. I think that we either do a **good** job, or a **bad** job. We work as we **should**, or do a poor job. There are no grey areas in the middle. Sometimes I redo my work so it will look **perfect**. I hate **mistakes**, mine and other people's—that's why I try to be organized and methodical. It's usually hard for me to request other people's help, to delegate tasks, because nobody can do the job as well as I can. I have a kind of internal judge that helps me discover what is being done in the wrong way so I can **correct** it. There is always one way of doing things, the "**right**" way. It's disappointing that many people don't understand this, both in my professional as well as in my personal life. They believe I think in "black and white," that I am too judgmental and that I criticize and get angry too often (Michael, Type One.)

Description of Type One

Ones are responsible, hard-working people who constantly try to improve themselves and the world around them.

At their best, they have a constant need for self-improvement, and they encourage others to grow, but they do so tolerantly and compassionately. Since they are accepting of themselves as whole human beings, including their less positive aspects, they can be accepting of others. They are visionaries who have a strong sense of purpose and strive for the ideal, but they also know what's humanly possible, and thus they are realistic. They are wise, discerning, fair, objective, honest, and have an open mind, ready to review even their own standards. They have integrity and hold high moral and ethical standards, but don't moralize to others: they teach by example. They are organized, methodical, productive, committed, and dedicated people who will put their best efforts to the work at hand. Although they are detail-oriented and extremely thorough in everything they do, they can maintain a big-picture sense and wisely make good decisions.

In the Stuckness Zone, an internal critical voice starts running inside them, and they become critical of themselves and others. They become perfectionistic and intolerant of mistakes, trying too hard to get everything the "right" way and to be right all the time. They compare reality to what it "should" or "must" be, and look for what doesn't fit. Their attention tends to go automatically to errors and mistakes, to what has been done incorrectly by them and others and consequently to what should be corrected. Sometimes the smallest flaw can ruin the whole for them, and they become "comma-counters." They act as if they knew the right way of doing almost everything. Black-and-white dominates their thinking: things are either good or bad, with no gray areas in the middle. This makes them rigid and inflexible. They cannot delegate, since nobody can do the work as perfectly as they will. Tension arises when they feel overburdened by too many responsibilities they feel they must undertake due to other people's carelessness. Anger arises since there are too many things to correct and too many people not following the rules and doing things the wrong way. Anger, however, is not always expressed directly, since they expect themselves to be self-controlled all the time. They thus become resentful and bitter, holding grudges for long periods and having difficulty in forgetting and forgiving. Although most of the time they will try to hold in and not express their anger, it is recognizable in their tense body language and facial expressions. Their perfectionistic and critical drive also pushes them to work too hard, with an inability to relax, enjoy, or have fun in life, making them too serious. It also causes them to take their and other people's efforts and hard work for granted, and also to moralize and preach, instead of teaching by example.

COACHING PROTOCOL FOR TYPE ONE

1. SET THE CLIMATE OF THE SESSION

Before you begin your coaching session with your client, check yourself:

Bring acceptance to the session
Ask yourself:
- Am I in a non-judgmental state?
- Does my specific personality type have any resistance with Type One?

"Turn on" your multimodal listening
It is extremely important that you use all the centers of intelligence (Head, Heart, Gut) during every coaching session. Be aware of "listening" actively with all three centers.

Listen with your Head center
- Pay attention to speaking style and language use.
- Analyze body language and posture.
- Analyze patterns and possibilities for interrupting them.

Listen with your Heart center
- Empathize.
- See the client as a human being, not as a "type."
- Look beyond the facade.
- Connect, in spite of any resistance that you may have. You are here to help the client grow.

Listen with your Gut center
- What kind of energy is the client bringing to the session?
- Is there a match between what the client says and the energy with which he or she says it?
- What does your intuition tell you regarding the last developments in this coaching process?
- "Listen to what people say but pay attention to what they *do*." (Madanes, 1995).

2. DEFINE THE CHALLENGE

Determine what the client wants to work on, what is the purpose of his or her pursuing coaching.

Typical challenges for Ones include:
- To be less critical of themselves and others, to be patient, and to reduce the suffering they cause to themselves and their relationships by relentlessly focusing on what needs correction.
- To become more tolerant, acceptant, and forgiving of others.
- To reduce stress, anger, resentment, and tension. To learn how to relax.

3. UNDERSTAND THE COACHEE'S MODEL OF THE WORLD AND HIS OR HER STUCKNESS ZONE

Ask yourself the following questions: Why is the client acting the way he does? What is shaping her behavior? What is his internal story? What are the filters through which she looks at and perceives the world? To what extent are the type fixations active and operative in this client?

Visualize potential
- responsible
- productive   WHILE...
- idealist
- hard-working
- realistic
- tolerant
- having integrity
- guiding by example

POSITIVE INTERRUPTION

STUCKNESS ZONE

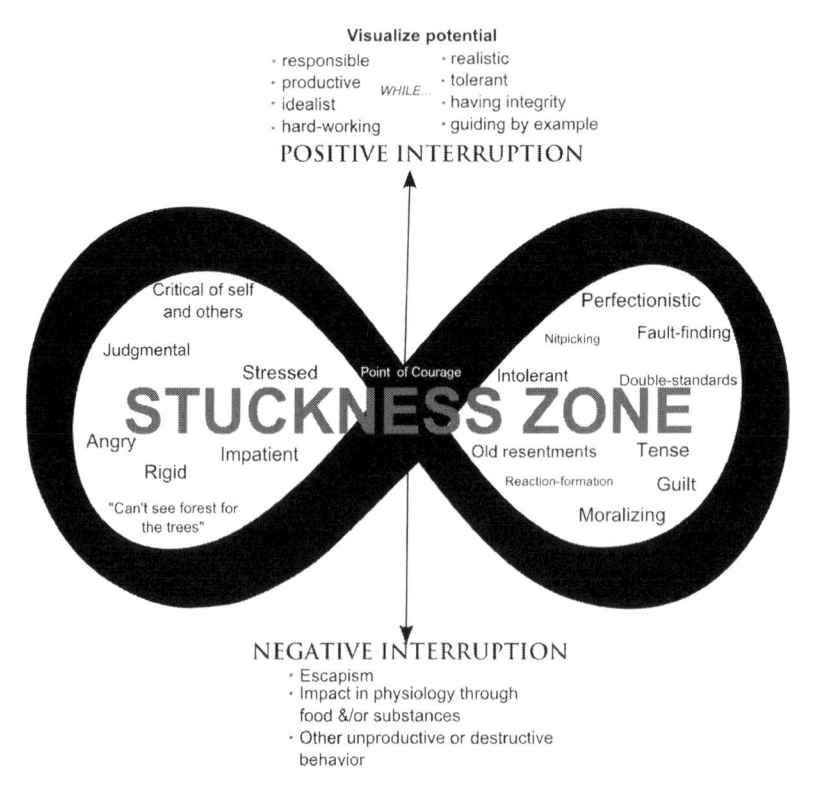

- Critical of self and others
- Judgmental
- Stressed
- Angry
- Impatient
- Rigid
- "Can't see forest for the trees"
- Point of Courage
- Perfectionistic
- Nitpicking
- Fault-finding
- Intolerant
- Double-standards
- Old resentments
- Tense
- Reaction-formation
- Guilt
- Moralizing

NEGATIVE INTERRUPTION
- Escapism
- Impact in physiology through food &/or substances
- Other unproductive or destructive behavior

Figure 3-1. Type One Stuckness Zone and exit strategy

When less aware or under stress, the attention of Type Ones gets hijacked/derailed by a quest for perfection. In this state they usually compare reality with an ideal they may have in mind, hence their extensive use of words such as "should" and "must," and a usually rigid body language.

4. BRING AWARENESS TO THE SIX HUMAN NEEDS

According to Human Needs Psychology, we all have six basic human needs (Madanes, 2009): Certainty, Variety, Love/Connection, Significance, Growth, and Contribution. These needs are not merely desires, but true drivers mobilizing our behavior.

Exercise for Type One: The six human needs. Look at the Stuckness Zone and from the whole range of behaviors there described, pick the most frequent ones: "What human needs are you trying to fulfill by engaging in these behaviors?"

Please score each need from 0 to 10.

Certainty. Does engaging in these behaviors make you feel certain? Give you a sense of security? Apart from these behaviors: Do you also know how to obtain certainty in a more positive way?

Variety. Does engaging in these behaviors bring you a sense of variety? Apart from these behaviors: Do you also know how to obtain variety in a more positive way?

Love/connection. Does engaging in these behaviors make you feel connected to others? Experience a sense of love?
Apart from these behaviors: Do you also know how to obtain love/connection in a more positive way?

Significance. Does engaging in these behaviors make you feel important? Special? Apart from these behaviors: Do you also know how to obtain significance in a more positive way?

Growth. Does engaging in these behaviors give you a sense of development, make you feel that you're growing? Apart from these behaviors: Do you also know how to obtain growth in a more positive way?

Contribution. Does engaging in these behaviors give you a sense of going beyond your own needs, of giving to others? Apart from these behaviors: Do you also know how to obtain contribution in a more positive way?

Coaching case study. Take as an example Danielle, one of our coachees, a Type One. According to her, the habit of criticizing her husband fulfills three of her human needs: Love/Connection (that's the way to demonstrate her love to him), Growth, and Contribution (she "makes" him a better person and obtains a sense of growth from correcting him). When in the Stuckness Zone, Ones tend to try to reform others so they become what the One thinks they *should* be. This is usually done through corrections and criticisms. Underlying this behavior is the attempt to fulfill specific human needs. But naturally, her ways of fulfilling her needs had a negative impact on her relationship, and the couple was on the brink of divorce. The breakthrough came when she became aware of the necessity to meet her human needs in more positive and constructive ways. Instead of trying to reform her loved ones, she began teaching by example, being nurturing and patient with their pace, and respecting the natural preferences of their personality types non-judgmentally.

One important point to take into account: pay special attention to the needs of Growth and Contribution. **Does the coachee meet these needs in healthy or in destructive ways?** As we integrate our personality, the needs of Growth and Contribution begin receiving high scores while also being met in positive and healthy ways. The reason for this is that when we move out of our Stuckness Zone, we act from new, conscious, chosen responses. This allows us to overcome our old habits and grow. This integration, in turn, will always bring greater contribution to others. In contrast, if we continue acting without awareness, out of our old patterns of reaction, we disempower ourselves and let our egos manage our lives. This always causes suffering to ourselves and to others.

5. PRODUCE LEVERAGE

The next step is to gain leverage by bringing awareness to the costs and suffering that the unhelpful patterns of the type are causing for the client.

Exercise for Type One: Gaining awareness of the costs of patterns
- How much does it cost you, in terms of your relationships, to be rigid, judgmental, and fault-finding?
- How much does it cost you, in terms of your health, to be tense and angry most of the time?
- How much does it cost you, in terms of your professional career and staff morale, to demand perfection, micromanaging others and

paying too much attention to details?
- How much does it cost you, in terms of your personal fulfillment and own sense of happiness, to be relentlessly critical of yourself?

6. PATTERN INTERRUPTION: BUILDING OUR ATTENTIONAL MUSCLES

TYPE ONE VISUALIZATION

Visualizations are a great tool for coaching in general and when doing personality-types coaching in particular. The following is a comprehensive visualization/meditation script for Type One. It encompasses working with the type's strengths and weaknesses, training attentional abilities through the Impartial Spectator, training conscious breathing, acceptance, and relaxation. In a single coaching session, you don't have to use them all. You can use these visualizations modularly, by selecting one or more of the sections that follow.

Script for Type One: Visualization/Meditation

Relaxation

Begin by finding a comfortable sitting position. Keep your spine straight in a natural way. Let your arms become loose. Lightly, with palms facing up or down, rest your hands on your lap. Take one deep breath, to begin relaxing your whole body. Inhale. . .Exhale. . . You can gently close your eyes and take another deep breath as a way to become centered and focused. Inhale. . .Exhale . . .

Training the Impartial Spectator

Let's begin by bringing awareness to the Impartial Spectator. Think of the Impartial Spectator as your friend who objectively watches your behavior from the outside. It helps you make wise decisions and allows you to regulate your automatic pilot.

The Impartial Spectator will do so by training your mind to be sensitive to the activity in your three centers of intelligence: the Body (our physical sensations), the Mind (thoughts, plans, future, past, images, ideas, imagination), and the Heart (feelings). Our breath, which symbolically represents our connection to our soul, will allow us to remain centered and to shift our attention from one center to the other. It will also help us to remain non-judgmental and to bring the qualities of gratitude, compassion, and acceptance to this exercise. Every time your mind wanders, you can use the moment to exercise those qualities of gratitude, compassion, and acceptance—for each one of those moments offers the opportunity to learn how to reorient our attention.

Begin by gently shifting your attention to your **Body** center of intelligence. Take a deep breath, and follow the path of the air in and out of the body. Do it slowly. Inhale again. . . and this time make the exhalation last a bit longer. Place your full attention on the path of the air getting in and out of your body, from beginning to end. Begin noticing your body sensations. Sense the contact points between your feet and the floor. What body sensations are in there right now? Move your attention to your back. Feel the support that the chair gives you. Stay with that sensation for a moment. Shift your attention to your hands. Focus on the contact point between the hands and your lap.

Place your hands over your chest, one over the other, and shift your attention to your **Heart** center of intelligence. What feelings do you have in this moment?

Now shift your attention to the **Head** center of intelligence. Is there a mental commentary about your feelings? Is there judgment or acceptance of your feelings? What is your mind saying about your feelings? What is it saying about this whole exercise? Serenely watch your mental discourse as it appears. Inhale. . .Exhale. . . Stay in the Head center, and now shift your attention to your memories. Imagine yourself watching an old black-and-white TV set on which your past history is being broadcast. You see yourself in the TV. Your life videotaped. Each stage of your life, on the screen, in slow motion. Nod when you actually see it. Inhale. . .Exhale. . . Still in the Head center, now move your attention to the future. Serenely reflect on each one of the following questions. Take a few moments as a pause between each question. What do you want your future to be like? How do you see yourself in the future? What plans do you have?

Visualization

Remain in the Head center, and you will now shift your attention to your imagination. Imagine yourself at the beach, at the sea shore, in slightly wet sand. Breath the air at the beach. Inhale. . .Exhale. . . Feel the wind. Listen to the waves in the sea. Feel the sand on your feet. Imagine yourself drawing an imaginary number eight, drawn horizontally, like the infinity symbol, in the slightly wet sand on the shore. Draw it slowwwly. Feel the contact point between your fingers and the sand.

Visualization of Stuckness Zone and costs

Now picture yourself putting all your problems and challenges *inside* that eight in the sand. One by one.

All my continuous attention to details and fear of making a mistake. All my perfectionism and constant measuring of things and people (including myself) against an ideal. All my "shoulds" and "musts." All my harshness and criticism against myself and against others. All the tension. All the anger. All the suffering.

Feel the tension and anger. Feel it in your belly as you see all the issues inside the eight in the sand. Feel the tension in your whole body. Stay there for a moment.

This eight in the sand represents our Stuckness Zone. The place we get stuck with negative focus and negative feelings.

"It's human" section

Every human being has issues that make him or her precisely that, human. It's a personal, tailor-made set of challenges in life. Watch your own personal challenges without judgments. If your mind passes a commentary, it's OK. Don't worry and try to do this exercise "right." If there is a judgment, just watch the judgment. Listen to its script. Watch it as it occurs, outside of you.

It's human to have judgments about our experience. It's OK. Bring your attention to your heart. Now, grab the judgments you just heard in your head, the mental comments, and put them there, in your heart. Use the energy of your heart to soften them and feel how it fills your whole body with compassion. Take a deep breath, and feel the energy of your heart throughout your whole body. Feel the acceptance.

Why does life bring you challenges? Life brings you challenges so you can overcome them, and allow the next level of plenitude and vitality to become available to you. They are precious opportunities to grow. Precious opportunities to discover the strengths *you already have* that simply need to be reactivated. The strengths that will help you overcome your challenges, the strengths that will help you move from stuckness to growth.

Inside of you there is a part that doesn't want to give up. That wants to live life at its fullest. It's the voice of your soul. The voice that wants to stand up to the voices of the ego and the personality—and become the best possible you. You've been there before, and that's what brought you up to this moment. This moment in which you are here struggling to become the best person you can be, standing up and not giving up to your personality, to your automatic thoughts. It's the real you, it's the strength of your soul.

At this point your attention may automatically go to create thoughts about your thoughts. It's OK. Simply keep breathing consciously, following the path of the air in and out of your body, and let your Impartial Spectator witness the activity of your mind non-judgmentally.

Visualization of strengths, potential, and personal power

Now please move your attention to that part of yourself that doesn't want to give up. Look at the drawing on the sand: exactly in the center of the eight there is a point: the intersection between the right side and the left side of the eight. Let's call it the *point of courage*. From that point, imagine yourself drawing an arrow up. An exit from the eight. An exit from the stuckness.

This arrow points to what is available outside the eight. This arrow points to your strengths and to your potential. To the future that is available to you in any given moment.

Let's see what's outside the eight.

I want you to think of any moment in the past in which you really felt relaxed, in which you felt acceptance for yourself and others. It can be any moment in which you felt light and you were playful. Bring it from any area of your life: you could have been by yourself, with a friend, with a group of friends, or with your family. In your personal or your professional life. Go to the past and bring back that moment. It could be a special moment or just a simple one. Feel it. Feel the relaxation of that moment in your whole body, especially in your neck and shoulders. Feel it also in your abdominal area.

Search your memories for that moment in which you were wise. Tolerant. Acceptant. Feel the relaxation of that moment in which you let go of correcting yourself and others. Everything flowed harmoniously and everything actually worked well and turned out well, without your correction and supervision. Take a deep breath and feel that moment.

Let's see what else is outside the eight.

I now want you to envision yourself in a new future. A future in which you are productive but serene. A future in which you are constantly growing and encouraging others to grow, but you do so tolerantly and compassionately. In which you accept yourself as a human being, including some less positive aspects. You are proud of being realistic and grounded, and that's because you can see yourself as a whole, in terms of *real*, not only *ideal*. A future in which you are in touch with your heart, and can forgive yourself and others for the mistakes human beings will naturally make. Please put your hands one over the other, and over your heart. Feel your heartbeat. Feel your humanity. Since you are human, you are allowed to rest and also have fun from time to time. This allows you to recharge your batteries and become more productive than when you drive yourself to exhaustion. Your realism makes you wiser, and your heart dissolves the anger, so plenty of energy gets liberated for productivity. Feel it. Feel how wisdom allows you to discern instead of judge. Wisdom also allows you to teach by example, and everyone can learn from your integrity and responsibility. Feel how much energy gets liberated from that, how much tension and anger gets dissolved. Since you are not afraid of making mistakes, you can admit them and learn from them. This helps you fulfill one of your true dreams: the one of growing as a person.

Bring that moment from the future, and feel it in your body, in the present moment. Feel it in your heart and in your mind. Feel the power of your mind, heart, and body working together and see what you can achieve, and most important: how all that is inside of you now and you *already* are the good person you always wanted to be.

Let's gently finish the meditation by slowly going back and watching the whole drawing in the sand.

Watch the eight, together with the point of courage and all the potential that is available *within* you.

End of visualization

I acknowledge you for your courage, for being here and trying to grow as a person, for trying to overcome yourself, for the efforts you do, for not giving up. The mere fact of your doing this exercise is a testimony to your inner strength and of your not giving up. I also want *you* to acknowledge yourself for your courage, for not giving up. And I want you to thank life for the challenges it brings you, for the many opportunities it brings you every day, so through them you can become in touch with your strengths, to grow and also to contribute to the world, to give to the world around you the gifts of your real self.

7. RE-PATTERNING: EXERCISES FOR FILTER FLEXING AND INTEGRATION

Black-and-White Thinking

"Black-and-White Thinking" is a distorting filter that may typically dominate Type Ones thinking in the Stuckness Zone. This filter causes Ones to think in dichotomous terms: things are either good or bad, right or wrong. Much of the rigidity and suffering of Type One is caused by this mechanism. In order to overcome this automatic tendency, Ones can incorporate the qualities of highly functioning Sevens: the ability to think in colors, in shades of gray. The ability to think more in percentages, in "degrees of," than in absolutes.

Exercise for Type One: Flexing the Black-and-White Filter
- What other possibilities do you see besides the two you mentioned?
- Is there an option in the middle?
- You said your boss is a bad person. Is there anything good you can find in this person? Every human being makes mistakes, so no one can really be *totally* perfect. Having said that, from 0–100 percent, what would you say: How "bad" is this person?

Finding the good

Finding and praising the good in people or things is usually an underdeveloped muscle in Ones in the Stuckness Zone.

Exercise for Type One: Finding the good. Look for the good in everything around you during one week. It can all be written in a two-column table: Column A will have all that comes under your radar that is perceived as needing correction and is about to be criticized. Column B will have everything that the people in your personal and professional life have done well during this week. To stretch it even further, it is possible to add a third column: How can I congratulate and say a nice thing to a person for the thing well done in column B?

Learn to relax

Ones on autopilot tend to overwhelm themselves with responsibilities. Guilt may arise if they allow themselves to be unproductive for even short periods of time. It's quite common to see Ones coming to coaching burned out after years of driving themselves too hard. Another underdeveloped muscle is the lack of ability to release tensions and relax and take things easy. This again can be obtained by integrating into Seven.

Exercise for Type One: Learning to relax. Ask yourself: How can you stop and "smell the roses" this week? Use the Type One organizing talent to rapidly schedule an appointment with yourself to simply relax and be with yourself. Otherwise this exercise will usually be hard for you to implement and will remain theoretical.

Develop your sense of humor

In the Stuckness Zone Ones become too serious, bitter, and easily irritable. The coach can help the One client flex this tendency by using humor. The benefits of humor have been well researched and its use is accepted and encouraged in a variety of therapeutic modalities. Humor provides an element of defiance of the client's rigid internal rules (Madanes, 1984 and 2006). Instead of dealing with the One's tendencies from an illness perspective and labeling the rigid internal norms as obsessions and compulsions, you can change the theme of the coaching and adopt a humorous perspective. Ones can access this resource by using their built-in connection to Type Seven.

Here are some directives the coach can use with Ones that emphasize an element of incongruity in order to counteract their overly serious nature and free them for new ways of relating to life and people (Madanes, 2010, personal communication):

Exercise for Type One: Using incongruity and humor
- Surprise your partner by dressing up like a clown.
- Get dressed for work and match the wrong colors, or wear something that has not been ironed and looks funny.
- In your next meeting at the office, deliberately give a wrong answer to something and tell a joke to the attendees.

Develop your creative muscles

If they spend too much time in the Stuckness Zone, where dichotomous Black-and-White Thinking dominates, Ones' creativity may suffer.
Exercise for Type One: Creativity.
During your interactions and activities this week:
- Ask as a Four (for deepening of perspective): What's the depth on this? What's the real meaning? What's beyond the obvious? What's beyond what I can catch with my senses?
- Ask as a Seven (for broadening of perspective): What are the opportunities here? How does all this connect with what I already know about this subject? What's the big picture? How would this look from a 1,000-foot altitude? From 10,000 feet?

Paying attention to the speaking style

Language is powerful: it's the vehicle that transports meaning. When we interpret reality through our filters, we put words to it. Therefore, if we are able to change the words that we attach to our experiences, we can indirectly impact our emotional states, since a big percentage of our emotions comes from our language. People are hypnotized by their own language patterns, creating blind spots that don't allow them to see reality accurately (Robbins and Madanes, 2005). By always using the same phrases and words to describe their experience, each personality type ends by not seeing what's in front of it. Literally, the description of reality becomes the *actual* reality. Those phrases and words are simply a manifestation of the underlying limiting beliefs that each type holds. Changing the speaking style can thus help us expand our frames of reference, allowing us to see the situations in our daily lives from many more angles.

It is important for coachees to develop the ability to become aware of when their personality mechanisms hijack their language, at the moment it occurs. For Type Ones in the Stuckness Zone, this manifests in demandingness and a judgmental discursive style. Also often present in their opinionated speaking style are conversations about responsibility and about "who's right."

Exercise for Type One: Flexing the discursive style. Pay attention to the use of words such as *should, must, correct/incorrect, responsible/irresponsible, good/bad, right/wrong.* Use more flexible wording instead.

Work with the Jungian preferences: integrating our less-dominant qualities

When coaching a Type One, it is very important to pay attention to his or her Jungian preferences. If a coachee has done an MBTI profile, ask for his or her four-letter type and discuss how Jungian preferences may play together with the coachee's Enneatype. Also, when clients get stuck in the lower side of their Jungian preference, we can use the same pattern interruption techniques described all through this book to help them shift out and grow. For a description of the Jungian preferences, please refer to Part I of this book.

Some examples of the usage of the Jungian preferences in coaching a Type One:
- Introverted Ones, who usually have a Nine wing, are quieter and more private. They are more intimate and reflective, needing more space and time to think about what's being said in the sessions. With them you'll have less eye contact and the sessions will move slowly, so don't overwhelm them with too much talking, insights, or homework (especially if you have a preference for Extraversion).
- The whole iNtuitive dimension in the MBTI is very illustrative of the development goals of Ones. Talk about it in your coaching sessions. Mention the importance of learning to watch and perceive the world from this angle: learning to look at the big picture and having less need to communicate facts in detail; developing a more figurative way of looking at situations; having an interest in what's possible instead of being too busy with the immediate and urgent; feeling more at ease with change.
- Another dimension that is very illustrative of the development goals of Ones is the Perceiving dimension. Here too, mention the importance of learning to watch the world from this angle and developing new abilities: to find pleasure in processing, not just in final results; to be spontaneous; to be flexible when the situation requires it; to adapt to changes; to see the necessity sometimes to gather more information before making important decisions; to relax and feel comfortable in some areas of life and leave a couple of things open and unplanned.

Between-Sessions Exercise for Type One: self-observation

During the week, actively engage in self-observing a particularly unhelpful pattern of your type. When you become aware of your patterns in real time, begin a spontaneous, one-cycle breath meditation. Follow the sequence described in Part II for observing the pattern and slowing it down. Share your insights with your coach in your next session.

TYPE TWO
THE HELPER

TWOS

I really enjoy being with other **people**. I have a special sense for perceiving other people's **needs**. If I sense that my boss or my colleagues need something, I cannot avoid intervening. I sometimes feel that I **devote** more time to others than I do to myself, so—despite the fact that there is no chance that you'll ever hear me say that in public—inside me it hurts when other people are **not grateful** to me [...] People say that I am very kind and that I have a **heart** of gold. It makes me **feel** good when people tell me that I am a **good person**. On the other hand, I've heard others tell me that I get **involved** too much, and that sometimes I am even intrusive. Intrusive?? In most cases I simply know better than the other what they truly need, and I **help** them because I **love** them. But when I need to ask for help, well, that's really hard for me...(Susan, Type Two)

Description of Type Two

Twos are people-oriented, warm, and keenly perceptive about the needs, wants, and feelings of others.

At their best, they are altruistic people who can quickly empathize with the needs of others. They are highly gregarious and know how to establish instant rapport with others. They are generous people who voluntarily help others as a selfless act of support and love—not to obtain something in return.

Although they are always ready to help others, they respect and are attuned to their own needs and know how to say no and how to set boundaries. Their giving is not at the expense of their own needs. They love working with people; they have high energy and are very expressive while also being gentle, compassionate, and sensitive.

They can truly listen empathically to another person and help him or her on their own terms: they are able to give their support in the way people want to receive it.

In the Stuckness Zone, an intense desire to be needed and become indispensable to others starts running inside them. An "I must give to be loved" belief dominates their thinking. Their attention tends to go automatically to detecting and anticipating the needs of others. They may become helpers, rescuers, and pleasers, trying to feel indispensable to too many people and projects, trying too hard to obtain approval, acceptance, and appreciation for their generous acts. (Although there is always some minimum degree of selectivity in their picking whom to help.) This makes them flatterers and makes them act receptively interested in others most of the time.

Sometimes they may act intrusively, as if forcing their help and advice on others, offering their insights when not asked. They may act as if they know better than you what you truly need. They can be controlling, possessive, manipulative, patronizing, and hostile, treating others with condescension and a "you-could-have-never-done-it-without-my-help" attitude.

They trap themselves in a triple way: **first**, it is hard for them to request and receive from others; **second**, they feel guilty about being selfish when they pay attention to their own needs; **third**, they expect others to do the same as they do for them (to divine their needs so they don't need to ask for things).

As a result, their personal needs become further repressed and unmet.

Anger builds inside since they feel they have dedicated too much to others while repressing their own needs, and they feel used, controlled, and unappreciated. Sudden emotional outbursts, upheavals, and accusations can be common. They can be confused regarding their own needs. Stress builds and mental, physical, emotional, and financial exhaustion arise since they have often dedicated all their available resources in their quest for approval, acceptance, and love from others.

COACHING PROTOCOL FOR TYPE TWO

1. SET THE CLIMATE OF THE SESSION

Before you begin your coaching session with your client, check yourself:

Bring acceptance to the session
Ask yourself:
- Am I in a non-judgmental state?
- Does my specific personality type have any resistance with type Two?

"Turn on" your multimodal listening
It is extremely important that you use all the centers of intelligence (Head, Heart, Gut) during every coaching session. Be aware of "listening" actively with all three centers.

Listen with your Head center
- Pay attention to speaking style and language use.
- Analyze body language and posture.
- Analyze patterns and possibilities for interrupting them.

Listen with your Heart center
- Empathize.
- See the client as a human being, not as a "type."
- Look beyond the facade.
- Connect, in spite of any resistance that you may have. You are here to help the client grow.

Listen with your Gut center
- What kind of energy is the client bringing to the session?
- Is there a match between what the client says and the energy with which he or she says it?
- What does your intuition tell you regarding the last developments in this coaching process?
- "Listen to what people say but pay attention to what they *do*." (Madanes, 1995).

2. DEFINE THE CHALLENGE

Determine what the client wants to work on, what is the purpose of his or her pursuing coaching.

Typical challenges for Twos include:
- To reduce stress and the suffering they cause to themselves by their giving pattern.
- To build their self-esteem and self-worth independently of their deeds to others and external approval and validation.
- To recognize their own needs and take care of them in an orderly way.
- To learn the value of introversion and of developing a rich inner life together with their usually dominant social life.
- To learn how to assert their will without guilt, setting boundaries and limits.

3. UNDERSTAND THE COACHEE'S MODEL OF THE WORLD AND HIS OR HER STUCKNESS ZONE

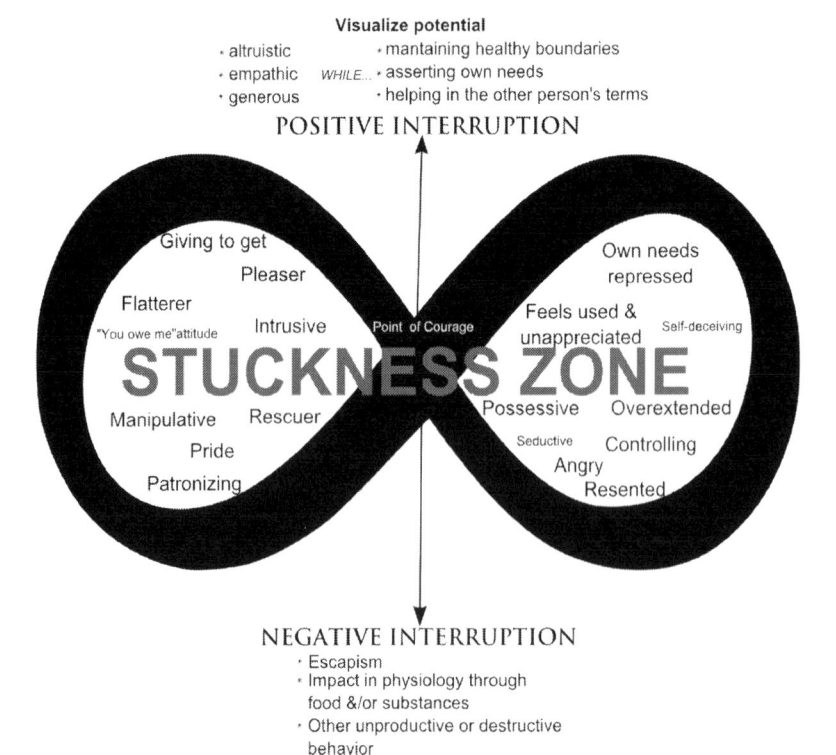

Visualize potential
- altruistic
- empathic   WHILE...
- generous
- mantaining healthy boundaries
- asserting own needs
- helping in the other person's terms

POSITIVE INTERRUPTION

STUCKNESS ZONE

Giving to get
Pleaser
Flatterer
"You owe me" attitude
Intrusive
Point of Courage
Manipulative
Rescuer
Pride
Patronizing

Own needs repressed
Feels used & unappreciated
Self-deceiving
Possessive
Overextended
Seductive
Controlling
Angry
Resented

NEGATIVE INTERRUPTION
- Escapism
- Impact in physiology through food &/or substances
- Other unproductive or destructive behavior

Ask yourself the following questions: Why is the client acting the way he does? What is shaping her behavior? What is his internal story? What are the filters through which she looks at and perceives the world? To what extent are the type fixations active and operative in this client?

When less aware or under stress, Type Two's attention gets hijacked/derailed by an intense desire to be needed and become indispensable to others. In this state they usually begin giving compulsively to others, but in an attempt to obtain something in return (which could be their love, friendship, etc.)

4. BRING AWARENESS TO THE SIX HUMAN NEEDS

According to Human Needs Psychology, we all have six basic human needs (Madanes, 2009): Certainty, Variety, Love/Connection, Significance, Growth, and Contribution. These needs are not merely desires, but true drivers mobilizing our behavior.

Exercise for Type Two: The six human needs. Look at the Stuckness Zone and from the whole range of behaviors there described, pick the most frequent ones: "What human needs are you trying to fulfill by engaging in these behaviors?"

Please score each need from 0 to 10.

Certainty. Does engaging in these behaviors make you feel certain? Give you a sense of security? Apart from these behaviors: Do you also know how to obtain certainty in a more positive way?

Variety. Does engaging in these behaviors bring you a sense of variety? Apart from these behaviors: Do you also know how to obtain variety in a more positive way?

Love/connection. Does engaging in these behaviors make you feel connected to others? Experience a sense of love?
Apart from these behaviors: Do you also know how to obtain love/connection in a more positive way?

Significance. Does engaging in these behaviors make you feel important? Special? Apart from these behaviors: Do you also know how to obtain significance in a more positive way?

Growth. Does engaging in these behaviors give you a sense of development, make you feel that you're growing? Apart from these behaviors: Do you also know how to obtain growth in a more positive way?

Contribution. Does engaging in these behaviors give you a sense of going beyond your own needs, of giving to others? Apart from these behaviors: Do you also know how to obtain contribution in a more positive way?

Coaching Case Study. Take, for example, Sonia, one of our coachees, a Type Two. According to her, helping others, even when they don't request it, allows her to fulfill three of the six human needs. The most important is Love/Connection: helping others help her cover her need to feel loved and appreciated. Second in importance is Significance: helping others make her feel special, since she feels she always "knows" what's better for the other person, and probably the other person would not be able to succeed without her help. By helping others she also fulfills her need for Variety: she feels that helping others is a vehicle to intrude into other people's lives whenever she wants. Since she is fulfilling those human needs in a negative way, she is not obtaining the recognition and appreciation from people she's so desperately seeking. People actually get a bit resentful of her continuous intrusiveness and unrequested help, and that hurts her relationships with others. The breakthrough came when Sonia realized that she could meet all her needs in a positive way. **That's possible only outside the Stuckness Zone: by abandoning the habit of giving to get and instead giving to others what they truly need, to the degree they need it, when they need it, and respecting their will and natural preferences of their personality type.**

One important point to take into account: pay special attention to the needs of Growth and Contribution. **Does the coachee meet these needs in healthy or in destructive ways?** As we integrate our personality, the needs of Growth and Contribution begin receiving high scores while also being met in positive and healthy ways. The reason for this is that when we move out of our Stuckness Zone, we act from new, conscious, chosen responses. This allows us to overcome our old habits and grow. This integration, in turn, will always bring greater contribution to others. In contrast, if we continue acting without awareness, out of our old patterns of reaction, we disempower ourselves and let our egos manage our lives. This always causes suffering to ourselves and to others.

5. PRODUCE LEVERAGE

The next step is to gain leverage by bringing awareness to the costs and suffering that the unhelpful patterns of the type are causing for the client.

Exercise for Type Two: Gaining awareness of the costs of patterns
- How much does it cost you, in terms of your relationships, to engage in the habit of giving to get?
- How much does it cost you, in terms of your health, to be exhausted physically and mentally, from overextending yourself in helping others?
- How much does it cost you, in terms of your professional career, to put a focus so exclusively on interpersonal relationships and the feelings of people, and sometimes neglecting other important aspects of the job?
- How much does it cost you, in terms of your personal fulfillment and own sense of happiness, to be relentlessly trying to obtain other people's approval?

6. PATTERN INTERRUPTION: BUILDING OUR ATTENTIONAL MUSCLES

TYPE TWO VISUALIZATION

Visualizations are a great tool for coaching in general and when doing personality-types coaching in particular. The following is a comprehensive visualization/meditation script for Type Two. It encompasses working with the type's strengths and weaknesses, training attentional abilities through the Impartial Spectator, training conscious breathing, acceptance, and relaxation. In a single coaching session, you don't have to use them all. You can use these visualizations modularly, by selecting one or more of the sections that follow.

Script for Type Two: Visualization/Meditation

Relaxation

Begin by finding a comfortable sitting position. Keep your spine straight in a natural way. Let your arms become loose. Lightly, with palms facing up or down, rest your hands on your lap. Take one deep breath, to begin relaxing your whole body. Inhale. . .Exhale. . . You can gently close your eyes and take another deep breath as a way to become centered and focused. Inhale. . .Exhale . . .

Training the Impartial Spectator

Let's begin by bringing awareness to the Impartial Spectator. Think of the Impartial Spectator as your friend who objectively watches your behavior from the outside. It helps you make wise decisions and allows you to regulate your automatic pilot.

The Impartial Spectator will do so by training your mind to be sensitive to the activity in your three centers of intelligence: the Body (our physical sensations), the Mind (thoughts, plans, future, past, images, ideas, imagination), and the Heart (feelings). Our breath, which symbolically represents our connection to our soul, will allow us to remain centered and to shift our attention from one center to the other. It will also help us to remain non-judgmental and to bring the qualities of gratitude, compassion, and acceptance to this exercise. Every time your mind wanders, you can use the moment to exercise those qualities of gratitude, compassion, and acceptance—for each one of those moments offers the opportunity to learn how to reorient our attention.

Begin by gently shifting your attention to your **Body** center of intelligence. Take a deep breath, and follow the path of the air in and out of the body. Do it slowly. Inhale again. . . and this time make the exhalation last a bit longer. Place your full attention on the path of the air getting in and out of your body, from beginning to end. Begin noticing your body sensations. Sense the contact points between your feet and the floor. What body sensations are in there right now? Move your attention to your back. Feel the support that the chair gives you. Stay with that sensation for a moment. Shift your attention to your hands. Focus on the contact point between the hands and your lap.

Place your hands over your chest, one over the other, and shift your attention to your **Heart** center of intelligence. What feelings do you have in this moment?

Now shift your attention to the **Head** center of intelligence. Is there a mental commentary about your feelings? Is there judgment or acceptance of your feelings? What is your mind saying about your feelings? What is it saying about this whole exercise? Serenely watch your mental discourse as it appears. Inhale. . .Exhale. . . Stay in the Head center, and now shift your attention to your memories. Imagine yourself watching an old black-and-white TV set on which your past history is being broadcast. You see yourself in the TV. Your life videotaped. Each stage of your life, on the screen, in slow motion. Nod when you actually see it. Inhale. . .Exhale. . . Still in the Head center, now move your attention to the future. Serenely reflect on each one of the following questions. Take a few moments as a pause between each question. What do you want your future to be like? How do you see yourself in the future? What plans do you have?

Visualization

Remain in the Head center, and you will now shift your attention to your imagination. Imagine yourself at the beach, at the sea shore, in slightly wet sand. Breath the air at the beach. Inhale. . .Exhale. . . Feel the wind. Listen to the waves in the sea. Feel the sand on your feet. Imagine yourself drawing an imaginary number eight, drawn horizontally, like the infinity symbol, in the slightly wet sand on the shore. Draw it slowwwly. Feel the contact point between your fingers and the sand.

Visualization of Stuckness Zone and costs

Now picture yourself putting all your problems and challenges *inside* that eight in the sand. One by one.

All my continuous attention to other people's needs while neglecting my own. All my physical exhaustion from overextending myself while trying to help even when not requested to. All my desperate attempts to gain others' approval and love. All my resentment for feeling unappreciated for all the good that I have done for others. All the anger. All the suffering.

Feel the tension and anger. Feel it in your belly as you see all the issues inside the eight in the sand. Feel the tension in your whole body. Stay there for a moment.

This eight in the sand represents our Stuckness Zone. The place we get stuck with negative focus and negative feelings.

"It's human" section

Every human being has issues that make him or her precisely that, human. It's a personal, tailor-made set of challenges in life. Watch your own personal challenges without judgments. If your mind passes a commentary, it's OK. Don't worry and try to do this exercise "right." If there is a judgment, just watch the judgment. Listen to its script. Watch it as it occurs, outside of you.

It's human to have judgments about our experience. It's OK. Bring your attention to your heart. Now, grab the judgments you just heard in your head, the mental comments, and put them there, in your heart. Use the energy of your heart to soften them and feel how it fills your whole body with compassion. Take a deep breath, and feel the energy of your heart throughout your whole body. Feel the acceptance.

Why does life bring you challenges? Life brings you challenges so you can overcome them, and allow the next level of plenitude and vitality to become available to you. They are precious opportunities to grow. Precious opportunities to discover the strengths *you already have* that simply need to be reactivated. The strengths that will help you overcome your challenges, the strengths that will help you move from stuckness to growth.

Inside of you there is a part that doesn't want to give up. That wants to live life at its fullest. It's the voice of your soul. The voice that wants to stand up to the voices of the ego and the personality—and become the best possible you. You've been there before, and that's what brought you up to this moment. This moment in which you are here struggling to become the best person you can be, standing up and not giving up to your personality, to your automatic thoughts. It's the real you, it's the strength of your soul.

At this point your attention may automatically go to create thoughts about your thoughts. It's OK. Simply keep breathing consciously, following the path of the air in and out of your body, and let your Impartial Spectator witness the activity of your mind non-judgmentally.

Visualization of strengths, potential, and personal power

Now please move your attention to that part of yourself that doesn't want to give up. Look at the drawing on the sand: exactly in the center of the eight there is a point: the intersection between the right side and the left side of the eight. Let's call it the *point of courage*. From that point, imagine yourself drawing an arrow up. An exit from the eight. An exit from the stuckness.

This arrow points to what is available outside the eight. This arrow points to your strengths and to your potential. To the future that is available to you in any given moment.

Let's see what's outside the eight.

I want you to think of any moment in the past in which you really felt unconditionally loved, regardless of what you did for others. Bring it from any area of your life: you could have been by yourself, with a friend, with a group of friends, or with your family. In your personal or your professional life. Go to the past and bring back that moment. It could be a special moment or just a simple one. Feel it. Feel the relaxation of that moment in your whole body.

Search your memories for that moment in which your self-worth was not dependent on others liking you. Feel the relaxation of that moment, in which you let go of needing the approval of others to feel good about yourself and about your life. Everything flowed harmoniously and everything actually worked well and turned out well, without your needing to take any action. Take a deep breath and feel that moment.

Let's see what else is outside the eight.

I now want you to envision yourself in a new future. A future in which you are supportive, loving, and empathic but serene. A future in which you are helpful and kind, but you are full of enthusiasm and vitality. A future in which you accept yourself as a human being, including your natural limitations. Please put your hands one over the other, and over your heart. Feel your heartbeat. Feel your humanity. Since you are human, you are allowed to rest and not feel that you must take care of everybody else's problems, all the time. This allows you to recharge your batteries and maintain your high energy, rather than driving yourself to exhaustion. Feel how much energy gets liberated from that, how much resentment and anger gets dissolved. Since you take care of your own needs, you don't give to others expecting something in return. This helps you fulfill one of your life dreams: the one of truly becoming a good, altruistic, generous person.

Bring that moment from the future, and feel it in your body, in the present moment. Feel it in your heart and in your mind. Feel the power of your mind, heart, and body working together and see what you can achieve, and most important: how all that is inside of you now and you *already* are the good person you always wanted to be.

Let's gently finish the meditation by slowly going back and watching the whole drawing in the sand.

Watch the eight, together with the point of courage and all the potential that is available *within* you.

End of visualization

I acknowledge you for your courage, for being here and trying to grow as a person, for trying to overcome yourself, for the efforts you do, for not giving up. The mere fact of your doing this exercise is a testimony to your inner strength and of your not giving up. I also want *you* to acknowledge yourself for your courage, for not giving up. And I want you to thank life for the challenges it brings you, for the many opportunities it brings you every day, so through them you can become in touch with your strengths, to grow and also to contribute to the world, to give to the world around you the gifts of your real self.

7. RE-PATTERNING: EXERCISES FOR FILTER FLEXING AND INTEGRATION

Learn to Relax

Twos on autopilot tend to overwhelm themselves with helping too many people while neglecting their own needs. Guilt may arise if they allow themselves to be unhelpful for even short periods of time. It is not uncommon to see Twos coming to coaching burned out after years of overextending themselves so much. To overcome this tendency, Twos can use the Type Four's frame of reference.

Exercise for Type Two: Learning to relax

Instead of trying to detect what others need, use your arrow to Four to ask: How do *I* feel now? What's going on inside myself? What do *I* need?

Develop your assertive muscles

If they spend too much time in the Stuckness Zone, where the giving-to-get thinking dominates, they may become pleasers and may feel selfish when saying "no." Twos' assertiveness may suffer and they may not maintain healthy boundaries in their relationships.

Exercise for Type Two: Healthy boundaries. During your activities and interactions this week,
- Using your arrow to Eight, ask: What do *I* want here? Connect to the grounded, solid, gut intelligence of healthy Eights. Bring that energy of determination to your interactions.
- Using your Three wing, ask: What are my goals? Use the business-like focus of healthy Threes when, in spite of your tiredness, you feel tempted to overextend yourself again and go to great lengths

for others, not attending to your own personal needs and derailing your own plans. Have a realistic and a bit more efficient look at your physical, emotional, and financial resources.
- Using your One wing, ask: How can I help people while responsibly attending to all my obligations? Check: Am I not attending to some of my family or job commitments in order to go help a third party? Am I keeping my word?

Paying attention to the speaking style

Language is powerful: it's the vehicle that transports meaning. When we interpret reality through our filters, we put words to it. Therefore, if we are able to change the words that we attach to our experiences, we can indirectly impact our emotional states, since a big percentage of our emotions comes from our language. People are hypnotized by their own language patterns, creating blind spots that don't allow them to see reality accurately (Robbins and Madanes, 2005). By always using the same phrases and words to describe their experience, each personality type ends by not seeing what's in front of it. Literally, the description of reality becomes the *actual* reality. Those phrases and words are simply a manifestation of the underlying limiting beliefs that each type holds. Changing the speaking style can thus help us expand our frames of reference, allowing us to see the situations in our daily lives from many more angles.

It is important for coachees to develop the ability to become aware of when their personality mechanisms hijack their language, at the moment it occurs. For Type Twos in the Stuckness Zone, this manifests in a discursive style that usually tends to be centered more on the other person: although participative in the conversation, the Two will share less about how she or he feels, and the conversation naturally gravitates to what the other needs, thinks, or feels.

Exercise for Type Two: Flexing the discursive style. Pay attention to the conversation topics and format. How much time have we been talking about you? And about my inner feelings and thoughts? Am I avoiding talking about my personal needs? Am I truly listening to what the other person really needs, or have I already decided what they need while they talk?

Work with the Jungian preferences: integrating our less-dominant qualities

When coaching a Type Two, it is very important to pay attention to his or her Jungian preferences. If a coachee has done an MBTI profile, ask for his or her four-letter type and discuss how Jungian preferences may play together with the coachee's Enneatype. Also, when clients get stuck in the lower side of their Jungian preference, we can use the same pattern interruption techniques described all through this book to help them shift out and grow. For a description of the Jungian preferences, please refer to Part I of this book.

Some examples of the usage of the Jungian preferences in coaching a Type Two:

- The whole Introversion dimension in Myers-Briggs is very illustrative of some development goals of Twos. Talk about it in your coaching sessions. Mention the importance of learning to watch and perceive the world from this angle: learning to be more reflective and inner oriented; developing the ability to take thoughts inside and process them, instead of instantly having Extravert thoughts; creating space and boundaries with people; developing a contemplative way of looking at situations; taking time to think things through thoroughly.
- Another dimension that is very useful for some development goals of Twos is Thinking. Here too, mention the importance of learning to watch the world from this angle: developing the ability to analyze situations in an impersonal manner; making decisions logically; weighing costs against expected benefits when taking action; asking logical questions and remaining task centered; analyzing cause and effect. All this is crucial in the development of Twos, since they have a clear Jungian preference for Feeling.

Between-Sessions Exercise for Type Two: self-observation

During the week, actively engage in self-observing a particularly unhelpful pattern of your type. When you become aware of your patterns in real time, begin a spontaneous, one-cycle breath meditation. Follow the sequence described in Part II for observing the pattern and slowing it down. Share your insights with your coach in your next session.

TYPE THREE
THE ACHIEVER

THREES

When I see other people content having second place, I can hardly understand them. Ever since I have had a memory of myself, I have always wanted to be **number one**. The **best**. And I **work** really hard to **achieve** it. In every area of my life, I try to be the best. Playing basketball with my friends, getting the **highest** grades in college. . .whatever. I work and work and work, at the expense of hours of sleep, if needed. I want to **be somebody** in this world. And I know that if I simply want it, I will be able to make it. I believe **image** is important. You can't look like a **loser** if you want to be somebody. You must know how to **project** the right image, one that will allow you to get **advancement** in your career. You need to be a true **professional**. At home they tell me I have no feelings. That's because they don't understand that when I am **busy** and **focused** on my next **target**, feelings can become an obstacle that doesn't let you get into action. When you have the level of **action** I have, it's sometimes hard to be demonstrative with your feelings. (Steven, Type Three.)

Description of Type Three

Threes are success and image-conscious, dynamic, self-driving people who want to excel and be the best they can.

At their best, they are driven to obtain excellence and can become exemplary and be role models in the areas they master. They are highly focused and know how to effectively set and meet goals. They want to bring out the best in themselves and are willing to keep sacrificing a great deal to achieve excellence, but at the same time they are accepting of themselves as they are. Their self-acceptance and confidence comes from within, not from the need to impress others and obtain external validation. They are sincere and realistic with themselves, and it is possible to see their heart together with their usually energetic attitude. They are inspirational and motivational in helping you achieve your goals, injecting hope in you that you are capable of attaining your potential. Although they are ambitious and are able to subordinate present needs in order to attain excellence in all they do, they know how to be supportive team players who can respectfully and inspirationally coach the other team members and inject hope in those who feel behind. They are hard workers, but work doesn't become everything for them; they are also committed to their family and friends. They are great communicators, receptive to people, personable and sociable, fast moving, fast learners, eager and enthusiastic, full of a go-ahead energy, entrepreneurial, efficient, practical, independent, ambitious, energetic, competent, persistent, and industrious.

In the Stuckness Zone, an intense desire to impress others starts running inside them. An "I must be and look successful" belief dominates their thinking. Consequently, their attention automatically goes in these two directions: on one hand, how to be successful; on the other, how to look successful.

In order to **be** successful, they believe they must work hard to get things done quickly and efficiently. Their attention automatically goes to tasks and goals, which in itself can be a good thing, but they can become overactive workaholics who never take a rest and are unable to slow down their tempo and pace. Work becomes their only focus. Their own feelings (and other people's feelings) are seen as distracting obstacles to their efficient, machine-like desired performance. Other people may be themselves seen as obstacles in their way to obtain their goals, and the Three begins playing more for himself or herself and less as a cooperative team player with others. They are tougher and impatient with people, especially if they perceive them as inefficient, incompetent, or hesitant. A strong competitive drive arises, and with it a desire to always be on top of others in as many aspects of life as possible, as if life was a game to be won. Failure is not an option for them. If they try to attain success "the faster the better," they may adopt a "the end justifies the means" frame of mind. They can become manipulative, unprincipled, and unscrupulous.

In order to **look** successful, they believe they must carefully cultivate a successful image and promote themselves. Their attention tends to go automatically to the way they look and how they are perceived by others. They may become image-conscious performers, trying too hard to mask their real self in order to be seen as successful and obtain external approval, acceptance, and appreciation for their achievements. They adopt the language of selling and self-promotion. This makes them chameleonic and makes them act adaptively to whatever they believe will win the admiration of others in every situation and context. They will try to project prestige, status, professionalism, beauty, or whatever their social context will value as ideal. In a parallel approach to their human "imperfections," they avoid talking about them and try to project an image of flawless functioning in as many areas of their life as possible.

Stress and emotional drain arise, since it is very difficult to maintain a perfect, "successful" image for periods as long as they do. Physical exhaustion arises from their busy, workaholic lifestyle.

COACHING PROTOCOL FOR TYPE THREE

1. SET THE CLIMATE OF THE SESSION

Before you begin your coaching session with your client, check yourself:

Bring acceptance to the session
Ask yourself:
- Am I in a non-judgmental state?
- Does my specific personality type have any resistance with Type Three?

"Turn on" your multimodal listening
It is extremely important that you use all the centers of intelligence (Head, Heart, Gut) during every coaching session. Be aware of "listening" actively with all three centers.
   Listen with your Head center
- Pay attention to speaking style and language use.
- Analyze body language and posture.

- Analyze patterns and possibilities for interrupting them.

Listen with your Heart center
- Empathize.
- See the client as a human being, not as a "type."
- Look beyond the facade.
- Connect, in spite of any resistance that you may have. You are here to help the client grow.

Listen with your Gut center
- What kind of energy is the client bringing to the session?
- Is there a match between what the client says and the energy with which he or she says it?
- What does your intuition tell you regarding the last developments in this coaching process?
- "Listen to what people say but pay attention to what they *do*." (Madanes, 1995).

2. DEFINE THE CHALLENGE

Determine what the client wants to work on, what is the purpose of his or her pursuing coaching.

Typical challenges for Threes include:
- to reduce stress and tension that arise from their drives to compete and constant need to prove themselves and impress others, in both their personal and professional lives.
- to learn to develop strategies to obtain their goals without burning out or ruining their relationships.
- to build their self-worth and self-esteem independently from their achievements and from external validation.

3. UNDERSTAND THE COACHEE'S MODEL OF THE WORLD AND HIS OR HER STUCKNESS ZONE

Ask yourself the following questions: Why is the client acting the way he does? What is shaping her behavior? What is his internal story? What are the filters through which she looks at and perceives the world? To what extent are the type fixations active and operative in this client?

From Stuckness to Growth

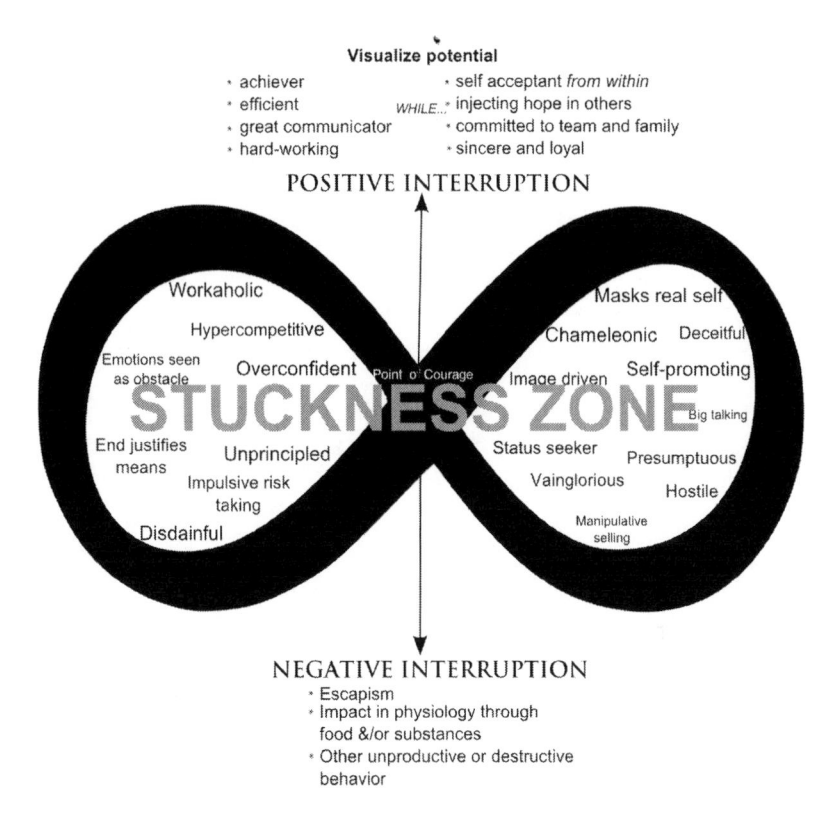

Visualize potential
- achiever
- efficient
- great communicator
- hard-working

WHILE...
- self acceptant *from within*
- injecting hope in others
- committed to team and family
- sincere and loyal

POSITIVE INTERRUPTION

STUCKNESS ZONE

- Workaholic
- Hypercompetitive
- Emotions seen as obstacle
- Overconfident
- Point o' Courage
- End justifies means
- Unprincipled
- Impulsive risk taking
- Disdainful
- Masks real self
- Chameleonic
- Deceitful
- Image driven
- Self-promoting
- Big talking
- Status seeker
- Presumptuous
- Vainglorious
- Hostile
- Manipulative selling

NEGATIVE INTERRUPTION
- Escapism
- Impact in physiology through food &/or substances
- Other unproductive or destructive behavior

When less aware or under stress, Type Three's attention gets hijacked/derailed by an intense desire to impress others that starts running inside them. An "I must be and look successful" belief dominates their thinking. Consequently, their attention automatically goes in these two directions: on one hand, how to *be* successful, on the other, how to *look* successful.

4. BRING AWARENESS TO THE SIX HUMAN NEEDS

According to Human Needs Psychology, we all have six basic human needs (Madanes, 2009): Certainty, Variety, Love/Connection, Significance, Growth, and Contribution. These needs are not merely desires, but true drivers mobilizing our behavior.

Exercise for Type Three: The six human needs. Look at the Stuckness Zone and from the whole range of behaviors there described,

pick the most frequent ones: "What human needs are you trying to fulfill by engaging in these behaviors?"
Please score each need from 0 to 10.

Certainty. Does engaging in these behaviors make you feel certain? Give you a sense of security? Apart from these behaviors: Do you also know how to obtain certainty in a more positive way?

Variety. Does engaging in these behaviors bring you a sense of variety? Apart from these behaviors: Do you also know how to obtain variety in a more positive way?

Love/connection. Does engaging in these behaviors make you feel connected to others? Experience a sense of love?
Apart from these behaviors: Do you also know how to obtain love/connection in a more positive way?

Significance. Does engaging in these behaviors make you feel important? Special? Apart from these behaviors: Do you also know how to obtain significance in a more positive way?

Growth. Does engaging in these behaviors give you a sense of development, make you feel that you're growing? Apart from these behaviors: Do you also know how to obtain growth in a more positive way?

Contribution. Does engaging in these behaviors give you a sense of going beyond your own needs, of giving to others? Apart from these behaviors: Do you also know how to obtain contribution in a more positive way?

Coaching case study. Take as an example Peter, one of our coachees, a Type Three. A production manager in a manufacturing company, he wants to be the best in what he does, "no matter the cost." His work being above everything else, it hurts his relationships with his wife at home and with his colleagues at the office. His workaholic behavior fulfills three of his human needs: Growth, Significance, and Certainty. *Growth*, because trying to excel in what he does makes him constantly best himself in order to achieve new peaks in his performance. *Significance*, because trying to be the best makes him feel superior to the rest. *Certainty*, because he is certain about achieving whatever he sets as a target to achieve, no matter what obstacles appear in his way ("I just *know* I can do it," he says.) He came to coaching in high physical exhaustion and with feelings of emptiness and lack of meaning in life. He now understands that satisfying his human needs in a negative way has a high cost and a negative impact in his life.

The breakthrough came when Peter achieved a balance between being excellent at what he does and taking care of his health and relationships. We used the same discipline he has for work to develop his underdeveloped emotional and relationship muscles. Peter realized that the things obtained "no matter the cost" didn't necessarily bring him to true "success." When he began to include activities and one-on-one times with his family in his weekly schedule, he discovered he could grow in other areas of his life, not only in his job, fulfilling the need of Growth in a positive way. With his team, instead of continuing with his competitive approach, Peter began coaching personally two of his employees, empowering them to become the best they can be. The results at the end of the first month were amazing: his department productivity grew 25 percent and team morale changed significantly. This was a major source of Significance for him. After implementing all these changes, he has a greater sense of Certainty than ever, precisely when he is ready *not* to pay any cost for obtaining the success he so much wants. This way he managed to fulfill all his dominant human needs in a positive and constructive way.

One important point to take into account: pay special attention to the needs of Growth and Contribution. Does the coachee meet these needs in healthy or in destructive ways?

As we integrate our personality, the needs of Growth and Contribution begin receiving high scores while also being met in positive and healthy ways. The reason for this is that when we move out of our Stuckness Zone, we act from new, conscious, chosen responses. This allows us to overcome our old habits and grow. This integration, in turn, always will bring greater contribution to others. In contrast, if we continue acting without awareness, out of our old patterns of reaction, we disempower ourselves and let our egos manage our lives. This always causes suffering to ourselves and to others.

5. PRODUCE LEVERAGE

The next step is to gain leverage by bringing awareness to the costs and suffering that the unhelpful patterns of the type are causing for the client.

Exercise for Type Three: Gaining awareness of the costs of patterns

- How much does it cost you, in terms of your relationships, to

repress your emotions and not dedicate enough time to family and friends?
- How much does it cost you, in terms of your health, to be workaholic and unable to slow down?
- How much does it cost you, in terms of your professional career, to be competitive and hostile and to find it hard to commit to the team's good?
- How much does it cost you, in terms of your personal fulfillment and own sense of happiness, to relentlessly mask your real self and project images chameleonically?

6. PATTERN INTERRUPTION: BUILDING OUR ATTENTIONAL MUSCLES

TYPE THREE VISUALIZATION

Visualizations are a great tool for coaching in general and when doing personality-types coaching in particular. The following is a comprehensive visualization/meditation script for Type Three. It encompasses working with the type's strengths and weaknesses, training attentional abilities through the Impartial Spectator, training conscious breathing, acceptance, and relaxation. In a single coaching session, you don't have to use them all. You can use these visualizations modularly, by selecting one or more of the sections that follow.

Script for Type Three: Visualization/Meditation

Relaxation

Begin by finding a comfortable sitting position. Keep your spine straight in a natural way. Let your arms become loose. Lightly, with palms facing up or down, rest your hands on your lap. Take one deep breath, to begin relaxing your whole body. Inhale. . .Exhale. . . You can gently close your eyes and take another deep breath as a way to become centered and focused. Inhale. . .Exhale . . .

Training the Impartial Spectator

Let's begin by bringing awareness to the Impartial Spectator. Think of the Impartial Spectator as your friend who objectively watches your behavior from the outside. It helps you make wise decisions and allows you to regulate your automatic pilot.

The Impartial Spectator will do so by training your mind to be sensitive to the activity in your three centers of intelligence: the Body (our physical sensations), the Mind (thoughts, plans, future, past, images, ideas, imagination), and the Heart (feelings). Our breath, which symbolically represents our connection to our soul, will allow us to remain centered and to shift our attention from one center to the other. It will also help us to remain non-judgmental and to bring the qualities of gratitude, compassion, and acceptance to this exercise. Every time your mind wanders, you can use the moment to exercise those qualities of gratitude, compassion, and acceptance—for each one of those moments offers the opportunity to learn how to reorient our attention.

Begin by gently shifting your attention to your **Body** center of intelligence. Take a deep breath, and follow the path of the air in and out of the body. Do it slowly. Inhale again. . . and this time make the exhalation last a bit longer. Place your full attention on the path of the air getting in and out of your body, from beginning to end. Begin noticing your body sensations. Sense the contact points between your feet and the floor. What body sensations are in there right now? Move your attention to your back. Feel the support that the chair gives you. Stay with that sensation for a moment. Shift your attention to your hands. Focus on the contact point between the hands and your lap.

Place your hands over your chest, one over the other, and shift your attention to your **Heart** center of intelligence. What feelings do you have in this moment?

Now shift your attention to the **Head** center of intelligence. Is there a mental commentary about your feelings? Is there judgment or acceptance of your feelings? What is your mind saying about your feelings? What is it saying about this whole exercise? Serenely watch your mental discourse as it appears. Inhale. . .Exhale. . . Stay in the Head center, and now shift your attention to your memories. Imagine yourself watching an old black-and-white TV set on which your past history is being broadcast. You see yourself in the TV. Your life videotaped. Each stage of your life, on the screen, in slow motion. Nod when you actually see it. Inhale. . .Exhale. . . Still in the Head center, now move your attention to the future. Serenely reflect on each one of the following questions. Take a few moments as a pause between each question. What do you want your future to be like?

How do you see yourself in the future? What plans do you have?

Visualization

Remain in the Head center, and you will now shift your attention to your imagination. Imagine yourself at the beach, at the sea shore, in slightly wet sand. Breath the air at the beach. Inhale. . .Exhale. . . Feel the wind. Listen to the waves in the sea. Feel the sand on your feet. Imagine yourself drawing an imaginary number eight, drawn horizontally, like the infinity symbol, in the slightly wet sand on the shore. Draw it slowwwly. Feel the contact point between your fingers and the sand.

Visualization of Stuckness Zone and costs

Now picture yourself putting all your problems and challenges *inside* that eight in the sand. One by one.

All my continuous attention to image and trying to mask my real self. All my self-enslaving behaviors of projecting the right image to impress others. All my competitive behavior and constant measuring of things and people (including myself) against external ideals of "success." All my hostility and impatience and lack of sensitivity towards others. All my exhaustion and burnout in trying to be the best. All the suffering.

Feel the tension and anger. Feel it in your belly as you see all the issues inside the eight in the sand. Feel the tension in your whole body. Stay there for a moment.

This eight in the sand represents our Stuckness Zone. The place we get stuck with negative focus and negative feelings.

"It's human" section

Every human being has issues that make him or her precisely that, human. It's a personal, tailor-made set of challenges in life. Watch your own personal challenges without judgments. If your mind passes a commentary, it's OK. Don't worry and try to do this exercise "right." If there is a judgment, just watch the judgment. Listen to its script. Watch it as it occurs, outside of you.

It's human to have judgments about our experience. It's OK. Bring your attention to your heart. Now, grab the judgments you just heard in your head, the mental comments, and put them there, in your heart. Use the energy of your heart to soften them and feel how it fills your whole body with compassion. Take a deep breath, and feel the energy of your heart throughout your whole body. Feel the acceptance.

Why does life bring you challenges? Life brings you challenges so you can overcome them, and allow the next level of plenitude and vitality to become available to you. They are precious opportunities to grow. Precious opportunities to discover the strengths *you already have* that simply need to be reactivated. The strengths that will help you overcome your challenges, the strengths that will help you move from stuckness to growth.

Inside of you there is a part that doesn't want to give up. That wants to live life at its fullest. It's the voice of your soul. The voice that wants to stand up to the voices of the ego and the personality—and become the best possible you. You've been there before, and that's what brought you up to this moment. This moment in which you are here struggling to become the best person you can be, standing up and not giving up to your personality, to your automatic thoughts. It's the real you, it's the strength of your soul.

At this point your attention may automatically go to create thoughts about your thoughts. It's OK. Simply keep breathing consciously, following the path of the air in and out of your body, and let your Impartial Spectator witness the activity of your mind non-judgmentally.

Visualization of strengths, potential, and personal power

Now please move your attention to that part of yourself that doesn't want to give up. Look at the drawing on the sand: exactly in the center of the eight there is a point: the intersection between the right side and the left side of the eight. Let's call it the *point of courage*. From that point, imagine yourself drawing an arrow up. An exit from the eight. An exit from the stuckness.

This arrow points to what is available outside the eight. This arrow points to your strengths and to your potential. To the future that is available to you in any given moment.

Let's see what's outside the eight.

I want you to think of any moment in the past in which you really felt self-acceptance, without the need to impress others. It can be any moment in which you felt comfortable dropping your masks. Bring it from any area of your life: you could have been by yourself, with a friend, with a group of friends, or with your family. In your personal or your professional life.

Go to the past and bring back that moment. It could be a special moment or just a simple one. Feel it. Feel the relaxation of that moment in your whole body.

Search your memories for that moment in which you were *truly* successful. Sincere. Receptive. Motivating. You were *yourself*. Feel the relaxation of that moment, in which you let go of trying to impress others to feel valuable. Everything flowed harmoniously and everything actually worked well and turned out well, without your doing anything, without impersonations, without depending on your being industrious or achieving something. Take a deep breath and feel that moment.

Let's see what else is outside the eight.

I now want you to envision yourself in a new future. A future in which you are exemplary and a mentor of others. A future in which you are constantly growing and encouraging others to grow, but you do so tolerantly and compassionately, injecting hope in others. In which you accept yourself as a human being, including some less positive aspects. In which you accept failure as a natural part of life, and don't feel the need to mask your failures in any way. Please put your hands one over the other, and over your heart. Feel your heartbeat. Feel your humanity. Since you are human, you are allowed to *fail* from time to time. Paradoxically, when you let go of the enslavement to projecting the right image, you have more emotional energies available, and you become more effective than ever. Since you are not afraid of failures, you can admit them and learn from them. You can drop your masks and be sincere. This helps you fulfill one of your true dreams: the one of truly becoming a successful human being.

Bring that moment from the future, and feel it in your body, in the present moment. Feel it in your heart and in your mind. Feel the power of your mind, heart, and body working together and see what you can achieve, and most important: feel how all that is inside of you now and you *already* are the succeful person you always wanted to be.

Let's gently finish the meditation by slowly going back and watching the whole drawing in the sand.

Watch the eight, together with the point of courage and all the potential that is available *within* you.

End of visualization

I acknowledge you for your courage, for being here and trying to grow as a person, for trying to overcome yourself, for the efforts you do, for not giving up. The mere fact of your doing this exercise is a testimony to your inner strength and of your not giving up. I also want *you* to acknowledge yourself for your courage, for not giving up. And I want you to thank life for the challenges it brings you, for the many opportunities it brings you every day, so through them you can become in touch with your strengths, to grow and also to contribute to the world, to give to the world around you the gifts of your real self.

7. RE-PATTERNING: EXERCISES FOR FILTER FLEXING AND INTEGRATION

Learning to relax

Threes on autopilot tend to overwhelm themselves with work. Fear may arise if they allow themselves to be unproductive for even short periods of time. It is not uncommon to see Threes coming to coaching burned out after years of driving themselves too hard. Using their connecting arrow to healthy Nines, Threes learn the value of flowing with life, independently of their actions and achievements, and any external validation they presently seek. It allows their machine to cool down and recharge for the next round in their typically busy life.

The value of commitment

Another underdeveloped muscle in their super-busy life is the Three's lack of ability to commit to family and colleagues. Many Threes come to Coaching because of imbalances in these areas. Ambition and a relentless drive to achieve success may cause the Three to see a spouse, kids, their colleagues or friends as potential obstacles in the way to their success. Their career and work become the most important thing for them. Their connecting arrow to Six can help in this respect. The *together*, the *we*, needs to be developed.

Exercise for Type Three: Learning the value of commitment. Ask as a Six: How can I show loyalty to my family today? How can I commit more? Do I have scheduled one-on-one times with my spouse or kids during the week (with cell phones off)? And at work, ask them to ask: What can I do at my job to make every member feel he or she is a valuable member of the team? How can we synergize together?

Paying attention to the speaking style

Language is powerful: it's the vehicle that transports meaning. When we interpret reality through our filters, we put words to it. Therefore, if we are able to change the words that we attach to our experiences, we can indirectly impact our emotional states, since a big percentage of our emotions comes from our language. People are hypnotized by their own language patterns, creating blind spots that don't allow them to see reality accurately (Robbins and Madanes, 2005). By always using the same phrases and words to describe their experience, each personality type ends by not seeing what's in front of it. Literally, the description of reality becomes the *actual* reality. Those phrases and words are simply a manifestation of the underlying limiting beliefs that each type holds. Changing the speaking style can thus help us expand our frames of reference, allowing us to see the situations in our daily lives from many more angles.

It is important for coachees to develop the ability to become aware of when their personality mechanisms hijack their language, when it is occurring. For Type Threes in the Stuckness Zone, this manifests in a confident discursive style that contains self-promotion, competitiveness, or put-downs (direct or indirect in the form of "jokes.")

Exercise for Type Three: Flexing the discursive style. Pay attention to the conversation topics and format: Am I using words and phrases to carefully cause an effect, to create a good impression? Am I playing roles, falsifying my emotions in this conversation? Am I talking too much about my work? About my career, credentials, and achievements? Do I feel uncomfortable when others mention their achievements and engage in a competitive dialog trying to best them?

Work with the Jungian preferences: integrating our less-dominant qualities

When coaching a Type Three, it is very important to pay attention to his or her Jungian preferences. If a coachee has done an MBTI profile, ask for his or her four-letter type and discuss how Jungian preferences may play together with the coachee's Enneatype. Also, when clients get stuck in the lower side of their Jungian preference, we can use the same pattern interruption techniques described all through this book to help them shift out and grow. For a description of the Jungian preferences, please refer to Part I of this book.

Some examples of the usage of the Jungian preferences in coaching a Type Three:

- The whole Feeling dimension in the MBTI is very illustrative for some development goals of Threes. Talk about it in your coaching sessions. Mention the importance of learning to watch and perceive the world from this angle: learning to recognize the personal needs of others; being receptive and learning to listen empathically to others; interacting in a more personal way instead of being business-like in excess; when making decisions, taking into account what impact the decisions will have on people.
- Another dimension that is very useful for some development goals of Threes is Perceiving. Here too, mention the importance of learning to watch the world from this angle: developing the ability to find pleasure in just processing, instead of obsessing with the achievement of the final results and the ability to be spontaneous and flexible when needed. Threes in the Stuckness Zone may go too fast, too mechanically in the direction of their next target, while having zero tolerance for anybody who happens to be in their way. Threes need to develop the ability in some areas of life to relax and feel comfortable, leaving a couple of things open and still unachieved.

Between-Sessions Exercise for Type Three: self-observation

During the week, actively engage in self-observing a particularly unhelpful pattern of your type. When you become aware of your patterns in real time, begin a spontaneous, one-cycle breath meditation. Follow the sequence described in Part II for observing the pattern and slowing it down. Share your insights with your coach in your next session.

TYPE FOUR
THE INDIVIDUALIST

FOURS

People are sometimes surprised by the speed with which my **mood** can swing. They tell me I am too **sensitive**, that I make people "walk on eggshells." I don't **feel** understood, listened to until the end. Yes, right, I have a bigger need to express my **feelings** than any other person I know. But that's because I experience things in a deeper way. I sometimes feel on an **emotional** rollercoaster. Since a very young age I have been told that I make a **drama** out of everything. To tell the truth, I prefer the drama, and to not live in a routine. Routine, the **ordinary**, feels like **death**. In the extremes, at the poles, it's much more attractive. I find daily life and ordinary people boring. I prefer the **special**, art, theater, films, music. The **imagined**, the **utopic**, the unexpected, the mysterious, the **unachievable**...(Tina, Type Four.)

Description of Type Four

Fours are introspective, emotionally profound people who can be original, creative, and imaginative.

At their best, they are the masters of introspection, emotionally skillful in understanding their own feelings and the complexity of their inner life. But they are also the masters of empathic listening; thus they are able to understand not only their own but other people's inner lives, needs, and suffering. They are tolerant of other people's moods and can offer compassionate and sensitive advice.

They can comprehend and know emotionally what another is experiencing and are able to take the other's perspective; they are able to spontaneously understand the other's internal frame of reference, *as if* the Four were the other person (without ever losing the "as if" condition, that is: they can sense the hurt or the pleasure of another as he senses it, but without ever losing the recognition that it is *as if* the Four were hurt or pleased). Their affective response is appropriate to what the other person needs to really be helped, and they listen more than they speak. Their empathy is empowering; they can show you how deep you are, how special you are. It is not debilitating sympathy or feeling sorry or having pity for the other. They are never drained from this kind of empathy; the opposite is true. Their growth is based not only on self-actualization, but also on their empathic contribution to others. This balance between their inner and outer focus makes them very consistent and adds stability and an element of objectivity to their lives.

They are perceptive and have emotional depth; they are warm, insightful, conscious, affirming, nurturing, and encouraging.

They are contemplative, reflective people interested in philosophy, spirituality, and the meaning and mysteries of life and existence. They look for answers to questions such as: What is life all about? Why are we here? Who am I? What is the meaning of it all? What is the reason to live? They take life as a journey and try to patiently find the answers to these questions with an open mind and heart.

They have a creative orientation and a very rich imagination. They have the ability to express and articulate themselves well, being creative, eloquent, and fluent in their use of words and metaphors. They can also express themselves through art. Their imagination allows them to arrange symbols in a way that they become a vehicle to communicate powerful emotions. They are refined and are drawn to aesthetics and know how to engage other people's aesthetic sensibilities. Although many Fours are artists, not all are, but most know how to use their imagination and skills in the creation of aesthetic objects, environments, or experiences, whatever their occupation.

They are creative but grounded. Imaginative but practical. They can embrace and accept the mundane and the ordinary as a part of life and remain creative within whatever mood they may be in, not exclusively in dark moods but also in stable or positive ones.

They are original and usually have new ways of seeing things, and they make distinct, unique contributions in whatever they do. They value sincerity and authenticity.

In the Stuckness Zone, an internal voice starts running inside them that focuses on what's missing or unavailable to them. This has an effect on both their relationship with themselves and their relationships with others and life in general.

In their relationship with themselves, they move from introspection to self-absorption, focusing mainly on their intense inner world, and they become preoccupied with their own emotions and life. They become moody, with rapid or even extreme changes in mood. They may alternate between persistent feelings of sadness, melancholy, and lack of motivation on one hand, and elevated energy levels on the other. They may become overwhelmed by their own feelings of incompletion, regret, and hopelessness. Their once healthy search for meaning is interrupted, and they may use their imagination to replace that search with fantasy and unrealistic ideals. Through their imagination they can live in an idealized past or in an idealized future. In the present moment they focus on the "half-empty glass." They become tragic, pessimistic, and negative. Their focus is on what they don't have or can't be, and on what others do have and are. Thus, feelings of envy may develop from that habit of comparing themselves to others. They may also become critical and judgmental towards the "half-full glass," that is, the things that they *do* have in life. Instead of insightfully *being* with their own feelings, they overreact emotionally to the story they themselves created. They may feel their emotions are unmanageable, they may wallow in self-reproach and shame, and become disillusioned, disheartened, and hypersensitive to criticism.

In their relationship with others, Fours want to find love and meaning through a deeply fulfilling relationship, but may unconsciously get caught in a search for their "ideal love." They may project ideal qualities onto others and relate with them through their imaginations. This intensifies their emotions and adds drama to their lives, since they maintain themselves in a state of longing, desiring the unattainable. If the relationship (or whatever they want to achieve) becomes a reality, they may withdraw and reject it, in order to long for it again and reintensify their emotions once again (or be looked after by the other party).

Feelings of specialness and a desire to be seen as special and unique arise, as if they were different from "normal" people. This can cause a sense of entitlement and elitism, as if they were exempt from the mundane obligations and tasks most people have. They may also make others feel they lack depth and substance, that they are flat, ordinary, unfashionable, or lack stylishness.

COACHING PROTOCOL FOR TYPE FOUR

1. SET THE CLIMATE OF THE SESSION

Before you begin your coaching session with your client, check yourself:

Bring acceptance to the session
Ask yourself:
- Am I in a non-judgmental state?
- Does my specific personality type have any resistance with Type Four?

"Turn on" your multimodal listening
It is extremely important that you use all the centers of intelligence (Head, Heart, Gut) during every coaching session. Be aware of "listening" actively with all three centers.

Listen with your Head center
- Pay attention to speaking style and language use.
- Analyze body language and posture.
- Analyze patterns and possibilities for interrupting them.

Listen with your Heart center
- Empathize.
- See the client as a human being, not as a "type."
- Look beyond the facade.
- Connect, in spite of any resistance that you may have. You are here to help the client grow.

Listen with your Gut center
- What kind of energy is the client bringing to the session?
- Is there a match between what the client says and the energy with which he or she says it?
- What does your intuition tell you regarding the last developments in this coaching process?
- "Listen to what people say but pay attention to what they *do*." (Madanes, 1995).

2. DEFINE THE CHALLENGE

Determine what the client wants to work on, what is the purpose of his or her pursuing coaching.
Typical challenges for Fours include:
- To reduce the suffering they cause in themselves by relentlessly focusing on the negative parts of their experience.
- To be creative and yet able to be fully functional in their daily life, to make things happen and give the world the gift of their creativity.
- To be able to enjoy the present moment and the gifts of life.
- To reclaim their emotional wisdom in order to be able to respond instead of react, so they can fully explore their inner richness and contribute to others' emotional well-being as well.

3. UNDERSTAND THE COACHEE'S MODEL OF THE WORLD AND HIS OR HER STUCKNESS ZONE

Ask yourself the following questions: Why is the client acting the way he does? What is shaping her behavior? What is his internal story? What are the filters through which she looks at and perceives the world? To what extent are the type fixations active and operative in this client?

When Type Fours are less aware or under stress, their attention gets hijacked/derailed by a voice that starts running inside focusing on what's missing or unavailable. This has an effect on both Fours' relationship with themselves and their relationships with others and life in general.

Visualize potential

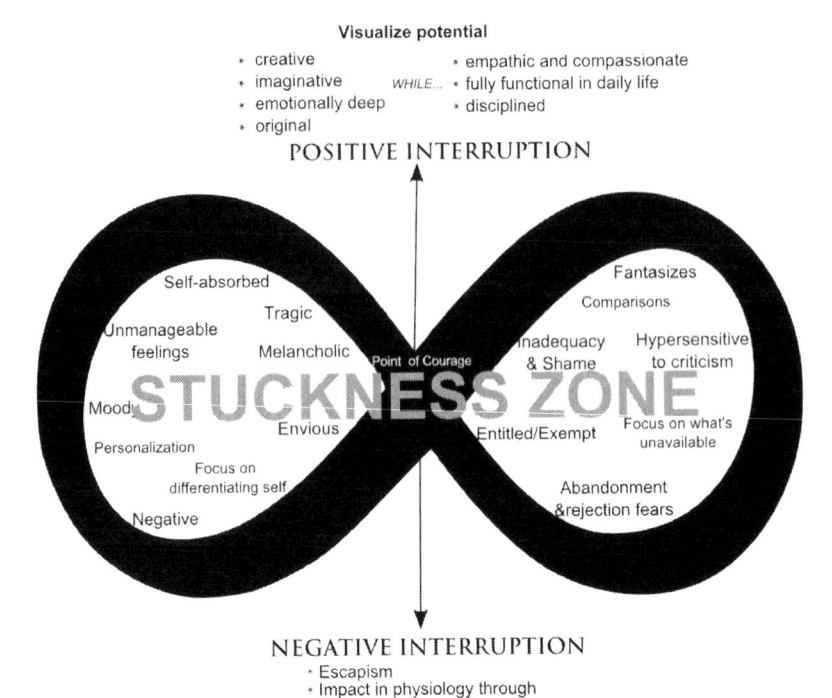

- creative
- imaginative
- emotionally deep
- original

WHILE...

- empathic and compassionate
- fully functional in daily life
- disciplined

POSITIVE INTERRUPTION

STUCKNESS ZONE

- Self-absorbed
- Tragic
- Unmanageable feelings
- Melancholic
- Moody
- Envious
- Personalization
- Focus on differentiating self
- Negative
- Point of Courage
- Fantasizes
- Comparisons
- Inadequacy & Shame
- Hypersensitive to criticism
- Entitled/Exempt
- Focus on what's unavailable
- Abandonment & rejection fears

NEGATIVE INTERRUPTION

- Escapism
- Impact in physiology through food &/or substances
- Other unproductive or destructive behavior

4. BRING AWARENESS TO THE SIX HUMAN NEEDS

According to Human Needs Psychology, we all have six basic human needs (Madanes, 2009): Certainty, Variety, Love/Connection, Significance, Growth, and Contribution. These needs are not merely desires, but true drivers mobilizing our behavior.

Exercise for Type Four: The six human needs. Look at the Stuckness Zone and from the whole range of behaviors there described, pick the most frequent ones: "What human needs are you trying to fulfill by engaging in these behaviors?"

Please score each need from 0 to 10.

Certainty. Does engaging in these behaviors make you feel certain? Give you a sense of security? Apart from these behaviors: Do you also know how to obtain certainty in a more positive way?

Variety. Does engaging in these behaviors bring you a sense of variety?

Apart from these behaviors: Do you also know how to obtain variety in a more positive way?

Love/connection. Does engaging in these behaviors make you feel connected to others? Experience a sense of love?
Apart from these behaviors: Do you also know how to obtain love/connection in a more positive way?

Significance. Does engaging in these behaviors make you feel important? Special? Apart from these behaviors: Do you also know how to obtain significance in a more positive way?

Growth. Does engaging in these behaviors give you a sense of development, make you feel that you're growing? Apart from these behaviors: Do you also know how to obtain growth in a more positive way?

Contribution. Does engaging in these behaviors give you a sense of going beyond your own needs, of giving to others? Apart from these behaviors: Do you also know how to obtain contribution in a more positive way?

Coaching case study. Take as an example Martha, one of our coachees, a Type Four, a book editor and copywriter. She came to coaching with a depressed mood but willing to work on her feelings of inadequacy and feeling different from most people. According to her, all these behaviors fulfill three of her human needs: Significance, Love/Connection, and Certainty. Martha is in the Stuckness Zone and all three needs are fulfilled in mostly negative ways. The first one, Significance, is fulfilled because she feels she is deeper than other people. She feels special. Her depressive mood is a way to Connect to herself, thus fulfilling the human need of Love/Connection. Her melancholic and depressive mood is also a place to which she has become accustomed to go, where a sense of Certainty is attained, a kind of "better the devil you know." When she keeps herself both depressed and having feelings of inadequacy, she also feels Certainty about her creativity: both emotions (depression and inadequacy) are perceived by her as necessary to guarantee a creative state. Many Fours in the Stuckness Zone hold this belief.

Martha came to coaching with persistent feelings of hopelessness and with great marital problems that were caused by her emotional instability. She understood the fact that keeping her negative habits in order to satisfy these three human needs was having a high cost in her life and relationships. The breakthrough for her came when she became aware of the necessity of meeting her human needs in more positive and constructive ways. We worked on overcoming the feelings of inadequacy by gradually helping Martha recover a fully functional daily life. Incorporating order and structure was not easy, but it brought rewards, and pretty quickly. Martha had great insights during that period. She described how her type had previously "convinced" her to keep herself depressed, only to get an *illusion* of creativity. She now felt self-actualized, and became a nurturing and affirming resource to her environment. Her marriage was revitalized (Love/Connection) and her creativity was expressed in her writings (Significance.) This way, incorporating structure and a healthy routine (Certainty) served to fulfill all three needs in a positive way.

One important point to take into account: pay special attention to the needs of Growth and Contribution. Does the coachee meet these needs in healthy or in destructive ways?

As we integrate our personality, the needs of Growth and Contribution begin receiving high scores while also being met in positive and healthy ways. The reason for this is that when we move out of our Stuckness Zone, we act from new, conscious, chosen responses. This allows us to overcome our old habits and grow. This integration, in turn, always will bring greater contribution to others. In contrast, if we continue acting without awareness, out of our old patterns of reaction, we disempower ourselves and let our egos manage our lives. This always causes suffering to ourselves and to others.

5. PRODUCE LEVERAGE

The next step is to gain leverage by bringing awareness to the costs and suffering that the unhelpful patterns of the type are causing for the client.

Exercise for Type Four: Gaining awareness of the costs of patterns

- How much does it cost you, in terms of your relationships, to be self-absorbed and dramatic?
- How much does it cost you, in terms of your health, to have extreme mood swings most of the time?
- How much does it cost you, in terms of your professional career, to feel inadequate and be hypersensitive to criticism?
- How much does it cost you, in terms of your personal fulfillment

and own sense of happiness, to constantly focus on what's missing and unavailable?

6. PATTERN INTERRUPTION: BUILDING OUR ATTENTIONAL MUSCLES

TYPE FOUR VISUALIZATION

Visualizations are a great tool for coaching in general and when doing personality-types coaching in particular. The following is a comprehensive visualization/meditation script for Type Four. It encompasses working with the type's strengths and weaknesses, training attentional abilities through the Impartial Spectator, training conscious breathing, acceptance, and relaxation. In a single coaching session, you don't have to use them all. You can use these visualizations modularly, by selecting one or more of the sections that follow.

Script for Type Four: Visualization/Meditation

Relaxation

Begin by finding a comfortable sitting position. Keep your spine straight in a natural way. Let your arms become loose. Lightly, with palms facing up or down, rest your hands on your lap. Take one deep breath, to begin relaxing your whole body. Inhale...Exhale... You can gently close your eyes and take another deep breath as a way to become centered and focused. Inhale...Exhale...

Training the Impartial Spectator

Let's begin by bringing awareness to the Impartial Spectator. Think of the Impartial Spectator as your friend who objectively watches your behavior from the outside. It helps you make wise decisions and allows you to regulate your automatic pilot.

The Impartial Spectator will do so by training your mind to be sensitive to the activity in your three centers of intelligence: the Body (our physical sensations), the Mind (thoughts, plans, future, past, images, ideas, imagination), and the Heart (feelings). Our breath, which symbolically represents our connection to our soul, will allow us to remain centered and to shift our attention from one center to the other. It will also help us to remain non-judgmental and to bring the qualities of gratitude, compassion, and acceptance to this exercise. Every time your mind wanders, you can use the moment to exercise those qualities of gratitude, compassion, and acceptance—for each one of those moments offers the opportunity to learn how to reorient our attention.

Begin by gently shifting your attention to your **Body** center of intelligence. Take a deep breath, and follow the path of the air in and out of the body. Do it slowly. Inhale again. . . and this time make the exhalation last a bit longer. Place your full attention on the path of the air getting in and out of your body, from beginning to end. Begin noticing your body sensations. Sense the contact points between your feet and the floor. What body sensations are in there right now? Move your attention to your back. Feel the support that the chair gives you. Stay with that sensation for a moment. Shift your attention to your hands. Focus on the contact point between the hands and your lap.

Place your hands over your chest, one over the other, and shift your attention to your **Heart** center of intelligence. What feelings do you have in this moment?

Now shift your attention to the **Head** center of intelligence. Is there a mental commentary about your feelings? Is there judgment or acceptance of your feelings? What is your mind saying about your feelings? What is it saying about this whole exercise? Serenely watch your mental discourse as it appears. Inhale. . .Exhale. . . Stay in the Head center, and now shift your attention to your memories. Imagine yourself watching an old black-and-white TV set on which your past history is being broadcast. You see yourself in the TV. Your life videotaped. Each stage of your life, on the screen, in slow motion. Nod when you actually see it. Inhale. . .Exhale. . . Still in the Head center, now move your attention to the future. Serenely reflect on each one of the following questions. Take a few moments as a pause between each question. What do you want your future to be like? How do you see yourself in the future? What plans do you have?

Visualization

Remain in the Head center, and you will now shift your attention to your imagination. Imagine yourself at the beach, at the sea shore, in slightly wet sand. Breath the air at the beach. Inhale. . .Exhale. . . Feel the wind. Listen to the waves in the sea. Feel the sand on your feet. Imagine yourself drawing an imaginary number eight, drawn horizontally, like the infinity symbol, in the slightly wet sand on the shore. Draw it slowwwly. Feel the contact point between your fingers and the sand.

Visualization of Stuckness Zone and costs

Now picture yourself putting all your problems and challenges *inside* that eight in the sand. One by one.

All my continuous attention to what's unavailable, to what's missing. All my feelings of shame and inadequacy. All my excessive occupation with myself, my self-absorption. My enslavement to trying to be special and different all the time; my letting my life pass by while focusing on what I don't have. All my fantasies and not being able to live in the present moment; all my self-inflicted pain due to my constant comparing of myself to others; all the envy. All the sadness. All the suffering.

Feel the sadness and anger. Feel it in your heart and in your body as you see all the issues inside the eight in the sand. Stay there for a moment.

This eight in the sand represents our Stuckness Zone. The place we get stuck with negative focus and negative feelings.

"It's human" section

Every human being has issues that make him or her precisely that, human. It's a personal, tailor-made set of challenges in life. Watch your own personal challenges without judgments. If your mind passes a commentary, it's OK. Don't worry and try to do this exercise "right." If there is a judgment, just watch the judgment. Listen to its script. Watch it as it occurs, outside of you.

It's human to have judgments about our experience. It's OK. Bring your attention to your heart. Now, grab the judgments you just heard in your head, the mental comments, and put them there, in your heart. Use the energy of your heart to soften them and feel how it fills your whole body with compassion. Take a deep breath, and feel the energy of your heart throughout your whole body. Feel the acceptance.

Why does life bring you challenges? Life brings you challenges so you can overcome them, and allow the next level of plenitude and vitality to become available to you. They are precious opportunities to grow. Precious opportunities to discover the strengths *you already have* that simply need to be reactivated. The strengths that will help you overcome your challenges, the strengths that will help you move from stuckness to growth.

Inside of you there is a part that doesn't want to give up. That wants to live life at its fullest. It's the voice of your soul. The voice that wants to stand up to the voices of the ego and the personality—and become the best possible you. You've been there before, and that's what brought you up to this moment. This moment in which you are here struggling to become the best person you can be, standing up and not giving up to your personality, to your automatic thoughts. It's the real you, it's the strength of your soul.

At this point your attention may automatically go to create thoughts about your thoughts. It's OK. Simply keep breathing consciously, following the path of the air in and out of your body, and let your Impartial Spectator witness the activity of your mind non-judgmentally.

Visualization of strengths, potential, and personal power

Now please move your attention to that part of yourself that doesn't want to give up. Look at the drawing on the sand: exactly in the center of the eight there is a point: the intersection between the right side and the left side of the eight. Let's call it the *point of courage*. From that point, imagine yourself drawing an arrow up. An exit from the eight. An exit from the stuckness.

This arrow points to what is available outside the eight. This arrow points to your strengths and to your potential. To the future that is available to you in any given moment.

Let's see what's outside the eight.

I want you to think of any moment in the past in which you really felt loved, in which you felt acceptance for yourself and others. It can be any moment in which you felt nothing was missing. Bring it from any area of your life: you could have been by yourself, with a friend, with a group of friends, or with your family. In your personal or your professional life. Go to the past and bring back that moment. It could be a special moment or just a simple one. Feel it. Feel the relaxation of that moment in your whole body.

Search your memories for that moment in which you were acceptant. Conscious. Affirming of yourself and others. Insightful. Spiritual. Feel the relaxation of that moment, in which you let go of trying to differentiate yourself. Everything flowed harmoniously and everything actually worked well and turned out well, without your intervention. Take a deep breath and feel that moment.

Let's see what else is outside the eight.

I now want you to envision yourself in a new future. A future in which you are creative, original and emotionally deep, but also serene. A future in which you know and self-actualize yourself and nurture and affirm others as well. In which you accept yourself as a human being, including some less positive aspects. In which you are truly in touch with your heart, and can forgive yourself and others for the mistakes human beings naturally make. Please put your hands one over the other, and over your heart. Feel your heartbeat. Feel your humanity. Since you are human, you are allowed to be non-original, non-creative, and doing mundane things from time to time. This allows you to recharge your batteries and become more original than when you drive yourself to emotional exhaustion. Your realism makes you deeper, and your heart dissolves the anger, so plenty of energy gets liberated for creativity. Feel how much energy gets liberated from that, how much sadness and anger gets dissolved. Paradoxically, since you let go of your attachment to a special identity as a cover to your real self, you fulfill one of your true dreams: the one of truly growing as a meaningful and truly unique human being.

Bring that moment from the future, and feel it in your body, in the present moment. Feel it in your heart and in your mind. Feel the power of your mind, heart, and body working together and see what you can achieve, and most important: how all that is inside of you now and you *already* are the good person you always wanted to be.

Let's gently finish the meditation by slowly going back and watching the whole drawing in the sand.

Watch the eight, together with the point of courage and all the potential that is available *within* you.

End of visualization

I acknowledge you for your courage, for being here and trying to grow as a person, for trying to overcome yourself, for the efforts you do, for not giving up. The mere fact of your doing this exercise is a testimony to your inner strength and of your not giving up. I also want *you* to acknowledge yourself for your courage, for not giving up. And I want you to thank life for the challenges it brings you, for the many opportunities it brings you every day, so through them you can become in touch with your strengths, to grow and also to contribute to the world, to give to the world around you the gifts of your real self.

7. RE-PATTERNING: EXERCISES FOR FILTER FLEXING AND INTEGRATION

Personalization Filter

"Personalization" is a cognitive distorting filter that may typically dominate Type Fours' thinking in the Stuckness Zone. It's a "jumping to conclusions" kind of filter. This filter causes Fours to interpret events happening around them as being always related to them. Anything happening around them is picked up and automatically personalized. For example, if their spouse tells them they don't feel like going out tonight, they may interpret that as: "My spouse doesn't love me anymore." Immediately after the activation of this distorting filter always comes an emotional reaction. Much of the suffering of Type Four is caused by this mechanism.

In order to overcome this automatic tendency, Fours can incorporate the qualities of highly functioning Ones: the ability to be grounded, realistic, to view an event "as is," without imagination attached to it.

Exercise for Type Four: ask "what" and "how" questions
- If you rely on your senses more than your imagination, what do you see? How can you re-interpret the situation?
- What are the concrete facts?
- My imagination is very rich but sometimes it doesn't serve me. The opposite seem to be true. Looks like I am at the service of my own imagination. So let's be practical: How can I simplify this situation into a black-and-white one, simple to understand, straightforward, uncomplex, so I can put some order in my head and in my heart?

Finding the good

Four's attentional focus tends to go to the unattainable and to what is missing. Through fantasy, this filter is a vehicle to escape from the present moment to the past or the future, leaving Fours miserable in the present. As a consequence, finding the good in people, events, or in themselves is usually an underdeveloped muscle in Fours in the Stuckness Zone.

Exercise for Type Four: Finding the good. Actively look for the good in everything around you during one week. It can all be written in a two column table: Column A will have all that comes under your radar that is perceived as negative. Column B will have everything that is going well in your life right now. To stretch it even further, it is possible to add a third column: How can I celebrate an item in column B (pick one and concentrate on its value and how you can manifest your appreciation and joy for having that.)

Paying attention to the speaking style

Language is powerful: it's the vehicle that transports meaning. When we interpret reality through our filters, we put words to it. Therefore, if we are able to change the words that we attach to our experiences, we can indirectly impact our emotional states, since a big percentage of our emotions comes from our language. People are hypnotized by their own language patterns, creating blind spots that don't allow them to see reality accurately (Robbins and Madanes, 2005). By always using the same phrases and words to describe their experience, each personality type ends by not seeing what's in front of it. Literally, the description of reality becomes the *actual* reality. Those phrases and words are simply a manifestation of the underlying limiting beliefs that each type holds. Changing the speaking style can thus help us expand our frames of reference, allowing us to see the situations in our daily lives from many more angles.

It is important for coachees to develop the ability to become aware of when their personality mechanisms hijack their language, at the moment it occurs. For Type Fours in the Stuckness Zone, this manifests in the following: 1. A discursive style that reflects self-absorption. 2. The inability to be factual and to communicate without interpretations. 3. The overuse of metaphorical language.

Exercise for Type Four: Flexing the discursive style #1 Pay attention to the conversation topics and format. What percentage of the time have I talked about myself? Am I being excessively self-involved? When the other person was talking, did I find points in the other's narrative from which I managed to make the conversation return back about myself again? Am I truly interested in the emotional needs of the other person, or just about sharing mine?

Another important issue in Fours' communicating style is separating facts from interpretation. When in the Stuckness Zone, their imagination filter is very active and they have difficulty adhering to mere facts without attaching an interpretation to those facts. Inside them, there is usually a subjective rearrangement of the facts.

Exercise for Type Four: Flexing the discursive style #2 Train yourself to ask: What happened? What are the facts? What's my interpretation of what happened? What's the story I am telling myself about what happened? Am I conscious of how my imagination works and what it says about objective events, or is it automatic and I am unaware of its mechanisms and dynamics?

Lastly, Fours are very good at using metaphorical language, but in the Stuckness Zone they overuse it. When integrating in Type One, they learn how to be straightforward in their communication: being factual and detail-oriented; being more action than philosophically oriented; using less colorful language and being more literal; instead of asking *why* questions, asking *what, how, will it work,* and *what has been done* questions.

Work with the Jungian preferences: Integrating our less-dominant qualities

When coaching a Type Four, it is very important to pay attention to his or her Jungian preferences. If a coachee has done an MBTI profile, ask for his or her four-letter type and discuss how Jungian preferences may play together with the coachee's Enneatype. Also, when clients get stuck in the lower side of their Jungian preference, we can use the same pattern interruption techniques described all through this book to help them shift out and grow. For a description of the Jungian preferences, please refer to Part I of this book.

Some examples of the usage of the Jungian preferences in coaching a Type Four:

- Although you'll find many Extraverted, social Fours, there is a high correlation between being a Four and Introversion (especially in the Fours with a Five wing). Take this into account, especially if you are an Extraverted coach. Slow your pace to match theirs. Introverts tend to be quieter and private. They are intimate and reflective, needing more space and time to think about what's being said in the sessions. With them you'll have less eye contact and the sessions will move slowly, so don't overwhelm them with too much or too fast talking. Match their pace by taking a deep breath from time to time, while deeply reflecting on what the Four coachee is saying and feeling.

- A dimension that is very useful for some development goals of Fours is Thinking. Here too, mention the importance of learning to watch the world from this angle: developing the ability to analyze situations in an impersonal manner; learning to make decisions logically; weighing costs against expected benefits when taking action; asking logical questions and remaining task centered; analyzing cause and effect. All this is crucial in the development of Fours, since they have a clear Jungian preference for Feeling.
- Another dimension that is very useful for some development goals of Fours is Sensing. Here too, mention the importance of learning to perceive the world *also* from this angle: being realistic and concrete; developing the ability to be practical, to channel what they feel into practical applications, to pause their imagination for a moment and look at things as they are; developing a need for clarity; considering good ideas that may seem non-original or non-creative to them instead of ruling them out automatically; being specific in their communication—asking specific questions, giving specific answers, communicating facts without interpretation. This work is easier with Fours who have a strong arrow to One.
- Pay attention to how active the Judging preference is in the Four coachee. The degree of operativeness of a healthy Judging dimension may indicate the degree of integration of the Four in Type One. Ask: Do you seek closure in your projects? Do you value structure and order? Can you responsibly attach to a schedule and a time frame? In the Stuckness Zone each of these questions is experienced by Fours as a limitation to creativity and there is much resistance to it. Paradoxically, when they are able to incorporate this element into their emotional arsenal, their creativity flourishes even more and reaches new heights—

something every Four wishes for and enjoys. Many famous Fours —musicians, writers, entrepreneurs, or whatever their occupation may be—are quite disciplined and achieve their healthiest state when incorporating a healthy measure of the J dimension into their lives.

Between-Sessions Exercise for Type Four: Self-observation
During the week, actively engage in self-observing a particularly unhelpful pattern of your type. When you become aware of your patterns in real time, begin a spontaneous, one-cycle breath meditation. Follow the sequence described in Part II for observing the pattern and slowing it down. Share your insights with your coach in your next session.

TYPE FIVE
THE INVESTIGATOR

FIVES

I've always enjoyed being by myself, spending time **alone**. Have not really enjoyed social gatherings. I've felt out of the picture, **observing** as a **spectator** from the side. Somehow, I can't **understand** most people; I see them busy with little and insignificant things. Talking about **irrelevant** things. I am not interested in that; I prefer a good book, something that is worth the investment of my **resources**. And being interrupted, intruded upon, that really bothers me a lot. I am very sensitive to **intrusions** into my **personal space**. At home I've been told I'm too isolated, that I get into the "cave" too often. That's actually true. I must **withdraw** from time to time to **recharge** my batteries. Especially after social events, after which I usually feel **drained**. The people around me appreciate my talents, in particular my **analytical** skills. But I've heard also that I'm **cold**, emotionally **unexpressive**. My boss also tells me I must get into action more quickly, instead of compulsively trying to always learn and **gather loads of preparatory materials**. The thing is, I actually really enjoy **learning**, challenging my **intellectual** abilities. (John, Type Five.)

Description of Type Five

Fives are perceptive and independent observers who have a predominantly cerebral approach to life.

At their best, they have a constant need to learn and expand their intellects. They are people motivated by the need to understand the world around them. They are stimulated by ideas and have strong analytical skills. They are perceptive, bright, logical; have the ability to concentrate; are innovative, scholarly, knowledgeable, nonconforming, and competent. They are the masters of observation and analysis. They have a perceptive eye and a strong, independent will, free from influence, that allows them to keep their distance and have a good, objective perspective on any problem. They are insightful, original thinkers who are great at formulating explanations, models, and theories in any area they may be interested in.

But their observational and analytical abilities don't convert them into passive observers who live in their heads and are emotionally distant from other people. They know how to convert their cerebral abilities and plans into action, and know how to "be in the arena," to act and live in the world like everybody else. Although private and usually introverted, with a preference for some quiet time alone every day and sometimes a low-key presence, they are socially engaged and connected to the world and have good social skills. Thus, they are not only observers but initiators and contributors. Although mainly stimulated by ideas and mental activities, they are also in touch with their feelings and their bodies, and know how to express their emotional side.

They are quietly strong; they are reflective and like to think before acting in order to take sensible action with good criteria. Their emotional detachment gives them the ability to remain calm even in stressful circumstances, when others may panic. This doesn't mean emotional repression or avoidance of feelings of empathy. To the contrary: it is the ability to remain serene and detached from the worries and restlessness of the mind, and the ability to keep their distance from the situation in order to calmly approach it.

They can become experts in their fields, and their intellectual growth is accompanied by a humble, relaxed attitude: they don't feel compelled to show that they know everything about a subject, and allow themselves to answer "I don't know" without feeling bad about it. In addition, they can recognize the limits of logic and are not afraid of challenging it and their own thoughts and mental constructs. Paradoxically, this is when they grow the most intellectually, since these attitudes help in keeping them curious and open-minded to new learning and possibilities.

In the Stuckness Zone, their mental activity gets intensified. They get more absorbed in their thoughts. This "living in their heads" disconnects them from their emotions. They may become more cold, evasive, nonresponsive, unaware of how they themselves feel, less able to connect emotionally with others or give support. They prefer to keep people more at a distance. Their relationships may suffer since they become more easily overwhelmed and drained, and get more sensitive to expectations and demands from others and to intrusions on their privacy. Not only do they want to stay distant and prevent their resources (time, energy, their attention, knowledge, money, etc.) from being drained by others, they also want to keep their distance by not needing others. They try to be self reliant. If necessary, they will keep their problems to themselves or will minimize their own needs in order to maintain their independence.

They become more passive observers, and have more difficulties in taking action. Their mental commentary may get more intense, as if running non-stop, as if everything requires their interpretation and explanation, and they lose focus. Action gets delayed by more preparation, more learning. Some of them direct their attention exclusively to ideas and information. There is the feeling that there is always more to study, observe, and figure out before taking action.

The habit of constant mental interpretation can make them more subjective and less open-minded and curious. They may interpret more than they research or experiment. In addition, from the observer position, they can sometimes look with disdain at the illogical, the "stupid" ways of others, the manifestation of emotions, or social conventions. They can be perceived as acting superior and snobbish towards other people.

Their adherence to logic and reductionism may be extreme, without awareness of the fact that logic may also be biased, and at the expense of excluding the emotional and sensorial from their analysis. They become less willing to challenge their own thoughts and push for less complex explanations of reality.

The habit of living in their heads also disconnects them from their bodies. Less time is dedicated to the sensorial and the physical in life, and they can become more sedentary and less aware of their own bodies. When they move to live in their heads they can feel alienated, empty, inadequate, not centered, tense, preoccupied, overwhelmed, angry, and lonely.

COACHING PROTOCOL FOR TYPE FIVE

1. SET THE CLIMATE OF THE SESSION

Before you begin your coaching session with your client, check yourself:

Bring acceptance to the session
Ask yourself:
- Am I in a non-judgmental state?
- Does my specific personality type have any resistance with Type Five?

"Turn on" your multimodal listening
It is extremely important that you use all the centers of intelligence (Head, Heart, Gut) during every coaching session. Be aware of "listening" actively with all three centers.

Listen with your Head center
- Pay attention to speaking style and language use.
- Analyze body language and posture.
- Analyze patterns and possibilities for interrupting them.

Listen with your Heart center
- Empathize.
- See the client as a human being, not as a "type."
- Look beyond the facade.
- Connect, in spite of any resistance that you may have. You are here to help the client grow.

Listen with your Gut center
- What kind of energy is the client bringing to the session?
- Is there a match between what the client says and the energy with which he or she says it?
- What does your intuition tell you regarding the last developments in this coaching process?

- "Listen to what people say but pay attention to what they *do*." (Madanes, 1995).

2. DEFINE THE CHALLENGE

Determine what the client wants to work on, what is the purpose of his or her pursuing coaching.
Typical challenges for Fives include:
- To trust not only their minds but also their instincts and hearts, in order to become more competent and more knowledgeable.
- To become more relaxed in social matters and less drained by social exchanges.
- To be able to put their ideas into action.
- To become more aware of their feelings, to be able to healthily express them, and to be more in touch with their own hearts.
- To reconnect with their bodies and the present moment, in order to balance their tendency to get lost in the labyrinths of their own minds.

3. UNDERSTAND THE COACHEE'S MODEL OF THE WORLD AND HIS OR HER STUCKNESS ZONE

Ask yourself the following questions: Why is the client acting the way he does? What is shaping her behavior? What is his internal story? What are the filters through which she looks at and perceives the world? To what extent are the type fixations active and operative in this client?

When Type Fives are less aware or under stress, their attention gets hijacked/derailed by an intense and excessive mental activity. They get disconnected from their emotions through this sort of "living in their heads." In this state they usually begin keeping people at a distance, and isolate themselves. There is also a growing difficulty in taking action.

Visualize potential

- knowledgeable
- analytical
- perceptive
- inventive

WHILE...

- open-minded
- taking quick action
- emotionally connected
- initiating and contributing

POSITIVE INTERRUPTION

↑

STUCKNESS ZONE

- Disconnects from emotions and body
- Cold
- Non-stop mental commentary
- Passive observer
- Isolated
- Over-prepares
- Difficulty taking action
- Point of Courage
- Hypersensitive to expectations, demands, intrusions
- Reductionistic
- Easily overwhelmed
- Avaricious
- Cynical
- Loses focus
- Disdainful
- Mental overload
- Subjective, less investigative, less open-minded

↓

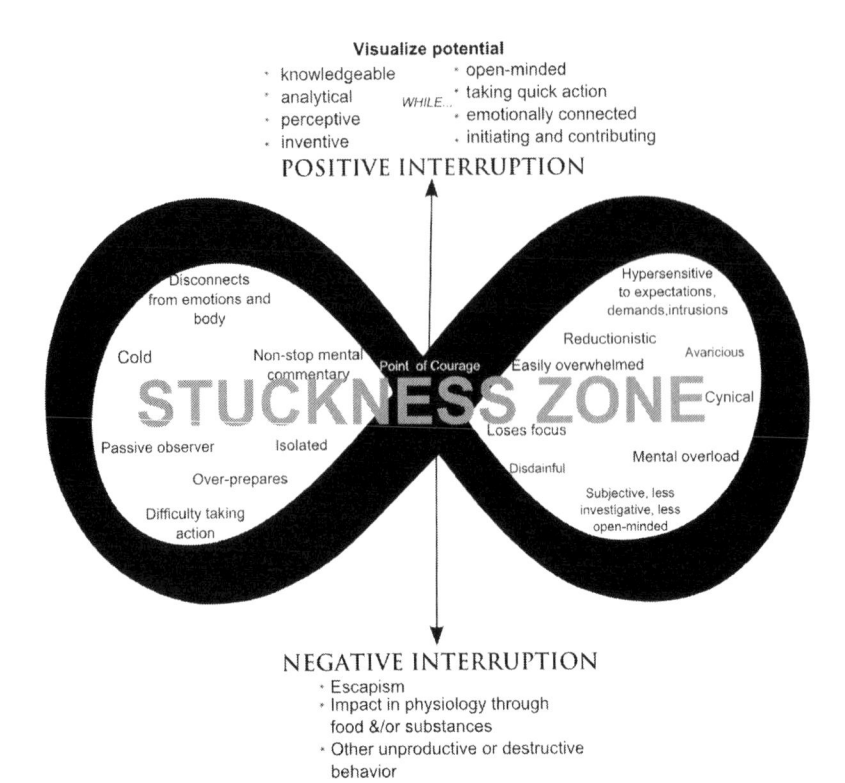

NEGATIVE INTERRUPTION
- Escapism
- Impact in physiology through food &/or substances
- Other unproductive or destructive behavior

4. BRING AWARENESS TO THE SIX HUMAN NEEDS

According to Human Needs Psychology, we all have six basic human needs (Madanes, 2009): Certainty, Variety, Love/Connection, Significance, Growth, and Contribution. These needs are not merely desires, but true drivers mobilizing our behavior.

Exercise for Type Five: The six human needs. Look at the Stuckness Zone and from the whole range of behaviors there described, pick the most frequent ones: "What human needs are you trying to fulfill by engaging in these behaviors?"

Please score each need from 0 to 10.

Certainty. Does engaging in these behaviors make you feel certain? Give you a sense of security? Apart from these behaviors: Do you also know how to obtain certainty in a more positive way?

Variety. Does engaging in these behaviors bring you a sense of variety?

Apart from these behaviors: Do you also know how to obtain variety in a more positive way?

Love/connection. Does engaging in these behaviors make you feel connected to others? Experience a sense of love?
Apart from these behaviors: Do you also know how to obtain love/connection in a more positive way?

Significance. Does engaging in these behaviors make you feel important? Special? Apart from these behaviors: Do you also know how to obtain significance in a more positive way?

Growth. Does engaging in these behaviors give you a sense of development, make you feel that you're growing? Apart from these behaviors: Do you also know how to obtain growth in a more positive way?

Contribution. Does engaging in these behaviors give you a sense of going beyond your own needs, of giving to others? Apart from these behaviors: Do you also know how to obtain contribution in a more positive way?

Coaching case study. Roberto, one of our coachees, a Type Five. He came to coaching to work on two challenges: the first, an intolerance for society in general that causes an inability to have a social life; the second, problems in his relationship due to lack of ability to express his deepest emotions.

According to him, each of these problems fulfills a different human need.

His social intolerance satisfies *Significance* in the following manner: very knowledgeable and academic, Roberto perceives the people around him as a "mass that are unable to think and reflect, that move all together as a group without the ability to think by themselves." When he perceives others this way, he has a sense of superiority. He distinguishes himself from the "mass" and observes it as an external observer and is proud to be a "freethinker." But this has turned him into a very isolated person.

On the other hand, his need for Certainty gets satisfied in the following way: Roberto believes that it isn't safe to manifest his emotions to others, even those closest to him. He prefers to protect his feelings and make sure he won't be hurt. Gaining Certainty in this negative way, his relationships got stuck.

The breakthrough came when Roberto realized he needed to satisfy his needs in a positive way. Roberto is a well-respected consumer behavior researcher, working in the marketing department of a big corporation. During our coaching sessions with him an idea came up that could fulfill his need for Significance in a positive way: since he has good writing abilities, why not share his talents with the world? Why not share with others his ability to see reality from a sociological perspective? Roberto began writing articles for a local newspaper, which became quite a success and brought him much recognition for his intellectual talents. We worked on how to inject compassion and tolerance into his views so his writings don't become ego-driven, Stuckness-Zone-like commentaries, but instead, the work of an intellectual contributing to the world to make it a better place. This helped him fulfill his need for Significance in a positive way.

On the other hand, he understood that, although it brought a sense of safety, his lack of emotional connection was having a big cost in his family relationships, especially with his wife, who has been very affected by this. Since this "muscle" was very untrained in Roberto, he slowly began to learn how to connect with his own feelings and safely express them. His wife participated in many sessions, and for her to know that her husband has a Type Five personality was a relief: she realized his behavior was not personal against her, or something that was "wrong," but just a part of her husband's type's challenges.

One important point to take into account: pay special attention to the needs of Growth and Contribution. Does the coachee meet these needs in healthy or in destructive ways?

As we integrate our personality, the needs of Growth and Contribution begin receiving high scores while also being met in positive and healthy ways. The reason for this is that when we move out of our Stuckness Zone, we act from new, conscious, chosen responses. This allows us to overcome our old habits and grow. This integration, in turn, always will bring greater contribution to others. In contrast, if we continue acting without awareness, out of our old patterns of reaction, we disempower ourselves and let our egos manage our lives. This always causes suffering to ourselves and to others.

5. PRODUCE LEVERAGE

The next step is to gain leverage by bringing awareness to the costs and suffering that the unhelpful patterns of the type are causing for the client.

Exercise for Type Five: Gaining awareness of the costs of patterns

- How much does it cost you, in terms of your relationships, to be cold, distant, and emotionally disconnected?
- How much does it cost you, in terms of your health, to "live in your head" and lack connection and awareness to your own body?
- How much does it cost you, in terms of your professional career, to overprepare and have difficulty putting your ideas into action?
- How much does it cost you, in terms of your personal fulfillment and own sense of happiness, to have a relentless mental commentary permanently activated and to disconnect yourself emotionally from other people?

6. PATTERN INTERRUPTION: BUILDING OUR ATTENTIONAL MUSCLES

TYPE FIVE VISUALIZATION

Visualizations are a great tool for coaching in general and when doing personality-types coaching in particular. The following is a comprehensive visualization/meditation script for Type Five. It encompasses working with the type's strengths and weaknesses, training attentional abilities through the Impartial Spectator, training conscious breathing, acceptance, and relaxation. In a single coaching session, you don't have to use them all. You can use these visualizations modularly, by selecting one or more of the sections that follow.

Script for Type Five: Visualization/Meditation

Relaxation

Begin by finding a comfortable sitting position. Keep your spine straight in a natural way. Let your arms become loose. Lightly, with palms facing up or down, rest your hands on your lap. Take one deep breath, to begin relaxing your whole body. Inhale. . .Exhale. . . You can gently close your eyes and take another deep breath as a way to become centered and focused. Inhale. . .Exhale . . .

Training the Impartial Spectator

Let's begin by bringing awareness to the Impartial Spectator. Think of the

Impartial Spectator as your friend who objectively watches your behavior from the outside. It helps you make wise decisions and allows you to regulate your automatic pilot.

The Impartial Spectator will do so by training your mind to be sensitive to the activity in your three centers of intelligence: the Body (our physical sensations), the Mind (thoughts, plans, future, past, images, ideas, imagination), and the Heart (feelings). Our breath, which symbolically represents our connection to our soul, will allow us to remain centered and to shift our attention from one center to the other. It will also help us to remain non-judgmental and to bring the qualities of gratitude, compassion, and acceptance to this exercise. Every time your mind wanders, you can use the moment to exercise those qualities of gratitude, compassion, and acceptance—for each one of those moments offers the opportunity to learn how to reorient our attention.

Begin by gently shifting your attention to your **Body** center of intelligence. Take a deep breath, and follow the path of the air in and out of the body. Do it slowly. Inhale again. . . and this time make the exhalation last a bit longer. Place your full attention on the path of the air getting in and out of your body, from beginning to end. Begin noticing your body sensations. Sense the contact points between your feet and the floor. What body sensations are in there right now? Move your attention to your back. Feel the support that the chair gives you. Stay with that sensation for a moment. Shift your attention to your hands. Focus on the contact point between the hands and your lap.

Place your hands over your chest, one over the other, and shift your attention to your **Heart** center of intelligence. What feelings do you have in this moment?

Now shift your attention to the **Head** center of intelligence. Is there a mental commentary about your feelings? Is there judgment or acceptance of your feelings? What is your mind saying about your feelings? What is it saying about this whole exercise? Serenely watch your mental discourse as it appears. Inhale. . .Exhale. . . Stay in the Head center, and now shift your attention to your memories. Imagine yourself watching an old black-and-white TV set on which your past history is being broadcast. You see yourself in the TV. Your life videotaped. Each stage of your life, on the screen, in slow motion. Nod when you actually see it. Inhale. . .Exhale. . . Still in the Head center, now move your attention to the future. Serenely reflect on each one of the following questions. Take a few moments as a pause between each question. What do you want your future to be like? How do you see yourself in the future? What plans do you have?

Visualization

Remain in the Head center, and you will now shift your attention to your imagination. Imagine yourself at the beach, at the sea shore, in slightly wet sand. Breath the air at the beach. Inhale. . .Exhale. . . Feel the wind. Listen to the waves in the sea. Feel the sand on your feet. Imagine yourself drawing an imaginary number eight, drawn horizontally, like the infinity symbol, in the slightly wet sand on the shore. Draw it slowwwly. Feel the contact point between your fingers and the sand.

Visualization of Stuckness Zone and costs

Now picture yourself putting all your problems and challenges *inside* that eight in the sand. One by one.

All my continuous attention and hypersensitivity to others' demands and expectations. All my reactions to what I perceive as intrusions on my privacy. All my continuous mental commentary; the feeling of my thoughts getting out of control, going on and on and on. My being drained by my permanent avoidance of society. All the fears. All the tension. All the suffering.

Feel the tension and anger. Feel it in your belly as you see all the issues inside the eight in the sand. Feel the tension in your whole body. Stay there for a moment.

This eight in the sand represents our Stuckness Zone. The place we get stuck with negative focus and negative feelings.

"It's human" section

Every human being has issues that make him or her precisely that, human. It's a personal, tailor-made set of challenges in life. Watch your own personal challenges without judgments. If your mind passes a commentary, it's OK. Don't worry and try to do this exercise "right." If there is a judgment, just watch the judgment. Listen to its script. Watch it as it occurs, outside of you.

It's human to have judgments about our experience. It's OK. Bring your attention to your heart. Now, grab the judgments you just heard in your head, the mental comments, and put them there, in your heart. Use the energy of your heart to soften them and feel how it fills your whole body with compassion. Take a deep breath, and feel the energy of your heart throughout your whole body. Feel the acceptance.

Why does life bring you challenges? Life brings you challenges so you can overcome them, and allow the next level of plenitude and vitality to become available to you. They are precious opportunities to grow. Precious opportunities to discover the strengths *you already have* that simply need to be reactivated. The strengths that will help you overcome your challenges, the strengths that will help you move from stuckness to growth.

Inside of you there is a part that doesn't want to give up. That wants to live life at its fullest. It's the voice of your soul. The voice that wants to stand up to the voices of the ego and the personality—and become the best possible you. You've been there before, and that's what brought you up to this moment. This moment in which you are here struggling to become the best person you can be, standing up and not giving up to your personality, to your automatic thoughts. It's the real you, it's the strength of your soul.

At this point your attention may automatically go to create thoughts about your thoughts. It's OK. Simply keep breathing consciously, following the path of the air in and out of your body, and let your Impartial Spectator witness the activity of your mind non-judgmentally.

Visualization of strengths, potential, and personal power

Now please move your attention to that part of yourself that doesn't want to give up. Look at the drawing on the sand: exactly in the center of the eight there is a point: the intersection between the right side and the left side of the eight. Let's call it the *point of courage*. From that point, imagine yourself drawing an arrow up. An exit from the eight. An exit from the stuckness.

This arrow points to what is available outside the eight. This arrow points to your strengths and to your potential. To the future that is available to you in any given moment.

Let's see what's outside the eight.

I want you to think of any moment in the past in which you really felt your mind relaxed, in which you felt acceptance for yourself and others. It can be any moment in which you felt light and you were playful. Bring it from any area of your life: you could have been by yourself, with a friend, with a group of friends, or with your family. In your personal or your professional life. Go to the past and bring that moment. It could be a special moment or just a simple one. Feel it. Feel the relaxation of that moment in your whole body.

Search your memories for that moment in which you were not only intelligent but wise. Tolerant. Acceptant. Feel the relaxation of that moment, in which you let go of your fears and of trying to prove you are intelligent and competent. Everything flowed harmoniously and everything actually worked well and turned out well, without your needing to do anything. Take a deep breath and feel that moment.

Let's see what else is outside the eight.

I now want you to envision yourself in a new future. A future in which you are perceptive and analytical while active and emotionally connected . A future in which you are sharing your talents with the world. In which you accept yourself as a human being, including some less positive aspects. In which you are in touch with your heart, and you can let go of any cynicism. Please put your hands one over the other, and over your heart. Feel your heartbeat. Feel your humanity. Since you are human, you are allowed to not be intelligent and knowledgeable from time to time. Walk. Take a deeep breath. Stretch. Connect to your body. This allows you to recharge your batteries and become smarter than when you drive yourself to exhaustion with constant mental activity. Your body processes and dissolves the fears, so plenty of energy gets liberated for renovated intellectual productivity. Feel it. Since you are not afraid of acknowledging your limitations, you are more open to learning than ever. This helps you fulfill one of your true dreams: having a deep understanding of the world and becoming a truly intelligent and wise person.

Bring that moment from the future, and feel it in your body, in the present moment. Feel it in your heart and in your mind. Feel the power of your mind, heart, and body working together and see what you can achieve, and most important: how all that is inside of you now and you *already* are the good person you always wanted to be.

Let's gently finish the meditation by slowly going back and watching the whole drawing in the sand.

Watch the eight, together with the point of courage and all the potential that is available *within* you.

End of visualization

I acknowledge you for your courage, for being here and trying to grow as a person, for trying to overcome yourself, for the efforts you do, for not giving up. The mere fact of your doing this exercise is a testimony of your inner strength and of your not giving up. I also want *you* to acknowledge yourself for your courage, for not giving up. And I want you to thank life for the challenges it brings you, for the many opportunities it brings you every day, so through them you can become in touch with your strengths, to grow and also to contribute to the world, to give to the world around you the gifts of your real self.

7. RE-PATTERNING: EXERCISES FOR FILTER FLEXING AND INTEGRATION

Exclusively-Logical Thinking

The "Exclusively-Logical Thinking" is a distorting filter that may typically dominate Type Five's thinking in the Stuckness Zone. Although being logical and centered is one of their strengths, this filter causes Fives to think *only* in logical terms. Explanations that don't follow a certain logic are thus automatically ruled out by the Five. Much of the defensiveness and suffering of Type Five is caused by this mechanism that makes them very reactive every time their logic is challenged.

When overused, their adherence to logic and reason in an attempt to remain objective may result instead in the opposite: reductionism and high subjectivity.

Exercise for Type Five: Flexing the Exclusively-Logical Thinking filter. In order to overcome this automatic tendency, ask yourself:

- What kind of logic am I using? Is it biased?
- Check your reasoning: are there underlying logical fallacies in it that may result in a misconception?
- Do I remain open-minded and investigative, or am I reducing complex issues to simple, one-sentence cause-and-effect explanations? Am I debating flexibly, or trying to impose a rigid model/view? What happens with things that I can't measure empirically? How do I approach them?

Finding the good

Finding and praising the good in people or society in general is usually an underdeveloped muscle in Fives in the Stuckness Zone.

Exercise for Type Five: Finding the good. Actively look for the good in everything around you during one week. It can all be written in a two column table: Column A will have all you perceive as stupid or irrational in others. Column B will have everything that the people in your personal and professional life have done well during this week.

Talk with the Five about the different intelligences people have and the latest research on the subject. This will help the Five do this exercise, and during the week find, for instance, *emotionally* intelligent people. Valuing EQ in others is a great way to connect Fives with their own hearts and feelings.

Learn to relax

Fives on autopilot tend to overwhelm themselves with mental activity. It is not uncommon to see Fives coming to coaching burned out after years of letting their minds totally dominate and overwhelm their being. Another underdeveloped muscle in Fives is the ability to connect to their bodies. This can be obtained by using their connection to Type Eight.

Exercise for Type Five: Learning to Relax. Ask yourself: What can I do with my body to physically interrupt the activity of my mind?

Many Fives are extremely sedentary. But even going out for a one-minute walk, for example, can produce a noticeable impact. Talk with the Five about what many researchers have found: that physical activity has an impact on short-term intellectual abilities and concentration. This means that when Fives connect to their bodies, they can improve their most valued resource. This is an incentive to all Fives and sometimes can be enough to motivate them to start. But remember to keep it simple in the beginning: this will prevent the autopilot response of "this is a waste of time" that many Fives may have when doing physical exercise.

Paying attention to the speaking style

Language is powerful: it's the vehicle that transports meaning. When we interpret reality through our filters, we put words to it. Therefore, if we are able to change the words that we attach to our experiences, we can indirectly impact our emotional states, since a big percentage of our emotions comes from our language. People are hypnotized by their own language patterns, creating blind spots that don't allow them to see reality accurately (Robbins and Madanes, 2005). By always using the same phrases and words to describe their experience, each personality type ends by not seeing what's in front of it. Literally, the description of reality becomes the *actual* reality. Those phrases and words are simply a manifestation of the underlying limiting beliefs that each type holds. Changing the speaking style can thus help us expand our frames of reference, allowing us to see the situations in our daily lives from many more angles.

It is important for coachees to develop the ability to become aware when their personality mechanisms hijack their language, at the moment it occurs. For Type Fives in the Stuckness Zone, this manifests in a tendency to speak *exclusively* about their ideas and areas of interest, and sometimes a certain disdain for light informal conversations or mundane subjects.

Exercise for Type Five: Flexing the discursive style. Pay attention to your conversation topics and format. How much time have you spent sharing your own ideas? Are you listening to the other side's ideas as well? Observe yourself from the outside: Are you talking exclusively in Head center language: logical terms, cause and effect, cost and benefit? Discussing theories, models, and systems? O rare you also including emotions-related issues in your narrative? What about body and action-related topics?

Another important point to pay attention to is that, since Fives' heads usually go very fast, they may have their words literally not matching the pace of the flow of ideas of their minds. Sometimes this results in sentences not completed until the end. Other times, the other person may not properly understand the Five, who has forgotten to explain some things that the Five was actually under the impression had already been explained. (Even though the thought happened in the Five's mind, he or she actually perceives it as if it had happened outside also.) This adds to a Five's already existing social awkwardness, so it is important for Fives in the Stuckness Zone to develop their communication abilities, and the coach should pay attention and be of help in these matters.

Work with the Jungian preferences: Integrating our less-dominant qualities

When coaching a Type Five, it is very important to pay attention to his or her Jungian preferences. If a coachee has done an MBTI profile, ask for his or her four-letter type and discuss how Jungian preferences may play together with the coachee's Enneatype. Also, when clients get stuck in the lower side of their Jungian preference, we can use the same pattern interruption techniques described all through this book to help them shift out and grow. For a description of the Jungian preferences, please refer to Part I of this book.

Some examples of the usage of the Jungian preferences in coaching a Type Five:

- Although you'll find many Extraverted, gregarious Fives, there is a high correlation between Fiveness and Introversion. Take this into account, especially if you are an Extraverted coach. Slow your pace to match theirs. Fives tend to be quiet and private and usually emotionally detached. They are intimate and reflective, needing more space and time to think about what's being said in the sessions. With them you'll have almost no eye contact and the sessions will move slowly, so don't overwhelm them with too much or too fast talking. Match their pace by taking a deep breath from time to time, while deeply reflecting on what the Five coachee is saying and feeling.
- The whole Feeling dimension in the MBTI is very illustrative for some development goals of Fives. Talk about it in your coaching sessions. Mention the importance of learning to watch and perceive the world from this angle: learning to recognize the personal needs of others; being receptive and learning to listen empathically to others; interacting in a more personal way instead of being logical in excess; when making decisions, taking into account other people's emotions and what impact the decisions will have on them.

Between-Sessions Exercise for Type Five: self-observation

During the week, actively engage in self-observing a particularly unhelpful pattern of your type. When you become aware of your patterns in real time, begin a spontaneous, one-cycle breath meditation. Follow the sequence described in Part II for observing the pattern and slowing it down. Share your insights with your coach in your next session.

TYPE SIX
THE LOYALIST

SIXES

People tell me I am too **tense**, that I jump from one **worry** to the next. Sometimes I do that, I kind of overwhelm myself, I try to **prepare** for so many **eventualities**. . .I sometimes feel exhausted because I can't prepare myself for all possible **dangers**. I feel a lot of **pressure**; every single day you hear about new dangers: accidents, illnesses, economic collapses, wars. There is no end to it. Maybe I'll go study and practice martial arts like my friend Jenny—she feels so much more **secure**. At least that's how it looks. At home they call me **"paranoid"**, all the time preparing for the **worst scenarios**. All I actually want is to feel prepared. I think that my **fear** and **suspiciousness** protect me. It's hard for me to **trust** others; I get into an endless loop of **checking** their **motives** and **intentions** (Linda, Type Six.)

Description of Type Six

Sixes are loyal, security-seeking, and hard-working people who can be very perceptive regarding potential problems and dangers and how to prepare for them.

At their best, they are efficient troubleshooters who have a keen eye for spotting and anticipating potential problems, but they do so with a calm and methodic approach. They are masters of problem-solving. Their highly developed analytical skills allow them to approach complex problems in an investigative, diligent, and non-anxious way in order to find solutions for things that don't work or to take preventive action for things they anticipate may not work in the future. They take charge of situations and take charge of themselves: they are proactive and not reactive—they don't react emotionally to their own anxieties or mental processes. They value the opinions of others and may take them into account—they are very good as team players—but they also trust themselves and their own heart and instincts, and know how to take action on them.

Their anticipation of dangers and problems doesn't make them overly fearful and anxious. They don't react to their perceptions, and as described by Fabien and Patricia Chabreuil, "their fear doesn't become their main focus of attention, they accept it but don't prolong it, amplify it, extend it to other circumstances, or project it to other people." When they are able to act this way, they are truly courageous—not simply brave nor trying to prove they are fearless. Seligman and Peterson's definition of Courage applies to them: "The ability to stand up for what is right in difficult situations." Also, their attentional range is quite wide, and includes not only potential problems but also what works and other positive dimensions of reality (what's uplifting, what is possible, what is inspiring, etc.) They have a good sense of humor and can be funny and ironical, sometimes laughing about themselves and their own fears.

They are loyal and are very committed to their families, jobs, friends, and communities. They are considerate, attentive, friendly, and thoughtful.

They are hard workers, dutiful, responsible, reliable, and persistent. They can persevere and maintain their course of action without regard to discouragement, opposition, or previous failure.

In spite of their active minds they know how to become quiet and simply relax into their body experience (by breathing consciously, for example). When they connect to their bodies they connect to the here and now, to the present moment, and they thus can take a break from their forecasting tendencies. This helps them as a powerful antidote to negative mental states.

In the Stuckness Zone, they begin to act more fearfully and anxiously, focusing their attention more exclusively on what could go wrong, what are the negative possibilities. Their minds produce a continuous chatter, sometimes of contradictory voices. They begin to react emotionally to their perceptions. They either fight (counterphobic) their fears or flee from them (phobic). Either way, they do it reactively. They turn tense and vigilant, and this may be visible on the outside or it may not. They become very focused on issues of certainty and security. Paradoxically, the more they focus on these, the less certain and secure they feel.

In their attempt to feel security and certainty, they trap themselves in a variety of ways.

In their personal lives:

First, they try to stay hypervigilant in order to scan for potential dangers and anticipate them. They overwhelm themselves with worst-case scenarios. This creates the habit of chronic worry and makes them feel exhausted, nervous, and anxious most of the time. They become negative and pessimistic.

Second, they become hyper-cautious and tense, in order to avoid any risk in their lives. This makes them indecisive, hesitant, and ambivalent, and it sometimes paralyzes them and prevents their taking charge and action. Their ambivalence makes them engage in contradictory behaviors.

Third, it is hard for them to trust their own guidance and judgments, so they become self-doubting and they disempower themselves. They may make themselves powerless in the face of their problems and challenges, and adopt an "I can't" mindset, falling into the habit of complaining. They may magnify and amplify small injuries or discomforts and overreact to minor obstacles with exaggerated expressions of emotion. Their self-esteem suffers as a consequence.

In their relationships:

First, they question the motives of others, cross-examining them, looking for meaning, motivations, intentions, double messages, and contradictions. They suspiciously doubt and test others and issues of trust/distrust arise in their relationships.

Second, they mismatch and play devil's advocate: given a certain argument, they take a position they don't necessarily agree with, just for the sake of argument or to test the quality of the arguments and identify weaknesses in them.

Third, they try to secure others' support by being loyal. In doing so, they become both obedient and rebellious against authority.

Fourth, they try to find certainty in systems, protocols, routines. They may become stubborn and dogmatic. They may also try to find certainty by asking for other people's advice and guidance.

COACHING PROTOCOL FOR TYPE SIX

1. SET THE CLIMATE OF THE SESSION

Before you begin your coaching session with your client, check yourself:

Bring acceptance to the session

Ask yourself:
- Am I in a non-judgmental state?
- Does my specific personality type have any resistance with Type Six?

"Turn on" your multimodal listening

It is extremely important that you use all the centers of intelligence (Head, Heart, Gut) during every coaching session. Be aware of "listening" actively with all three centers.

Listen with your Head center
- Pay attention to speaking style and language use.
- Analyze body language and posture.
- Analyze patterns and possibilities for interrupting them.

Listen with your Heart center
- Empathize.
- See the client as a human being, not as a "type."
- Look beyond the facade.
- Connect, in spite of any resistance that you may have. You are here to help the client grow.

Listen with your Gut center
- What kind of energy is the client bringing to the session?
- Is there a match between what the client says and the energy with which he or she says it?
- What does your intuition tell you regarding the last developments in this coaching process?
- "Listen to what people say but pay attention to what they *do*." (Madanes, 1995).

2. DEFINE THE CHALLENGE

Typical challenges for Sixes include:
- To be more confident in themselves and to follow their own guidance. To build a healthy self-esteem.
- To become more relaxed, less emotionally reactive.
- To learn how to trust in themselves, in other people, and in life in general.

3. UNDERSTAND THE COACHEE'S MODEL OF THE WORLD AND HIS OR HER STUCKNESS ZONE

Ask yourself the following questions: Why is the client acting the way he does? What is shaping her behavior? What is his internal story? What are the filters through which she looks at and perceives the world? To what extent are the type fixations active and operative in this client?

When Type Sixes are less aware or under stress, their attention gets hijacked/derailed by an intense desire to be safe and obtain certainty. In this state they usually begin preparing compulsively for worst-case scenarios.

4. BRING AWARENESS TO THE SIX HUMAN NEEDS

According to Human Needs Psychology, we all have six basic human needs (Madanes, 2009): Certainty, Variety, Love/Connection, Significance, Growth, and Contribution. These needs are not merely desires, but true drivers mobilizing our behavior.

Exercise for Type Six: The six human needs. Look at the Stuckness Zone and from the whole range of behaviors there described, pick the most frequent ones: "What human needs are you trying to fulfill by engaging in these behaviors?"

Please score each need from 0 to 10.

Certainty. Does engaging in these behaviors make you feel certain? Give you a sense of security? Apart from these behaviors: Do you also know how to obtain certainty in a more positive way?

Visualize potential

- problem-solver
- takes preventive action
- loyal and commited
- dutiful

WHILE...

- friendly and serene
- not prolonging / amplifying / projecting / extending fears
- having a wide attentional range

POSITIVE INTERRUPTION

STUCKNESS ZONE

- Fearful
- Unmanageable thoughts
- Anxious
- Obedient/rebellious
- Fight/Flight
- Point of Courage
- Hyper-vigilant
- Overreactive/ Magnifying/ Catastrophizing
- Distrustful/ Suspicious
- Projecting
- Pessimistic
- Indecisive
- Opinion "shop around"
- Self-doubting
- Ambivalent
- Mismatching
- Complaining
- Disempowering "I can't" approach
- Devil's advocate
- "Us against them" mindset
- Dogmatic

NEGATIVE INTERRUPTION

- Escapism
- Impact in physiology through food &/or substances
- Other unproductive or destructive behavior

Variety. Does engaging in these behaviors bring you a sense of variety? Apart from these behaviors: Do you also know how to obtain variety in a more positive way?

Love/connection. Does engaging in these behaviors make you feel connected to others? Experience a sense of love?
Apart from these behaviors: Do you also know how to obtain love/connection in a more positive way?

Significance. Does engaging in these behaviors make you feel important? Special? Apart from these behaviors: Do you also know how to obtain significance in a more positive way?

Growth. Does engaging in these behaviors give you a sense of development, make you feel that you're growing? Apart from these behaviors: Do you also know how to obtain growth in a more positive way?

Contribution. Does engaging in these behaviors give you a sense of going beyond your own needs, of giving to others? Apart from these behaviors: Do you also know how to obtain contribution in a more positive way?

Coaching case study. Take as an example Adrianne, one of our coachees, a Type Six. She came to coaching because of her suffering with constant and high levels of anxiety, and for feeling incapable of resolving her own problems. The present situation helps her fulfill two human needs: Certainty and Significance. In our sessions we discovered she is very afraid of changes in her life, so she keeps them away by avoiding challenges and doing as little as possible. Sticking with the devil she knows gives her a sense of Certainty. On the other hand, having problems is a way for her to feel special and obtain Significance. (Remember that the need for Significance can also be fulfilled by having problems or being the *worst* at something.) The fulfillment of her needs in a negative way has left her with high costs in her personal and professional life. The breakthrough occurred when she began to be aware of her personality mechanisms. She was able to interrupt the patterns and look for positive ways to fulfill her needs. She decided to return to college to finish a degree that years ago she wasn't able to complete. She was passionate about having a degree in social work, but due to family pressure (her father preferred that she study business), she quit. She now is focused on obtaining a degree that will ensure the possibility of working in an area she is passionate about. Her enthusiasm about this area makes her feel confident that she will be able to make a good living. This move gave her an enormous sense of Certainty. Also, it allowed for the possibility to succeed at something and achieve something valuable to her, thus obtaining Significance in a positive way.

One important point to take into account: pay special attention to the needs of Growth and Contribution. Does the coachee meet these needs in healthy or in destructive ways?

As we integrate our personality, the needs of Growth and Contribution begin receiving high scores while also being met in positive and healthy ways. The reason for this is that when we move out of our Stuckness Zone, we act from new, conscious, chosen responses. This allows us to overcome our old habits and grow. This integration, in turn, always will bring greater contribution to others. In contrast, if we continue acting without awareness, out of our old patterns of reaction, we disempower ourselves and let our egos manage our lives. This always causes suffering to ourselves and to others.

5. PRODUCE LEVERAGE

The next step is to gain leverage by bringing awareness to the costs and suffering that the unhelpful patterns of the type are causing for the client.

Exercise for Type Six: Gaining awareness of the costs of patterns

- How much does it cost you, in terms of your relationships, to be fearful, suspicious, and mismatching?
- How much does it cost you, in terms of your health, to be tense and hypervigilant most of the time?
- How much does it cost you, in terms of your professional career, to be indecisive, ambivalent, self-doubting, and pessimistic?
- How much does it cost you, in terms of your personal fulfillment and own sense of happiness, to be constantly anxious and unable to live in the present moment?

6. PATTERN INTERRUPTION: BUILDING OUR ATTENTIONAL MUSCLES

TYPE SIX VISUALIZATION

Visualizations are a great tool for coaching in general and when doing personality-types coaching in particular. The following is a comprehensive visualization/meditation script for Type Six. It encompasses working with the type's strengths and weaknesses, training attentional abilities through the Impartial Spectator, training conscious breathing, acceptance, and relaxation. In a single coaching session, you don't have to use them all. You can use these visualizations modularly, by selecting one or more of the sections that follow.

Script for Type Six: Visualization/Meditation

Relaxation

Begin by finding a comfortable sitting position. Keep your spine straight in a natural way. Let your arms become loose. Lightly, with palms facing up or down, rest your hands on your lap. Take one deep breath, to begin relaxing your whole body. Inhale. . .Exhale. . . You can gently close your eyes and take another deep breath as a way to become centered and focused. Inhale. . .Exhale . . .

Training the Impartial Spectator

Let's begin by bringing awareness to the Impartial Spectator. Think of the Impartial Spectator as your friend who objectively watches your behavior from the outside. It helps you make wise decisions and allows you to regulate your automatic pilot.

The Impartial Spectator will do so by training your mind to be sensitive to the activity in your three centers of intelligence: the Body (our physical sensations), the Mind (thoughts, plans, future, past, images, ideas, imagination), and the Heart (feelings). Our breath, which symbolically represents our connection to our soul, will allow us to remain centered and to shift our attention from one center to the other. It will also help us to remain non-judgmental and to bring the qualities of gratitude, compassion, and acceptance to this exercise. Every time your mind wanders, you can use the moment to exercise those qualities of gratitude, compassion, and acceptance—for each one of those moments offers the opportunity to learn how to reorient our attention.

Begin by gently shifting your attention to your **Body** center of intelligence. Take a deep breath, and follow the path of the air in and out of the body. Do it slowly. Inhale again. . . and this time make the exhalation last a bit longer. Place your full attention on the path of the air getting in and out of your body, from beginning to end. Begin noticing your body sensations. Sense the contact points between your feet and the floor. What body sensations are in there right now? Move your attention to your back. Feel the support that the chair gives you. Stay with that sensation for a moment. Shift your attention to your hands. Focus on the contact point between the hands and your lap.

Place your hands over your chest, one over the other, and shift your attention to your **Heart** center of intelligence. What feelings do you have in this moment?

Now shift your attention to the **Head** center of intelligence. Is there a mental commentary about your feelings? Is there judgment or acceptance of your feelings? What is your mind saying about your feelings? What is it saying about this whole exercise? Serenely watch your mental discourse as it appears. Inhale...Exhale... Stay in the Head center, and now shift your attention to your memories. Imagine yourself watching an old black-and-white TV set on which your past history is being broadcast. You see yourself in the TV. Your life videotaped. Each stage of your life, on the screen, in slow motion. Nod when you actually see it. Inhale...Exhale... Still in the Head center, now move your attention to the future. Serenely reflect on each one of the following questions. Take a few moments as a pause between each question. What do you want your future to be like? How do you see yourself in the future? What plans do you have?

Visualization

Remain in the Head center, and you will now shift your attention to your imagination. Imagine yourself at the beach, at the sea shore, in slightly wet sand. Breath the air at the beach. Inhale...Exhale... Feel the wind. Listen to the waves in the sea. Feel the sand on your feet. Imagine yourself drawing an imaginary number eight, drawn horizontally, like the infinity symbol, in the slightly wet sand on the shore. Draw it slowwwly. Feel the contact point between your fingers and the sand.

Visualization of Stuckness Zone and costs

Now picture yourself putting all your problems and challenges *inside* that eight in the sand. One by one.

All my continuous fears in so many areas of my life. All my permanent attention to what could go wrong, and the enslavement of trying to be hypervigilant and prepared for everything. All the exhaustion and stress that result from my catastrophizing even minor events. All my self-doubts, my ambivalence and indecision. My inability to trust others or myself. My unmanageable thoughts and the constant chatter in my head. All the anxiety and the pressure. All the suffering.

Feel the pressure and the tension in your whole body. Stay there for a moment.

This eight in the sand represents our Stuckness Zone. The place we get stuck with negative focus and negative feelings.

"It's human" section

Every human being has issues that make him or her precisely that, human. It's a personal, tailor-made set of challenges in life. Watch your own personal challenges without judgments. If your mind passes a commentary, it's OK. Don't worry and try to do this exercise "right." If there is a judgment, just watch the judgment. Listen to its script. Watch it as it occurs, outside of you.

It's human to have judgments about our experience. It's OK. Bring your attention to your heart. Now, grab the judgments you just heard in your head, the mental comments, and put them there, in your heart. Use the energy of your heart to soften them and feel how it fills your whole body with compassion. Take a deep breath, and feel the energy of your heart throughout your whole body. Feel the acceptance.

Why does life bring you challenges? Life brings you challenges so you can overcome them, and allow the next level of plenitude and vitality to become available to you. They are precious opportunities to grow. Precious opportunities to discover the strengths *you already have* that simply need to be reactivated. The strengths that will help you overcome your challenges, the strengths that will help you move from stuckness to growth.

Inside of you there is a part that doesn't want to give up. That wants to live life at its fullest. It's the voice of your soul. The voice that wants to stand up to the voices of the ego and the personality—and become the best possible you. You've been there before, and that's what brought you up to this moment. This moment in which you are here struggling to become the best person you can be, standing up and not giving up to your personality, to your automatic thoughts. It's the real you, it's the strength of your soul.

At this point your attention may automatically go to create thoughts about your thoughts. It's OK. Simply keep breathing consciously, following the path of the air in and out of your body, and let your Impartial Spectator witness the activity of your mind non-judgmentally.

Visualization of strengths, potential, and personal power

Now please move your attention to that part of yourself that doesn't want to give up. Look at the drawing on the sand: exactly in the center of the eight there is a point: the intersection between the right side and the left side of the eight. Let's call it the *point of courage*. From that point, imagine yourself drawing an arrow up. An exit from the stuckness.

This arrow points to what is available outside the eight. This arrow points to your strengths and to your potential. To the future that is available to you in any given moment.

Let's see what's outside the eight.

I want you to think of any moment in the past in which you really felt relaxed, in which you felt acceptance for yourself and others. It can be any moment in which you felt at peace, grounded and serene. Bring it from any area of your life: you could have been by yourself, with a friend, with a group of friends, or with your family. In your personal or your professional life. Go to the past and bring back that moment. It could be a special moment or just a simple one. Feel it. Feel the relaxation of that moment in your whole body.

Search your memories for that moment in which you were courageous. Feel the relaxation of that moment in which you let go of reacting to your own fears. Everything flowed harmoniously and everything actually worked well and turned out well, without your intervention or monitoring. Take a deep breath and feel that moment.

Let's see what else is outside the eight.

I now want you to envision yourself in a new future. A future in which you are proactive but serene. A future in which you are not only empowering yourself but also others. In which you embrace life and all of its aspects, including some less positive aspects. Please put your hands one over the other, and over your heart. Feel your heartbeat. Feel your humanity. Since you are human, you are allowed to relax and also have fun from time to time. This allows you to recharge your batteries and become more productive than when you activate your mind in a way that drives you to exhaustion. Your realism makes you moderate in your thoughts, feelings, and actions. And your groundedness dissolves the fear, so plenty of resources get liberated. Feel it. Feel how your stability and composure allow you to feel centered. This helps you fulfill one of your true dreams: truly feeling secure in the world, trusting life and flowing with your destiny.

Bring that moment from the future, and feel it in your body, in the present moment. Feel it in your heart and in your mind. Feel the power of your mind, heart, and body working together and see what you can achieve, and most important: how all that is inside of you now and you *already* are the person you always wanted to be.

Let's gently finish the meditation by slowly going back and watching the whole drawing in the sand. Watch the eight, together with the point of courage and all the potential that is available *within* you.

End of visualization

I acknowledge you for your courage, for being here and trying to grow as a person, for trying to overcome yourself, for the efforts you do, for not giving up. The mere fact of your doing this exercise is a testimony to your inner strength and of your not giving up. I also want *you* to acknowledge yourself for your courage, for not giving up. And I want you to thank life for the challenges it brings you, for the many opportunities it brings you every day, so through them you can become in touch with your strengths, to grow and also to contribute to the world, to give to the world around you the gifts of your real self.

7. RE-PATTERNING: EXERCISES FOR FILTER FLEXING AND INTEGRATION

Flexing the Six's Distorting Filters

Sixes in the Stuckness Zone have many cognitive distorting filters that are activated without awareness and through which reality is perceived. They can all operate simultaneously, or a few at a time, or even singly. These filters are as follows: (After the descriptions there is an exercise to observe and flex the filters.)

"Ignoring the Good" filter

When Sixes are in the Stuckness Zone, there is a tendency to interpret events in a way that ignores good things that may have happened. It requires a conscious attentional effort for them to take a new look at reality and look for the positive.

"Amplification/Catastrophization" filter

Another perceptual filter that is very active in Sixes in the Stuckness Zone is the Amplification filter. With their overreactivity, a minor situation can be blown out of proportion, usually causing a disproportionate emotional reaction. Minor frustrations are perceived as *hopelessly problematic*. It's as if they hold a magnifying glass through which they filter all their experience. Shortcomings and problems are amplified and at the same time, as with the "Ignoring the Good" filter, the importance of positive aspects is minimized or directly omitted.

"Blame" filter

Dr. Viktor Frankl, a disciple of Freud and Adler and father of the psychological school of Logotherapy, defined proactivity as our ability to be responsible for our own life, rather than making context, other people, or outside circumstances responsible for it. In the Stuckness Zone, the "Blame" filter gets activated and Sixes view reality in exactly the opposite way: they place responsibility and culpability for almost anything in their lives outside of themselves. When things go wrong, they may adopt a victim stance and shift responsibility to something or someone outside of themselves. This is an extremely disempowering filter that in the end causes much suffering to the Six. In the Stuckness Zone it is common to see this filter combined with the "Amplification" filter: for instance, a minor external event may cause the Six to feel like a victim of the situation (Blame), and an exaggerated emotional response may follow (Amplification.)

"Slippery Slope" filter

Sixes in the Stuckness Zone tend to focus on worst-case scenarios. When doing this, they usually use the "Slippery Slope" filter. This prevents their perceiving any middle ground: the situation is perceived as if having an "uninterrupted transition" from what is happening now to total disaster. Events will continue to slide in the same negative direction until the worst scenario is reached. Things will get worse. They will often predict that events will unfold in a very specific way, in a series of intermediate events, with a mechanism of connection leading from today's situation to their worst scenario. There is always danger ahead.
As in the other filters, the emotional reactions that follow these mental scenarios are usually intense, leaving the Six with a higher sense of stress, anxiety, and despair.

"Mind-reading" filter

In the Stuckness Zone, Sixes may assume they know for sure what other people think and what their intentions are. They seem to discern precisely what others believe about them and what they intend to do, as if they had telepathic, extrasensory means to do that. They quickly jump to conclusions, automatically assuming others' thoughts and intentions will be negative (and sometimes the worst) in nature, in spite of the fact that the Six will not have sufficient (if any) evidence for that conclusion. The effects of the "Mind-reading" filter on the Six's relationships can be damaging, especially when combined with other cognitive distortions such as Blame, Amplification, and Ignoring the Good.

Exercise for Type Six: Flexing the filters. Actively look for the presence of the distorting filters in your interpretations of reality during the week. It can all be written in a three-column table: Column A will have all events on your radar that triggered an emotional response. Column B will have the interpretation you gave to the event, and Column C will have your emotional response to that interpretation. In column D, identify what type of filter you used in interpreting the event. And in Column E, identify alternative interpretation(s) that could have been given, or what action you could take instead of jumping to conclusions. Examples can be found in the following table:

Event	Interpretation	Emotional Reaction	Filter(s) used	Alternative action, interpretation
My friend Diana is not returning my calls.	"I complain too much and she probably thinks I am an unbearable person. She doesn't like to talk with me as before. Our friendship will fall apart."	Disillusioned Abandoned Ignored Unrequited Anxious Agitated	Mind reading Amplification Ignoring the good Slippery slope	She's been very busy lately dealing with her new position. I'll call her to check.

Paying attention to the speaking style

Language is powerful: it's the vehicle that transports meaning. When we interpret reality through our filters, we put words to it. Therefore, if we are able to change the words that we attach to our experiences, we can indirectly impact our emotional states, since a big percentage of our emotions comes from our language. People are hypnotized by their own language patterns, creating blind spots that don't allow them to see reality accurately (Robbins and Madanes, 2005.) By always using the same phrases and words to describe their experience, each personality type ends by not seeing what's in front of it. Literally, the description of reality becomes the *actual* reality. Those phrases and words are simply a manifestation of the underlying limiting beliefs that each type holds. Changing the speaking style can thus help us expand our frames of reference, allowing us to see the situations in our daily lives from many more angles.

The following are very useful language-based exercises with Sixes.

Exercise # 1 - Conversation topics and format. Pay attention to your conversation topics and format. Am I empowering other people, or the situation, while disempowering myself? Do I make others capable while I stick to an "I can't" approach? Pay attention to small hassles in everyday life: How do I react to them and what language do I use to describe those hassles? Do I exaggerate? To what degree?

Exercise # 2 – Exaggerations. Exaggerations are a form of lying (Madanes, 1995). Consider the application of this definition to yourself. Sixes are loyal people who are very sensitive to all forms of lying, and they dislike being even remotely perceived as liars by others.

Exercise # 3 - "At cause" vs. "at effect". Another important distinction in working with your language patterns is NLP's being "at cause" vs. "at effect" idea. When you are "at cause" you take responsibility for your life. When you are "at effect" you place the responsibility for your well-being on others.

Exercise # 4 - Excuses vs. choice/responsibility. Pay attention: Is my language plagued with excuses? Do I tend to blame external factors? Practice the language of *choice* and *responsibility:* What do *I* think about this? What do *I* believe about this? What choices do *I* have? How can *I* take responsibility for this? What can *I* personally do to advance towards the desired results and make things happen?

Exercise # 5 - Labels and blame. Some Sixes in the Stuckness Zone become dogmatic or rigid, and have a linguistic tendency to negatively label others whom they see as deviant from the norms of the group or community. Absolute or unalterable words may be attached to themselves or someone else, in an emotional and blaming language. Pay attention to your language. Am I being persecutory? Am I being ideologically patrolling? Does my language give me a sense of belonging, power, or superiority at the expense of other members of the group, community, or society? Does my language reflect that my own group (my company, my department, my soccer team, etc.) is centrally important, and that all others are measured in relation to my own?

Work with the Jungian preferences: Integrating our less-dominant qualities

When coaching a Type Six, it is very important to pay attention to his or her Jungian preferences. If a coachee has done an MBTI profile, ask for his or her four-letter type and discuss how Jungian preferences may play together with the coachee's Enneatype. Also, when clients get stuck in the lower side of their Jungian preference, we can use the same pattern interruption techniques described all through this book to help them shift out and grow. For a description of the Jungian preferences, please refer to Part I of this book.

Some examples of the usage of the Jungian preferences in coaching a Type Six:

- Introverted Sixes, who tend to have a Five wing, are more quiet and private. They tend to have a rich internal world and hyper-busy heads. Their intense mental activity is not always perceived from the outside. Many introverted Sixes have difficulty in expressing their emotions in a *clear* way: discuss with them the value of training the Extraversion "muscle" and learning how to articulate what's on their minds.
- iNtuitive Sixes tend to be imaginative, conceptual, and original. When in the Stuckness Zone, they have difficulty being in the here and now and are busy imagining future scenarios of what could go wrong. They may jump to conclusions quickly, reading between the lines and speculating about what might happen. Discuss the

Sensing dimension with them, and the importance of following a sensible sequence of logic instead of jumping to whatever scenario their iNtuition may take them to; be factual—notice "what is" instead of "what might be"; ask "What are the facts?", "What resources are available?", "What worked in the past when we (or others) faced a similar problem?", "How can we solve this in a practical way?"; give more room to your senses and less to your imagination.
- Sensing Sixes tend to be classic, conservative, and traditionalist. When in the Stuckness Zone they have higher chances than iNtuiting Sixes of becoming dogmatic and rigid. Discuss the iNtuiting dimension and the importance of opening their minds to be tolerant of other people's preferences and styles as well; to consider many possibilities instead of "one right and proven way"; to develop their creativity and look beyond the obvious; to develop the ability of not being afraid to change; to look for the big picture, the connections between data and underlying patterns.
- Sixes in the Stuckness Zone may also tend to organize their lifestyle in a too rigid and constricting way. They may plan too much and too far ahead, and give too much weight to structure in their lives. Another dimension that is very useful to help Sixes in this regard is Perceiving. Here too, mention the importance of learning to watch the world from this angle: developing the ability to be spontaneous; the ability to be flexible when the situation requires it; the ability to adapt to changes; the ability in some areas of the Six's life to relax and feel comfortable with leaving a couple of things open and unplanned, to learn how to flow, to learn that uncertainty is a fact of life and of being human.

Between-Sessions Exercise for Type Six: Self-observation
During the week, actively engage in self-observing a particularly unhelpful pattern of your type. When you become aware of your patterns in real time, begin a spontaneous, one-cycle breath meditation. Follow the sequence described in Part II for observing the pattern and slowing it down. Share your insights with your coach in your next session.

TYPE SEVEN
THE ENTHUSIAST

SEVENS

I am an **optimistic** person; I love **life**. At home they tell me, "Wake up darling, life is not all roses, it's not like the movies, come down to earth." As if I don't know that. . . I try to be in an **uplifting** state, and simply can't stand **boring**, annoying people who come with their mental rigidity, everything in black and white. . .or that they want to tell me what to do. I don't like when others try to **limit** me. I prefer **spontaneity**, **flexibility**. If I am in the company of depressing people, I fly[...] I am making **plans** all the time. I **enjoy** that. I tend to load my schedule with a million things, but I don't always end up doing all that, all those things that I myself planned. I think most of the time in terms of **opportunity**, of **possibilities**. If I get **enthusiastic** about something, I can work really hard. But in those aspects of the job that become routine, I get bored and get stuck. It's easier for me to initiate, but harder to follow up or bring closure. I paid a big price for my lack of perseverance. Sometimes when I must complete a task until the end, I feel **trapped**. Feel as if I have no **freedom**. I like the joy of having everything **open** and in process[...] I love life and sometimes I have a feeling as if I don't have enough **energy** for all the things I want to do. There is so much that life has to offer, and I sometimes catch myself running from here to there, as if trying not to miss anything. I recognize that yes, that can be quite draining. My attention is easily **distracted** and I tend to **jump** from one thing to another, and it's hard for me to **concentrate** on doing just one thing and being disciplined. I get bored, and boredom is frightening. I immediately look for ways to **escape**." (Miri, Type Seven.)

Description of Type Seven

Sevens are optimistic, energetic, possibilities-oriented people who appreciate life and want to live it to its fullest.

At their best, they are multitalented people who learn fast and have many abilities in many diverse areas. They are the masters of brainstorming. They have curious and agile minds and can quickly generate new ideas. Their minds are especially great at finding associations, interconnections, and interrelationships between seemingly unconnected events, and they use this ability to see patterns where most people would miss them. They are ingenious, creative, and imaginative. They are "big picture" planners who can multitask and work on many projects at the same time, but they are also focused and disciplined and know how to bring a project to completion. Although their minds are agile and fast, they can pause and make decisions with serenity.

They are endowed with a love for life and a natural optimism and enthusiasm that are highly contagious. They are high-spirited, positive, adventurous, and upbeat and can motivate others with their energy. They can naturally look for the good in everything that happens in their life and in the lives of the people around them. They teach us how to appreciate the simplest things in life. How to be fascinated and obtain joy from daily and minor events, and learn to be satisfied and happy in the present moment. They are happy because they can also accept life's difficulties, frustrations, and pain without reacting to them or resisting them or trying to escape from them. This also makes them resilient—they know how to accept a crisis and turn it into a challenge, into an opportunity. They also know how to recover and "bounce back" from stress and crises.

They are fun to be around, are great conversationalists, and usually are the "life of the party" with their energetic sense of humor and entertaining storytelling. They can be charming, cheerful, and playful.

In the Stuckness Zone, an intense desire to maintain a sense of happiness and well-being starts running inside them. An "I must keep myself busy and excited" belief dominates their thinking. Consequently, their attention automatically goes to seeking variety and finding new possibilities and new sources of stimulation on one hand, and to the avoidance of negative emotions, pain, frustration, and boredom on the other. Since staying in motion is so important to them, special emphasis is put on defending their freedom and independence against anything or anyone they perceive as limiting or restrictive to them.

They become restless and less focused. They become interested in too many things, as if trying not to miss anything on the spectrum of possibilities that life has to offer, jumping from one track to another as if they couldn't say no to themselves. They keep planning for more activities and want to keep their options open, thus creating an inability to narrow their focus. As a result, they have a problem with commitment and completion. They start projects and don't have the discipline or the patience to complete them. They feel trapped and lose interest in a project once they have already started and the initial excitement is gone. As a result of their overextending themselves, their lack of focus and lack of discipline, their many talents may become wasted (or not fully developed to their potential), and their many dreams may not come to realization.

Their planning habit can backfire on them: the more they plan, the more they live in the future, and consequently the less they can feel joy in the present moment or appreciate what they do have. Anger and frustration arise from this, as they can't feel truly content in spite of their multiple activities, distractions, and busy schedules. Anxiety builds and they turn to even more planning and busier schedules in the hope of finding new pleasurable things and activities that will lessen that anxiety. They become escapists: self-indulgent, self-centered, bitter, uninhibited, impulsive, infantile, insensitive, and demanding.

Stress and emotional drain arise since it is very difficult to maintain a "happy," "negativity-free" life for long periods as they try to do. Physical, financial, and emotional exhaustion arise from their busy, hyperactive lifestyle.

COACHING PROTOCOL FOR TYPE SEVEN

1. SET THE CLIMATE OF THE SESSION

Before you begin your coaching session with your client, check yourself:

Bring acceptance to the session
Ask yourself:
- Am I in a non-judgmental state?
- Does my specific personality type have any resistance with Type Seven?

"Turn on" your multimodal listening
It is extremely important that you use all the centers of intelligence (Head, Heart, Gut) during every coaching session. Be aware of "listening" actively with all three centers.

Listen with your Head center
- Pay attention to speaking style and language use.
- Analyze body language and posture.
- Analyze patterns and possibilities for interrupting them.

Listen with your Heart center
- Empathize.
- See the client as a human being, not as a "type."
- Look beyond the facade.
- Connect, in spite of any resistance that you may have. You are here to help the client grow.

Listen with your Gut center
- What kind of energy is the client bringing to the session?
- Is there a match between what the client says and the energy with which he or she says it?
- What does your intuition tell you regarding the last developments in this coaching process?
- "Listen to what people say but pay attention to what they *do*." (Madanes, 1995).

2. DEFINE THE CHALLENGE

Determine what the client wants to work on, what is the purpose of his or her pursuing coaching.

Typical challenges for Sevens include:
- to learn how to focus and be disciplined towards the completion of their goals.
- to learn how to focus to capitalize on their many talents, and to develop their abilities to their potential.
- to recover their natural ability to appreciate the present and love life without the need for constant activity and stimulation.

3. UNDERSTAND THE COACHEE'S MODEL OF THE WORLD AND HIS OR HER STUCKNESS ZONE

Ask yourself the following questions: Why is the client acting the way he does? What is shaping her behavior? What is his internal story? What are the filters through which she looks at and perceives the world? To what extent are the type fixations active and operative in this client?

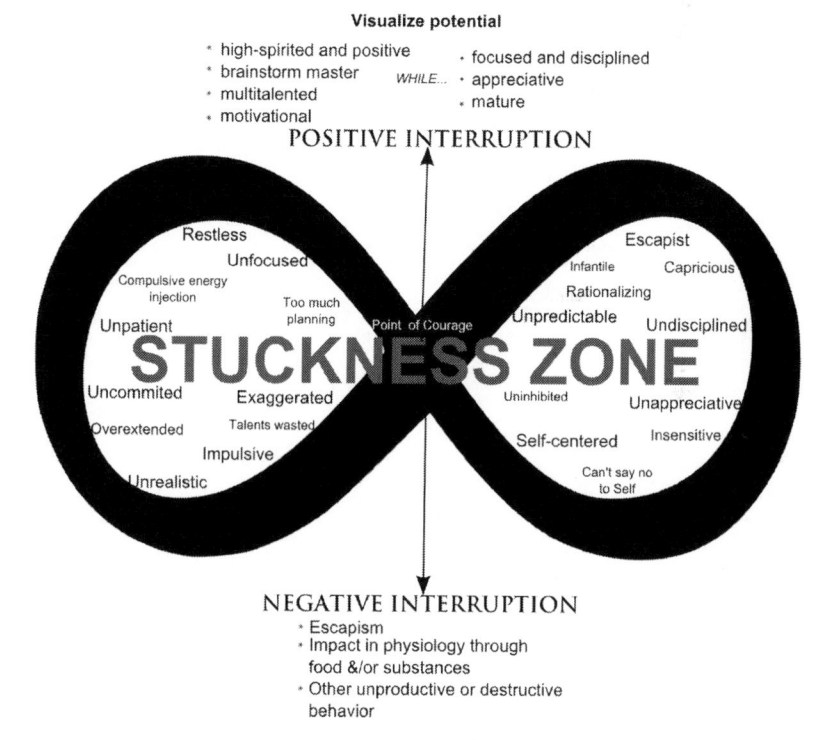

Visualize potential

- high-spirited and positive
- brainstorm master
- multitalented
- motivational

WHILE...

- focused and disciplined
- appreciative
- mature

POSITIVE INTERRUPTION

Restless
Unfocused
Compulsive energy injection
Too much planning
Unpatient
Point of Courage
Uncommited
Exaggerated
Overextended
Talents wasted
Impulsive
Unrealistic

Escapist
Infantile
Capricious
Rationalizing
Unpredictable
Undisciplined
Uninhibited
Unappreciative
Self-centered
Insensitive
Can't say no to Self

STUCKNESS ZONE

NEGATIVE INTERRUPTION
- Escapism
- Impact in physiology through food &/or substances
- Other unproductive or destructive behavior

When Type Sevens are less aware or under stress, their attention gets hijacked/derailed by an intense desire to maintain a sense of happiness and well-being. In this state a Seven's attention automatically goes to seeking variety and finding new possibilities and new sources of stimulation on one hand, and to the avoidance of negative emotions, pain, frustration, and boredom on the other.

4. BRING AWARENESS TO THE SIX HUMAN NEEDS

According to Human Needs Psychology, we all have six basic human needs (Madanes, 2009): Certainty, Variety, Love/Connection, Significance, Growth, and Contribution. These needs are not merely desires, but true drivers mobilizing our behavior.

Exercise for Type Seven: The six human needs. Look at the Stuckness Zone and from the whole range of behaviors there described, pick the most frequent ones: "What human needs are you trying to fulfill by engaging in these behaviors?"

Please score each need from 0 to 10.

Certainty. Does engaging in these behaviors make you feel certain? Give you a sense of security? Apart from these behaviors: Do you also know how to obtain certainty in a more positive way?

Variety. Does engaging in these behaviors bring you a sense of variety? Apart from these behaviors: Do you also know how to obtain variety in a more positive way?

Love/connection. Does engaging in these behaviors make you feel connected to others? Experience a sense of love? Apart from these behaviors: Do you also know how to obtain love/connection in a more positive way?

Significance. Does engaging in these behaviors make you feel important? Special? Apart from these behaviors: Do you also know how to obtain significance in a more positive way?

Growth. Does engaging in these behaviors give you a sense of development, make you feel that you're growing? Apart from these behaviors: Do you also know how to obtain growth in a more positive way?

Contribution. Does engaging in these behaviors give you a sense of going beyond your own needs, of giving to others? Apart from these behaviors: Do you know how to obtain contribution in a positive way?

Coaching case study. Take as an example Carl, one of our coachees, a Type Seven. He came to coaching to work on problems in his marriage. His main complaint was that he perceived marriage as a limiting routine. He identified his strong need for Variety, which led him to a very disorganized financial life recognizable by its escapism, overspending, and debt. This was causing constant fights with his wife and they were considering a divorce. The breakthrough came when Carl identified this strong Variety need and then worked to find ways to satisfy it in a positive way. Using Type Seven's innate strengths, he began reorienting his attention towards trying to appreciate the simplest things in life. He began to recover his natural strength of being able to be in the present moment, to be fascinated by everyday life. Embracing life with all that it has to offer, including some darker parts of it, allowed him to flow with certain difficulties in his marriage instead of trying to escape from them.

One important point to take into account: pay special attention to the needs of Growth and Contribution. Does the coachee meet these needs in healthy or in destructive ways? As we integrate our personality, the needs for Growth and Contribution begin receiving high scores while also being met in positive and healthy ways. The reason for this is that when we move out of our Stuckness Zone, we act from new, conscious, chosen responses. This allows us to overcome our old habits and grow. This integration, in turn, will always bring greater contribution to others. In contrast, if we continue acting without awareness, out of our old patterns of reaction, we disempower ourselves and let our egos manage our lives. This always causes suffering to ourselves and to others.

5. PRODUCE LEVERAGE

The next step is to gain leverage by bringing awareness to the costs and suffering that the unhelpful patterns of the type are causing for the client.

Exercise for Type Seven: Gaining awareness of the costs of patterns

- How much does it cost you, in terms of your relationships, to be self-centered, self-indulgent, and uncommitted?
- How much does it cost you, in terms of your health, to be whimsical, unable to say "no" to yourself, and overextend and exhaust yourself?
- How much does it cost you, in terms of your professional career, to

be unfocused, undisciplined, unable to follow up, and unrealistic?
- How much does it cost you, in terms of your personal fulfillment and own sense of happiness, to be restless and unable to live in the present moment?

6. PATTERN INTERRUPTION: BUILDING OUR ATTENTIONAL MUSCLES

TYPE SEVEN VISUALIZATION

Visualizations are a great tool for coaching in general and when doing personality-types coaching in particular. The following is a comprehensive visualization/meditation script for Type Seven. It encompasses working with the type's strengths and weaknesses, training attentional abilities through the Impartial Spectator, training conscious breathing, acceptance, and relaxation. In a single coaching session, you don't have to use them all. You can use these visualizations modularly, by selecting one or more of the sections that follow.

Script for Type Seven: Visualization/Meditation

Relaxation

Begin by finding a comfortable sitting position. Keep your spine straight in a natural way. Let your arms become loose. Lightly, with palms facing up or down, rest your hands on your lap. Take one deep breath, to begin relaxing your whole body. Inhale. . .Exhale. . . You can gently close your eyes and take another deep breath as a way to become centered and focused. Inhale. . .Exhale . . .

Training the Impartial Spectator

Let's begin by bringing awareness to the Impartial Spectator. Think of the Impartial Spectator as your friend who objectively watches your behavior from the outside. It helps you make wise decisions and allows you to regulate your automatic pilot.

The Impartial Spectator will do so by training your mind to be sensitive to the activity in your three centers of intelligence: the Body (our physical sensations), the Mind (thoughts, plans, future, past, images, ideas, imagination), and the Heart (feelings). Our breath, which symbolically represents our connection to our soul, will allow us to remain centered and to shift our attention from one center to the other. It will also help us to remain non-judgmental and to bring the qualities of gratitude, compassion, and acceptance to this exercise. Every time your mind wanders, you can use the moment to exercise those qualities of gratitude, compassion, and acceptance—for each one of those moments offers the opportunity to learn how to reorient our attention.

Begin by gently shifting your attention to your **Body** center of intelligence. Take a deep breath, and follow the path of the air in and out of the body. Do it slowly. Inhale again. . . and this time make the exhalation last a bit longer. Place your full attention on the path of the air getting in and out of your body, from beginning to end. Begin noticing your body sensations. Sense the contact points between your feet and the floor. What body sensations are in there right now? Move your attention to your back. Feel the support that the chair gives you. Stay with that sensation for a moment. Shift your attention to your hands. Focus on the contact point between the hands and your lap.

Place your hands over your chest, one over the other, and shift your attention to your **Heart** center of intelligence. What feelings do you have in this moment?

Now shift your attention to the **Head** center of intelligence. Is there a mental commentary about your feelings? Is there judgment or acceptance of your feelings? What is your mind saying about your feelings? What is it saying about this whole exercise? Serenely watch your mental discourse as it appears. Inhale. . .Exhale. . . Stay in the Head center, and now shift your attention to your memories. Imagine yourself watching an old black-and-white TV set on which your past history is being broadcast. You see yourself in the TV. Your life videotaped. Each stage of your life, on the screen, in slow motion. Nod when you actually see it. Inhale. . .Exhale. . . Still in the Head center, now move your attention to the future. Serenely reflect on each one of the following questions. Take a few moments as a pause between each question. What do you want your future to be like? How do you see yourself in the future? What plans do you have?

Visualization

Remain in the Head center, and you will now shift your attention to your imagination. Imagine yourself at the beach, at the sea shore, in slightly wet sand. Breath the air at the beach. Inhale. . .Exhale. . . Feel the wind. Listen to the waves in the sea. Feel the sand on your feet. Imagine yourself drawing an imaginary number eight, drawn horizontally, like the infinity symbol, in the slightly wet sand on the shore. Draw it slowwwly. Feel the contact point between your fingers and the sand.

Visualization of Stuckness Zone and costs

Now picture yourself putting all your problems and challenges *inside* that eight in the sand. One by one.

All my continuous focusing and unfocusing of my attention in so many different directions. All my exhaustion due to running in so many directions because of being unable to say "no" to myself. All the costs I've paid in my life because of my impulsiveness. My being tired of having happiness, somehow, always avoiding me. All my anxieties. All the suffering.

Feel the tension and anger. Feel it in your belly as you see all the issues inside the eight in the sand. Feel the tension in your whole body. Stay there for a moment.

This eight in the sand represents our Stuckness Zone. The place we get stuck with negative focus and negative feelings.

"It's human" section

Every human being has issues that make him or her precisely that, human. It's a personal, tailor-made set of challenges in life. Watch your own personal challenges without judgments. If your mind passes a commentary, it's OK. Don't worry and try to do this exercise "right." If there is a judgment, just watch the judgment. Listen to its script. Watch it as it occurs, outside of you.

It's human to have judgments about our experience. It's OK. Bring your attention to your heart. Now, grab the judgments you just heard in your head, the mental comments, and put them there, in your heart. Use the energy of your heart to soften them and feel how it fills your whole body with compassion. Take a deep breath, and feel the energy of your heart throughout your whole body. Feel the acceptance.

Why does life bring you challenges? Life brings you challenges so you can overcome them, and allow the next level of plenitude and vitality to become available to you. They are precious opportunities to grow. Precious opportunities to discover the strengths *you already have* that simply need to be reactivated. The strengths that will help you overcome your challenges, the strengths that will help you move from stuckness to growth.

Inside of you there is a part that doesn't want to give up. That wants to live life at its fullest. It's the voice of your soul. The voice that wants to stand up to the voices of the ego and the personality—and become the best possible you. You've been there before, and that's what brought you up to this moment. This moment in which you are here struggling to become the best person you can be, standing up and not giving up to your personality, to your automatic thoughts. It's the real you, it's the strength of your soul.

At this point your attention may automatically go to create thoughts about your thoughts. It's OK. Simply keep breathing consciously, following the path of the air in and out of your body, and let your Impartial Spectator witness the activity of your mind non-judgmentally.

Visualization of strengths, potential, and personal power

Now please move your attention to that part of yourself that doesn't want to give up. Look at the drawing on the sand: exactly in the center of the eight there is a point: the intersection between the right side and the left side of the eight. Let's call it the *point of courage*. From that point, imagine yourself drawing an arrow up. An exit from the eight. An exit from the stuckness.

This arrow points to what is available outside the eight. This arrow points to your strengths and to your potential. To the future that is available to you in any given moment.

Let's see what's outside the eight.

I want you to think of any moment in the past in which you felt really serene, in which you felt acceptance for yourself, others and reality "as is". It can be any moment in which you felt focused and yet playful. Bring it from any area of your life: you could have been by yourself, with a friend, with a group of friends, or with your family. In your personal or your professional life. Go to the past and bring back that moment. It could be a special moment or just a simple one. Feel it. Feel the relaxation of that moment in your whole body.

Search your memories for that moment in which you were appreciative. Mature. Patient. Happy. Feel the relaxation of that moment in which you let go of running after things that promised "more" excitement. Everything flowed harmoniously and everything actually worked well and turned out well, without your trying to "inject" energy. Take a deep breath and feel that moment.

Let's see what else is outside the eight.

I now want you to envision yourself in a new future. A future in which you are high-spirited but realistic. A future in which you love life and empower others with your contagious optimism, but you do so compassionately, with tolerance for the pace of others. In which you accept yourself as a human being in this world, including some less positive aspects of yourself and life as a whole. In which you are in touch with your heart, and can forgive yourself and others for the mistakes human beings will naturally make. Please put your hands one over the other, and over your heart. Feel your heartbeat. Feel your humanity. Feel how much energy gets liberated from that, how much tension and anxiety gets dissolved. Since you are not afraid of looking at life in its entirety, including its painful or less positive aspects, you can recognize the magnificence of it, and become fascinated. This helps you fulfill one of your true dreams: to truly becoming a happy person.

Bring that moment from the future, and feel it in your body, in the present moment. Feel it in your heart and in your mind. Feel the power of your mind, heart, and body working together and see what you can achieve, and most important: how all that is inside of you now and you *already* are the happy person you always wanted to be.

Let's gently finish the meditation by slowly going back and watching the whole drawing in the sand. Watch the eight, together with the point of courage and all the potential that is available *within* you.

End of visualization

I acknowledge you for your courage, for being here and trying to grow as a person, for trying to overcome yourself, for the efforts you do, for not giving up. The mere fact of your doing this exercise is a testimony to your inner strength and of your not giving up. I also want *you* to acknowledge yourself for your courage, for not giving up. And I want you to thank life for the challenges it brings you, for the many opportunities it brings you every day, so through them you can become in touch with your strengths, to grow and also to contribute to the world, to give to the world around you the gifts of your real self.

7. RE-PATTERNING: EXERCISES FOR FILTER FLEXING AND INTEGRATION

Minimization Filter

While in Type Six we saw that one of its cognitive distorting filters was "Amplification/Catastrophization"— the perception of reality through a magnifying glass, overreacting emotionally to events in a disproportionate manner — in Type Seven we see a filter that works in exactly the opposite way: minimizing events, shrinking their importance to a degree that allows the Seven to stay "happy" and go on with his or her life. Much of the suffering of Type Seven is caused by this mechanism, and it's a strong drive behind their escapisms in the Stuckness Zone. In order to overcome this automatic tendency, Sevens can use their connection to One and their Eight wing and incorporate their ability to be grounded, centered, to see reality in a concrete way, "as is."

Exercise for Type Seven: Flexing the Minimization filter
- What are the facts?
- Is this a stressful or painful event for me? Am I trying to escape, to minimize pain by trying to look through an optimistic lens? Is this the objective reality or am I forcing a positive, wishful interpretation onto it?

Learn to relax

Sevens on autopilot tend to overwhelm themselves with activities and plans. Boredom and frustration may arise if they allow themselves to be inactive for even short periods of time. It is not uncommon to see Sevens coming to coaching burned out after years of overextending themselves too hard. An underdeveloped muscle is the ability to appreciate the simplest things. In the Stuckness Zone they go after better, higher, more refined experiences with the expectation that those will bring the sought after "happiness." The emotion of ecstasy may be confused with happiness. When they use their connection to Five, they discover the value of quiet. Of introspection. When Sevens are able to stop and interrupt their pattern of restlessness, they become truly enlightened. As a Five, they can focus on something, see it from so many angles, and find true joy from their observations. They become appreciators.

Exercise for Type Seven: Learning to relax. Take some time in nature to focus your attention on something. To find the abundance of colors in, for example, a single tree. To learn how to take a moment (a few seconds in the beginning) to contemplate as if time was unhurried.

Develop your willpower

If they spend too much time in the Stuckness Zone being impulsive and self-indulgent, Sevens' willpower may suffer. As they become interested in too many things, jumping from one track to another, they lose focus and the ability to patiently work towards a goal. Sadly, this results in their many talents becoming wasted (or not fully developed to their potential) and their many dreams not coming to realization. Dr. Enrique Rojas, in his book *La Conquista de la Voluntad,* brings a quote from Kant's *Anthropology* that can be useful when coaching a Seven: "Deny yourself the pleasure of fun, but not in the stoic sense of wanting to completely ignore it, but in the finely epicurean sense of having a project which will bring even greater pleasure, that in turn will make you richer, in spite of your having to give up your immediate satisfaction." This notion can be a powerful motivator for Sevens. Sevens will be ready to make sacrifices when their perception is that they are going for a greater pleasure than today's.

Exercise for Type Seven: Developing willpower. Ask yourself: Am I giving up too quickly in my weekly tasks? How frequently do I get distracted? What happens exactly at the moment of distraction? Acknowledge anything that can derail you out of your target: a body sensation, a feeling, a thought. Write down everything in detail and discuss it in your next coaching session.
- Becoming more the "owners" of ourselves requires that we actively train ourselves into gradually higher levels of self-discipline. Do I persevere? How far can I look? Is it worth it to indulge my habit of avoiding important responsibilities by escaping into nonsense distractions that, as time goes by, will explain my failure to realize my deepest dreams? Can I say "no" to myself? Do I become tyrannized by wishes of all sorts: physical, mental, and emotional?
- Use your arrow to Five to develop an awareness of your resources:

Is this distraction that I am embarking on going to be taxing on my resources? Is it going to misuse my energies, my time, my money? Other people's resources? Develop a cost-benefit awareness. Ask: Is it worth it? Weigh the consequences by looking at the long-term.

Paying attention to the speaking style

Language is powerful: it's the vehicle that transports meaning. When we interpret reality through our filters, we put words to it. Therefore, if we are able to change the words that we attach to our experiences, we can indirectly impact our emotional states, since a big percentage of our emotions comes from our language. People are hypnotized by their own language patterns, creating blind spots that don't allow them to see reality accurately (Robbins and Madanes, 2005). By always using the same phrases and words to describe their experience, each personality type ends by not seeing what's in front of it. Literally, the description of reality becomes the *actual* reality. Those phrases and words are simply a manifestation of the underlying limiting beliefs that each type holds. Changing the speaking style can thus help us expand our frames of reference, allowing us to see the situations in our daily lives from many more angles.

It is important for coachees to develop the ability to become aware of when their personality mechanisms hijack their language, at the moment it occurs. For Type Sevens in the Stuckness Zone, this may manifest in a discursive style that reflects their wish to maintain themselves "up."

Exercise for Type Seven: Flexing the discursive style
- Pay attention to the use of words such as "fun," "enjoy," "boring," "slow," "interesting." How frequently do you use them?
- Pay attention to your conversation topics and format. How much time have we been talking about the things that particularly interest *me*? Pay attention to your breathing during the conversation. Am I truly listening to what the other person is saying? How frequently have I interrupted the other person? Am I talking too much? Too fast? How many "bracketed comments" have I inserted in the middle of my sentences? Was it necessary to deliver all that information in order for the message to be conveyed? Use your arrow to Five to be more short and precise in your communication,

avoiding exaggerations. Are my hand gestures adding too much "spice" to my message? Remember that obligating yourself to entertain in *every* conversation leaves you drained afterwards. Pay attention to the topics: Am I unconsciously avoiding talking about my inner feelings and thoughts? Am I avoiding talking about my deepest fears?

Work with the Jungian preferences: Integrating our less-dominant qualities

When coaching a Type Seven, it is very important to pay attention to his or her Jungian preferences. If a coachee has done an MBTI profile, ask for his or her four-letter type and discuss how Jungian preferences may play together with the coachee's Enneatype. Also, when clients get stuck in the lower side of their Jungian preference, we can use the same pattern interruption techniques described all through this book to help them shift out and grow. For a description of the Jungian preferences, please refer to Part I of this book.

Some examples of the usage of the Jungian preferences in coaching a Type Seven:

- The whole dimension of Introversion in the MBTI is very illustrative for some development goals of Sevens. Mention the importance of learning to watch and perceive the world from this angle: learning to be more reflective and inner oriented; developing the ability to take thoughts inside and process them instead of instantly having Extravert thoughts; creating space and boundaries with people; developing a contemplative way of looking at situations; taking time to think things thoroughly. This work is easier when there is a strong and operative arrow to Type Five.
- Another dimension that is very useful for some development goals of Sevens is Judging. In the Stuckness Zone, a little structure may make Sevens may feel trapped, suffocated. So here too, mention the importance of flexing this tendency and learning to watch the world from this angle: developing the ability to find pleasure *also* in closure, not only in processing; to follow a project until the very

end before moving on to something else; to be on time and respect the other's time; to plan and commit to a time frame; to create and maintain structure; to be organized and unclutter the environment (and the mind).

Between-Sessions Exercise for Type Seven: self-observation

During the week, actively engage in self-observing a particularly unhelpful pattern of your type. When you become aware of your patterns in real time, begin a spontaneous, one-cycle breath meditation. Follow the sequence described in Part II for observing the pattern and slowing it down. Share your insights with your coach in your next session.

TYPE EIGHT
THE CHALLENGER

EIGHTS

I think that to succeed in life you have to be **strong** and know how to **defend** yourself. If you are going to look **weak,** anybody can just treat you as a doormat. The world is not an easy place. You see **injustice** and lies everywhere. People with nice talk, nice manners, but at the bottom line: deeply unjust. The **truth** gets twisted and manipulated. I like people who talk **straight** and to the point, people who can put their cards on the table. I like knowing whom I am doing business with [...] **Independence** is important. You can't depend on others; you have to grow up and take care of yourself. (Mike, Type Eight.)

Description of Type Eight

Eights are strong, direct, and power-oriented people who are natural leaders.

At their best, they have a constant need for taking the initiative and making things happen. They face challenges head-on and encounter trouble with firmness. They are strong, decisive, determined, industrious, entrepreneurial, persistent, and tenacious. Their groundedness makes them realistic and practical, people with very good intuition.

They have a very strong tendency to independence and self-sufficiency, always preferring to be in the lead rather than being a follower. They have a very strong will, and in pursuing their vision they don't let social conventions or the opinions of others pressure them. They are honest and direct, don't adapt to the expectations of others, and don't let others' criticisms influence them or change their mind.

They are charismatic leaders whom others look up to and follow. They are quiet yet strong, and they may have a powerful presence even when silent. Paradoxically, the less they use and display their power when they could have used it, the stronger they are perceived by others.

Although they are strong and may seem hardened and rock-like at times, they have deep feelings and they use whatever power they may have to magnanimously help and protect the weak. They strive for justice and truth, and make those in their circle of trust feel well protected.

In the Stuckness Zone, they begin perceiving life as a battle. This causes them to automatically focus their attention on issues of power and control. This focus determines their approach to life, as follows:

First, they believe they must harden themselves and at the same time hide their vulnerabilities in order not to be taken advantage of. In their attempts to avoid being perceived as weak, they neither negotiate nor back down from their decisions. This results in a "my way or the highway" attitude. They want to be feared and respected. They may adopt an accountability frame of mind and become revengeful against those they perceive as enemies. At the same time, they will only respect worthy opponents—those who stand their ground.

Second, they may feel compelled to dominate and control their environment "before it controls them." They try to impose order and structure on every area of their life.

Third, their communication is direct, straightforward and often blunt, abrupt, confrontational, aggressive and "in your face." They may have a sharp antisocial attitude. Anger and its direct expression is a hallmark of Eights under stress. Denying and bullying attitudes may be present too.

Fourth, an "all-or-nothing" tendency dominates their thinking (especially regarding power issues): you are either respected or disrespected, strong or weak, independent or dependent, dominating or controlled, trusted or not trusted.

As a result of the above-mentioned four points, Eights will often advance in their quest for independence and strength, but often at too high a price. Their personal and professional relationships will inevitably suffer.

And their excesses exact a toll on their bodies as well: they become too tense, angry, reactive, and driven to exhaustion.

COACHING PROTOCOL FOR TYPE EIGHT

1. SET THE CLIMATE OF THE SESSION

Before you begin your coaching session with your client, check yourself:

Bring acceptance to the session
Ask yourself:
- Am I in a non-judgmental state?
- Does my specific personality type have any resistance with Type Eight?

"Turn on" your multimodal listening
It is extremely important that you use all the centers of intelligence (Head, Heart, Gut) during every coaching session. Be aware of "listening" actively with all three centers.

Listen with your Head center
- Pay attention to speaking style and language use.
- Analyze body language and posture.
- Analyze patterns and possibilities for interrupting them.

Listen with your Heart center
- Empathize.
- See the client as a human being, not as a "type."
- Look beyond the facade.
- Connect, in spite of any resistance that you may have. You are here to help the client grow.

Listen with your Gut center
- What kind of energy is the client bringing to the session?
- Is there a match between what the client says and the energy with which he or she says it?
- What does your intuition tell you regarding the last developments in this coaching process?
- "Listen to what people say but pay attention to what they *do*." (Madanes, 1995).

2. DEFINE THE CHALLENGE

Determine what the client wants to work on, what is the purpose of his or her pursuing coaching.

Typical challenges for Eights include:
- To be less reactive and to learn to filter their communications.
- To advance their projects by becoming more patient, better listeners to others' points of view.
- To find healthier ways to process their anger.
- To learn to negotiate and back down at times, to preserve their relationships (especially when nothing important is at stake).
- To learn how to relax in order to avoid an excessive lifestyle that can affect their health.

3. UNDERSTAND THE COACHEE'S MODEL OF THE WORLD AND HIS OR HER STUCKNESS ZONE

Ask yourself the following questions: Why is the client acting the way he does? What is shaping her behavior? What is his internal story? What are the filters through which she looks at and perceives the world? To what extent are the type fixations active and operative in this client?

When Type Eights are less aware or under stress, their attention gets hijacked/derailed by their perception of life as a battle in which you either survive or are destroyed. In this state their attention goes automatically to issues of power and control.

4. BRING AWARENESS TO THE SIX HUMAN NEEDS

According to Human Needs Psychology, we all have six basic human needs (Madanes, 2009): Certainty, Variety, Love/Connection, Significance, Growth, and Contribution. These needs are not merely desires, but true drivers mobilizing our behavior.

Exercise for Type Eight: **The six human needs.** Look at the Stuckness Zone and from the whole range of behaviors there described, pick the most frequent ones: "What human needs are you trying to fulfill by engaging in these behaviors?"

Please score each need from 0 to 10.

Certainty. Does engaging in these behaviors make you feel certain?

From Stuckness to Growth

Visualize potential
- leader
- builder   WHILE...
- entrepreneurial

- calmly powerful
- protecting
- empowering

POSITIVE INTERRUPTION

STUCKNESS ZONE

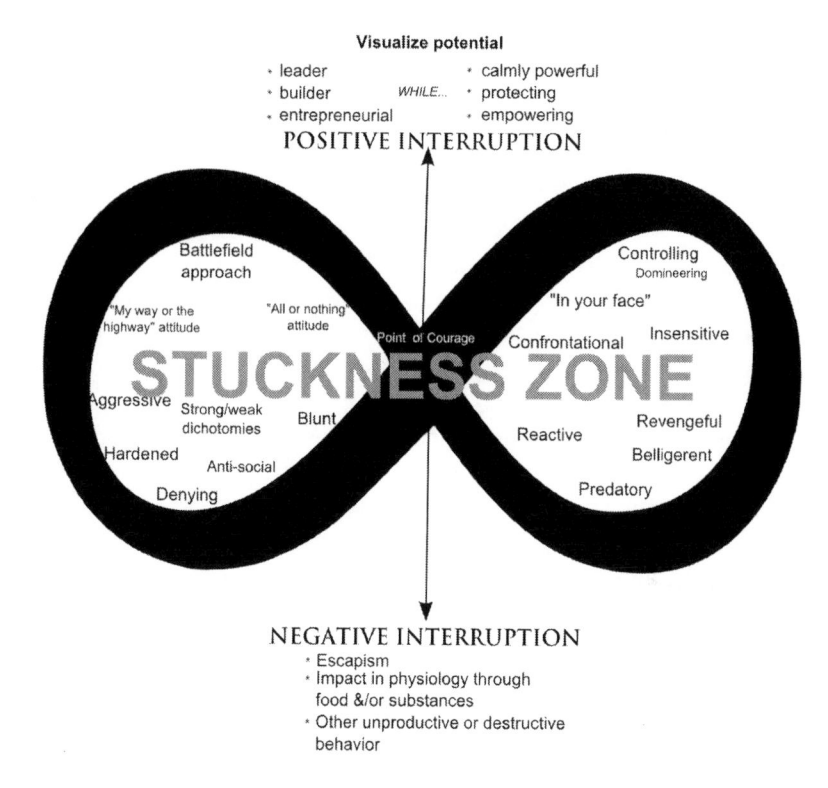

- Battlefield approach
- "My way or the highway" attitude
- "All or nothing" attitude
- Point of Courage
- Aggressive
- Strong/weak dichotomies
- Blunt
- Hardened
- Anti-social
- Denying

- Controlling
- Domineering
- "In your face"
- Confrontational
- Insensitive
- Reactive
- Revengeful
- Belligerent
- Predatory

NEGATIVE INTERRUPTION
- Escapism
- Impact in physiology through food &/or substances
- Other unproductive or destructive behavior

Give you a sense of security? Apart from these behaviors: Do you also know how to obtain certainty in a more positive way?

Variety. Does engaging in these behaviors bring you a sense of variety? Apart from these behaviors: Do you also know how to obtain variety in a more positive way?

Love/connection. Does engaging in these behaviors make you feel connected to others? Experience a sense of love? Apart from these behaviors: Do you also know how to obtain love/connection in a more positive way?

Significance. Does engaging in these behaviors make you feel important? Special? Apart from these behaviors: Do you also know how to obtain significance in a more positive way?

Growth. Does engaging in these behaviors give you a sense of development, make you feel that you're growing? Apart from these behaviors: Do you know how to obtain growth in a more positive way?

Contribution. Does engaging in these behaviors give you a sense of going beyond your own needs, of giving to others? Apart from these behaviors: Do you also know how to obtain contribution in a more positive way?

Coaching case study. Take as an example George, one of our coachees, a Type Eight. He comes from a family that went through very tough economic times; he saw his father sinking in debt and his business collapsing. Today George owns a small business that is rapidly expanding. He devotes most of his time to his business, in order to satisfy his strong need for *Significance*. He came to coaching due to feelings of constant exhaustion, and a crisis with his family due to his almost total devotion to the business. Another need that he tries to satisfy through his business is the need for *Certainty*. It's hard for him to trust his employees, and through the years he has not been able to delegate enough, keeping him hypervigilant and, in turn, stressed. He gave himself Certainty by not trusting anyone. The breakthrough came when George identified these strong needs and the fact he was satisfying them in negative ways. To find positive, alternative ways to fulfill his needs, George first rediscovered his strong connection to Type Two, and his ever-present need to make a contribution to his community. He became more involved in community issues, and accepted an *ad honorem* position in one of the community's religious institutions. The institution's administration had long been requesting him to accept that position, because they believed he could be of great help due to his leadership abilities. This became a major source of *Significance* for George, opening the door to the awareness that Significance can be obtained through other means too, not only through his business. This in turn led him to a more balanced life, in spite of his still devoting much time to his business, and also to his looking for ways to be with his family more. He began by asking his wife to come with him on many of his business trips. He also asked his son to take over one department of the business. He gradually began trusting him and other loyal employees. This helped him fulfill his need for Certainty in a positive way, and became a path of integration towards a more relaxed and centered life.

One important point to take into account: pay special attention to the needs of Growth and Contribution. Does the coachee meet these needs in healthy or in destructive ways? As we integrate our personality, the needs of Growth and Contribution begin receiving high scores while also being met in positive and healthy ways. The reason for this is that when we move out of our Stuckness Zone, we act from new, conscious, chosen responses. This allows us to overcome our old habits and grow. This integration, in turn, will always bring greater contribution to others. In contrast, if we continue acting without awareness, out of our old patterns of reaction, we disempower ourselves and let our egos manage our lives. This always causes suffering to ourselves and to others.

5. PRODUCE LEVERAGE

The next step is to gain leverage by bringing awareness to the costs and suffering that the unhelpful patterns of the type are causing for the client.

Exercise for Type Eight: Gaining awareness of the costs of patterns
- How much does it cost you, in terms of your relationships, to be insensitive, revengeful, and controlling?
- How much does it cost you, in terms of your health, to be reactive and angry most of the time?
- How much does it cost you, in terms of your professional career, to have a battlefield approach—being blunt and anti-social, and having a constant confrontational attitude?
- How much does it cost you, in terms of your personal fulfillment and own sense of happiness, to be unable to connect to your own vulnerabilities?

6. PATTERN INTERRUPTION: BUILDING OUR ATTENTIONAL MUSCLES

TYPE EIGHT VISUALIZATION

Visualizations are a great tool for coaching in general and when doing personality-types coaching in particular. The following is a comprehensive visualization/meditation script for Type Eight. It encompasses working with the type's strengths and weaknesses, training attentional abilities through the Impartial Spectator, training conscious breathing, acceptance, and relaxation. In a single coaching session, you don't have to use them all. You can use these visualizations modularly, by selecting one or more of the sections that follow.

Script for Type Eight: Visualization/Meditation

Relaxation

Begin by finding a comfortable sitting position. Keep your spine straight in a natural way. Let your arms become loose. Lightly, with palms facing up or down, rest your hands on your lap. Take one deep breath, to begin relaxing your whole body. Inhale. . .Exhale. . . You can gently close your eyes and take another deep breath as a way to become centered and focused. Inhale. . .Exhale . . .

Training the Impartial Spectator

Let's begin by bringing awareness to the Impartial Spectator. Think of the Impartial Spectator as your friend who objectively watches your behavior from the outside. It helps you make wise decisions and allows you to regulate your automatic pilot.

The Impartial Spectator will do so by training your mind to be sensitive to the activity in your three centers of intelligence: the Body (our physical sensations), the Mind (thoughts, plans, future, past, images, ideas, imagination), and the Heart (feelings). Our breath, which symbolically represents our connection to our soul, will allow us to remain centered and to shift our attention from one center to the other. It will also help us to remain non-judgmental and to bring the qualities of gratitude, compassion, and acceptance to this exercise. Every time your mind wanders, you can use the moment to exercise those qualities of gratitude, compassion, and acceptance—for each one of those moments offers the opportunity to learn how to reorient our attention.

Begin by gently shifting your attention to your **Body** center of intelligence. Take a deep breath, and follow the path of the air in and out of the body. Do it slowly. Inhale again. . . and this time make the exhalation last a bit longer. Place your full attention on the path of the air getting in and out of your body, from beginning to end. Begin noticing your body sensations. Sense the contact points between your feet and the floor. What body sensations are in there right now? Move your attention to your back. Feel the support that the chair gives you. Stay with that sensation for a moment. Shift your attention to your hands. Focus on the contact point between the hands and your lap.

Place your hands over your chest, one over the other, and shift your attention to your **Heart** center of intelligence: What feelings do you have in this moment?

Now shift your attention to the **Head** center of intelligence. Is there a mental commentary about your feelings? Is there judgment or acceptance of your feelings? What is your mind saying about your feelings? What is it saying about this whole exercise? Serenely watch your mental discourse as it appears. Inhale...Exhale... Stay in the Head center, and now shift your attention to your memories. Imagine yourself watching an old black-and-white TV set on which your past history is being broadcast. You see yourself in the TV. Your life videotaped. Each stage of your life, on the screen, in slow motion. Nod when you actually see it. Inhale...Exhale... Still in the Head center, now move your attention to the future. Serenely reflect on each one of the following questions. Take a few moments as a pause between each question. What do you want your future to be like? How do you see yourself in the future? What plans do you have?

Visualization

Remain in the Head center, and you will now shift your attention to your imagination. Imagine yourself at the beach, at the sea shore, in slightly wet sand. Breath the air at the beach. Inhale...Exhale... Feel the wind. Listen to the waves in the sea. Feel the sand on your feet. Imagine yourself drawing an imaginary number eight, drawn horizontally, like the infinity symbol, in the slightly wet sand on the shore. Draw it slowwwly. Feel the contact point between your fingers and the sand.

Visualization of Stuckness Zone and costs

Now picture yourself putting all your problems and challenges *inside* that eight in the sand. One by one.

All my continuous attempts to impose control over everything and everyone and my fear of looking vulnerable. All my enslavement to maintaining a strong armor, and the tiredness and exhaustion that result from not being able to let my guard down. My constant hiding of my deepest emotions. Keeping all my anger inside, my constant holding of an accountability mindset, and my seeking revenge. My fear inside for not being able to trust anybody. All the tension. All the suffering.

Feel the tension and anger. Feel it in your belly as you see all the issues inside the eight in the sand. Feel the tension in your whole body. Stay there for a moment.

This eight in the sand represents our Stuckness Zone. The place we get stuck with negative focus and negative feelings.

"It's human" section

Every human being has issues that make him or her precisely that, human. It's a personal, tailor-made set of challenges in life. Watch your own personal challenges without judgments. If your mind passes a commentary, it's OK. Don't worry and try to do this exercise "right." If there is a judgment, just watch the judgment. Listen to its script. Watch it as it occurs, outside of you.

It's human to have judgments about our experience. It's OK. Bring your attention to your heart. Now, grab the judgments you just heard in your head, the mental comments, and put them there, in your heart. Use the energy of your heart to soften them and feel how it fills your whole body with compassion. Take a deep breath, and feel the energy of your heart throughout your whole body. Feel the acceptance.

Why does life bring you challenges? Life brings you challenges so you can overcome them, and allow the next level of plenitude and vitality to become available to you. They are precious opportunities to grow. Precious opportunities to discover the strengths *you already have* that simply need to be reactivated. The strengths that will help you overcome your challenges, the strengths that will help you move from stuckness to growth.

Inside of you there is a part that doesn't want to give up. That wants to live life at its fullest. It's the voice of your soul. The voice that wants to stand up to the voices of the ego and the personality—and become the best possible you. You've been there before, and that's what brought you up to this moment. This moment in which you are here struggling to become the best person you can be, standing up and not giving up to your personality, to your automatic thoughts. It's the real you, it's the strength of your soul.

At this point your attention may automatically go to create thoughts about your thoughts. It's OK. Simply keep breathing consciously, following the path of the air in and out of your body, and let your Impartial Spectator witness the activity of your mind non-judgmentally.

Visualization of strengths, potential, and personal power

Now please move your attention to that part of yourself that doesn't want to give up. Look at the drawing on the sand: exactly in the center of the eight there is a point: the intersection between the right side and the left side of the eight. Let's call it the *point of courage*. From that point, imagine yourself drawing an arrow up. An exit from the eight. An exit from the stuckness.

This arrow points to what is available outside the eight. This arrow points to your strengths and to your potential. To the future that is available to you in any given moment.

Let's see what's outside the eight.

I want you to think of any moment in the past in which you felt really relaxed, in which you felt acceptance for yourself and others. It can be any moment in which you felt light and serene.

Bring it from any area of your life: you could have been by yourself, with a friend, with a group of friends, or with your family. In your personal or your professional life. Go to the past and bring back that moment. It could be a special moment or just a simple one. Feel it. Feel the relaxation of that moment in your whole body.

Search your memories for that moment in which you were calmly powerful. Tolerant. Feel the relaxation of that moment in which you let go of perceiving life as survival. Everything flowed harmoniously and everything actually worked well and turned out well, without your doing anything. Take a deep breath and feel that moment.

Let's see what else is outside the eight.

I now want you to envision yourself in a new future. A future in which you are productive but serene. A future in which you are constantly building something important and you lead others to good and constructive causes, and you do so tolerantly and compassionately. In which you accept yourself as a human being, including some less positive aspects. In which you are in touch with your heart. Please put your hands one over the other, and over your heart. Feel your heartbeat. Feel your humanity. Since you are human, you are allowed to have and sense vulnerabilities. That doesn't make you less safe. It just makes you more human. Your heart dissolves the anger, so plenty of energy gets liberated for healthy productivity. Feel it. Since you are not afraid of having vulnerabilities like everybody else, you can admit them and learn from them. This helps you fulfill one of your true dreams: truly becoming a strong person.

Bring that moment from the future, and feel it in your body, in the present moment. Feel it in your heart and in your mind. Feel the power of your mind, heart, and body working together and see what you can achieve, and most important: how all that is inside of you now and you *already* are the good person you always wanted to be.

Let's gently finish the meditation by slowly going back and watching the whole drawing in the sand.

Watch the eight, together with the point of courage and all the potential that is available *within* you.

End of visualization

I acknowledge you for your courage, for being here and trying to grow as a person, for trying to overcome yourself, for the efforts you do, for not giving up. The mere fact of your doing this exercise is a testimony of your inner strength and of your not giving up. I also want you to acknowledge yourself for your courage, for not giving up. And I want you to thank life for the challenges it brings you, for the many opportunities it brings you every day, so through them you can become in touch with your strengths, to grow and also to contribute to the world, to give to the world around you the gifts of your real self.

7. RE-PATTERNING: EXERCISES FOR FILTER FLEXING AND INTEGRATION

Black-and-White Thinking

"Black-and-White Thinking" is a cognitive distorting filter that may typically dominate Type Eight thinking in the Stuckness Zone. This filter causes Eights to think in dichotomous terms. This filter is also used by Type One, but here the Eight puts much emphasis on dichotomies regarding strength and power: you are either strong or weak, controlling or controlled, exploiting or exploited, courageous or cowardly; "you are either my friend or my enemy." Much of the rigidity and suffering of Type Eight is caused by this mechanism. In order to overcome this automatic tendency, Eights can use their Seven wing to incorporate the qualities of highly functioning Sevens: the ability to think in colors, in shades of gray.

The ability to think more in percentages, in "degrees of," than in absolutes.

Exercise for Type Eight: Flexing the Black-and-White filter
- What other possibilities do you see besides the two you mentioned?
- Is there an option in the middle?
- People can fail from time to time. Forgiveness is a mechanism that exists in life precisely to compensate for those human errors. Check your reactivity. Ask yourself: When I perceive an action as being disloyal to me, am I jumping to conclusions too quickly? Use your connection to Five to bring criteria and objectivity. From 0 to 100 percent, what would you say: How "disloyal" has this person become?

Learn to relax

Eights on autopilot tend to overwhelm themselves with controlling their work and projects. Fear may arise if they allow themselves to be non-controlling for even short periods of time. It is not uncommon to see Eights coming to coaching burned out after years of driving themselves too hard. An underdeveloped muscle in Eights is the ability to release tensions and know how to relax and take things easy. This can be obtained by using their Seven and Nine wings.

Exercise for Type Eight: Learning to relax. Ask yourself: How can I stop and "smell the roses" this week? How can I laugh at my mistakes?
Many Eights find peace in nature. Consider making a weekly trip to a quiet place in nature where you can connect with yourself and quiet your tense body.

Open your Heart

If they spend too much time in the Stuckness Zone, where their battlefield mentality dominates, Eights may become hardened and lose connection with their own hearts. In terms of the Enneagram Triads, they may spend too much time in their bodies and heads, and no time in their hearts. Connecting with their deepest emotions and vulnerabilities is perhaps the most difficult challenge for the Eight coachee, so be patient and non-judgmental, and adapt yourself to his or her pace. Provide a safe place and find the appropriate timing for your interventions.

Exercise for Type Eight: Opening the Heart
- For many people, anger is a secondary emotion. They may resort to anger to protect other vulnerable feelings. In other words, every time they have an emotion they think will make them look vulnerable if they were to show it, they cover it up with anger. Ask yourself: Can I perceive what emotion I feel right *before* my anger erupts? Use a precise word to describe that emotion: Is it worry? Disappointment? Sadness? Fear? Humiliation?
- Ask as a Two: What does this person feel? Stay there for a moment. Empathize. Understand. Then ask: How can I help? What can I give? What else can I give? Allow your well-guarded heart and generosity to manifest on the outside.

Paying attention to the speaking style

Language is powerful: it's the vehicle that transports meaning. When we interpret reality through our filters, we put words to it. Therefore, if we are able to change the words that we attach to our experiences, we can indirectly impact our emotional states, since a big percentage of our emotions comes from our language. People are hypnotized by their own language patterns, creating blind spots that don't allow them to see reality accurately (Robbins and Madanes, 2005). By always using the same phrases and words to describe their experience, each personality type ends by not seeing what's in front of it. Literally, the description of reality becomes the *actual* reality. Those phrases and words are simply a manifestation of the underlying limiting beliefs that each type holds. Changing the speaking style can thus help us expand our frames of reference, allowing us to see the situations in our daily lives from many more angles.

It is important for coachees to develop the ability to become aware of when their personality mechanisms hijack their language, at the moment it occurs. For Type Eights in the Stuckness Zone, this manifests in their attempt to control the conversations.

Exercise for Type Eight: Flexing the discursive style
- Pay attention to the use of words that put in motion your strong/weak dichotomies: "war," "coward," "crybaby," "strength," "power," and the like, and use more flexible wording instead.

Avoid the use of profanity as a way to make your messages more shocking and intense.
- Pay attention to the conversation topics and format. Am I being or sounding commanding? Use your Seven wing to *equalize* between you and your conversation partner. Am I considering other people's opinions or just my own? Use your Nine wing to open yourself to actively listen to *everyone's* point of view.
- Am I being impatient? Am I rushing my conversation partner to present their "bottom line"? Use your Nine wing to bring calmness to your interactions.
- Use your Nine wing to add a bit of diplomacy to your powerful speaking style. There is an English proverb that says: "Politeness costs nothing." A related Spanish expression, *"Lo cortes no quita lo valiente,"* goes a little beyond that point, meaning that you can have enough valor to do whatever necessary while dealing with the matter as politely as possible. Eights' language is sometimes too abrupt, too blunt, too shocking, and it doesn't serve their purposes well. Paradoxically, the less they use and display bluntness and aggressive language, when they could have used it, the stronger they are perceived by others. Out of the Stuckness Zone they may have a powerful presence even when silent.

Work with the Jungian preferences: Integrating our less-dominant qualities

When coaching a Type Eight, it is very important to pay attention to his or her Jungian preferences. If a coachee has done an MBTI profile, ask for his or her four-letter type and discuss how Jungian preferences may play together with the coachee's Enneatype. Also, when clients get stuck in the lower side of their Jungian preference, we can use the same pattern interruption techniques described all through this book to help them shift out and grow. For a description of the Jungian preferences, please refer to Part I of this book.

Some examples of the usage of the Jungian preferences in coaching a Type Eight:
- When you are coaching Eights, it will become almost immediately

clear to you whether they are Extraverts or Introverts. Eights with a Seven Wing tend to be Extraverts, while Eights with a Nine wing tend to be Introverts. The latter are more quiet and private, and tend to be less blunt in their style. They are more intimate and reflective, needing more space and time to think about what's being said in the sessions. With them the sessions will move slowly, so don't overwhelm them with too much talking or too many insights.

- The whole Feeling dimension is very illustrative for some development goals of Eights. Talk about it in your coaching sessions. Mention the importance of learning to watch and perceive the world from this angle: learning to recognize the personal needs of others; being receptive and learning to listen empathically to others; learning to canalize their search for justice towards meaningful personal and social values; interacting in a more interpersonal way instead of being distant; when making decisions, taking into account other people's emotions and what impact the decisions will have on them.
- Another dimension that is very useful for some development goals of Eights is Perceiving. Here too, mention the importance of learning to watch the world from this angle: developing the ability to flow, to develop flexibility when the situation requires it, instead of being too strict and rigid; finding pleasure in process itself, not just final results; developing the ability to be spontaneous, to adapt to changes, to recognize the necessity sometimes to gather more information before making important decisions, to relax and feel comfortable in some areas of life, leaving a couple of things flowing and not under their control.

Between-Sessions Exercise for Type Eight: self-observation

During the week, actively engage in self-observing a particularly unhelpful pattern of your type. When you become aware of your patterns in real time, begin a spontaneous, one-cycle breath meditation. Follow the sequence described in Part II for observing the pattern and slowing it down. Share your insights with your coach in your next session.

TYPE NINE
THE PEACEMAKER

NINES

People tell me I am an **easygoing** person, easy to live with. That I am **non-judgmental, accepting.** At home I've heard that I'm a little **dreamy, spacey**. . .Everyone tries to speed me up. I dislike it when **others** try to accelerate me; I become **stubbornly** slower. I usually like to do things at my **pace**, at my rhythm. No **rush**. When others get **nervous**, I automatically go slower. It's very important for me to be **asked for** things in an **appropriate** manner. I don't like aggressiveness and lack of **harmony** between people. My father says I need to learn how to stand my ground, that I say "yes" when inside I mean "no." Maybe he's right, **I don't know**. . .I just don't like fights, conflicts. I truly believe that by **talking** about everything, everything can be solved. There is no need to bring senseless friction into all we do (Tom, Type Nine.)

Description of Type Nine

Nines are easygoing, relaxed, and stable people who have an orientation towards the peaceful and the harmonious.

At their best, they are easygoing, receptive, adaptive, and flexible. They are emotionally stable, good-natured, slow to anger, relaxed, and diplomatic. Although not very demonstrative or expressive emotionally, they are kind, warm, supportive, and likable.

They have a quiet, stable nature and have a strong need for harmony in both their internal life and their relationships. Although they look serene and stable and are usually modest and keep a low profile, they are very active and dynamic, achieving the goals they set for themselves in a gentle, non-anxious style. They are present and fully engaged in their lives. They are nice to people, but know how to keep their boundaries and respect their own priorities, desires, and needs.

They are masters of mediation and conflict resolution: they possess the necessary skills for making all parties in a conflict feel heard and their perspective understood. They are good listeners and accept people as they are. They are able to understand different perspectives simultaneously. They are firm yet relaxed and diplomatic, treating others respectfully. They are good communicators and know how to tactfully guide the parties in a conflict without making them defensive. They are highly creative, and when a full resolution is not possible, they know how to bring the parties to "agree to disagree," whereby all parties tolerate but don't accept the opposing position, but at least remain on amicable terms while continuing to disagree (or recognize that further conflict is unnecessary, ineffective, or undesirable).

They have a spiritual quality that gives them a sense of being one with life. From this quality many characteristics emerge.

First, they have a faith in life and the Universe, and that everything that happens is for the good of the person. They also believe that "when you want something, all the Universe conspires in helping you to achieve it."

Second, they are patient and have endurance under difficult circumstances, persevering in the face of delay or provocation without acting in a negative way. They exhibit forbearance when under strain, especially when faced with long-term difficulties. Their patience also allows them to function effectively during crises, acting without agitation or disturbance and bringing calm to an anxious environment.

Third, they have equanimity, a deep awareness and acceptance of the present moment, that allows them to appreciate the simplest things in life.

Fourth, they empower others by simply accepting and encouraging them to develop themselves and giving them freedom to choose their growth path.

Although they are spiritual people, they remain deeply grounded, and realistic, and they can take quick action based on their instincts.

In the Stuckness Zone, they begin to have a strong desire to maintain an internal and external sense of peace (sometimes at any cost). Their focus of attention shifts more exclusively to things that can alter their sense of quiet.

To maintain their external sense of peace, they focus automatically on how to avoid conflict and tension. They begin to accommodate their own agenda to other people's requests and demands, merging themselves and sometimes almost disappearing in the process. They may say "yes" just to please other people, when they really mean "no." They don't take strong positions because they prefer not to upset others. Although they may look outwardly nice, they may begin acting passive-aggressively, becoming stubborn and internally refusing to act.

To maintain their internal sense of peace, they try to maintain their life as free from changes as possible, and as comfortable as possible. They want to hold to routines and not be moved from them. They can become passive and unpretentious. Their healthy modesty degenerates into an "I don't count" mentality. They perceive themselves as not important, as if their participation in the world doesn't count. They forget themselves and become invisible while acquiring other people's agendas.

In order to maintain peace they try to dissociate from anything disturbing, including their own emotions, thoughts, and experiences. Since reality and life usually present us with daily annoyances and disturbances, they may begin to numb themselves in order to avoid them. Many fall into distracting and anesthetizing habits like overeating, watching TV, or spending hours at the computer with no clear purpose. It's like escaping into sleep. They lose track of time and begin living with low self-awareness.

This automatic focus on keeping internal/external peace usually leaves them confused and with low energy, with difficulties in taking action in the important areas of their lives. Since nothing seems either really important or urgent to them, they give everything the same importance, losing the ability to prioritize or make decisions effectively. Inessentials and small comforts replace real priorities. Problems may accumulate and they may become indifferent to them, and a "problems-will-take-care-of-themselves" mentality sets in.

COACHING PROTOCOL FOR TYPE NINE

1. SET THE CLIMATE OF THE SESSION

Before you begin your coaching session with your client, check yourself:

Bring acceptance to the session

Ask yourself:
- Am I in a non-judgmental state?
- Does my specific personality type have any resistance with Type Nine?

"Turn on" your multimodal listening

It is extremely important that you use all the centers of intelligence (Head, Heart, Gut) during every coaching session. Be aware of "listening" actively with all three centers.

Listen with your Head center
- Pay attention to speaking style and language use.
- Analyze body language and posture.
- Analyze patterns and possibilities for interrupting them.

Listen with your Heart center
- Empathize.
- See the client as a human being, not as a "type."
- Look beyond the facade.
- Connect, in spite of any resistance that you may have. You are here to help the client grow.

Listen with your Gut center
- What kind of energy is the client bringing to the session?
- Is there a match between what the client says and the energy with which he or she says it?
- What does your intuition tell you regarding the last developments in this coaching process?
- "Listen to what people say but pay attention to what they *do*." (Madanes, 1995).

2. DEFINE THE CHALLENGE

Determine what the client wants to work on, what is the purpose of his or her pursuing coaching.

Typical challenges for Nines include:
- To take charge of their lives and begin advancing their own agenda.
- To give conflict a healthy place in their lives and learn how to effectively deal with it.
- To become clear and effective in their decision-making and goal-setting processes.
- To become more aware, present, and engaged in their lives.

3. UNDERSTAND THE COACHEE'S MODEL OF THE WORLD AND HIS OR HER STUCKNESS ZONE

Ask yourself the following questions: Why is the client acting the way he does? What is shaping her behavior? What is his internal story? What are the filters through which she looks at and perceives the world? To what extent are the type fixations active and operative in this client?

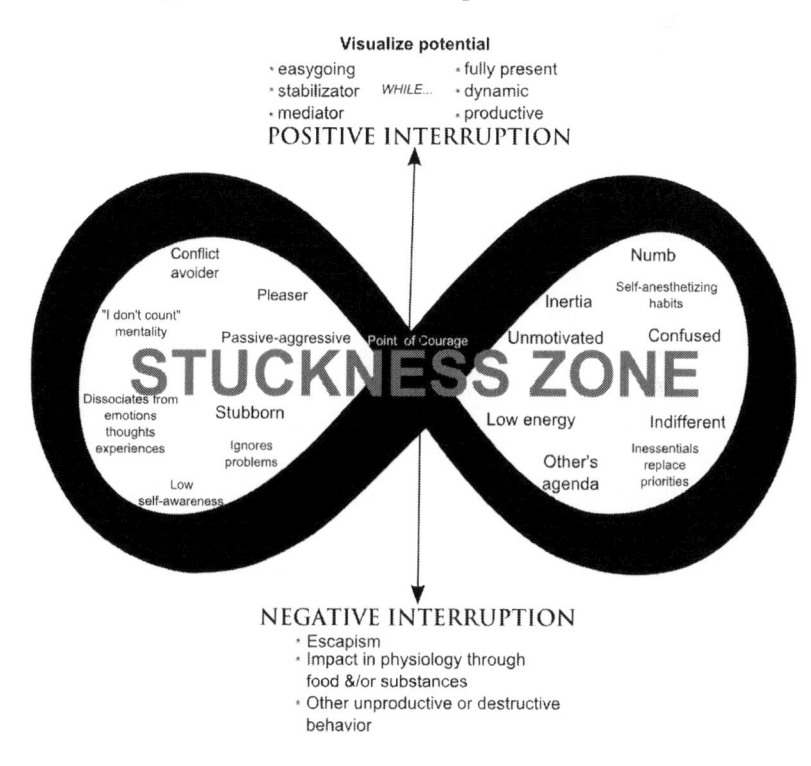

Visualize potential
- easygoing
- stabilizator   WHILE...
- mediator
- fully present
- dynamic
- productive

POSITIVE INTERRUPTION

STUCKNESS ZONE

- Conflict avoider
- "I don't count" mentality
- Pleaser
- Passive-aggressive
- Point of Courage
- Dissociates from emotions thoughts experiences
- Stubborn
- Ignores problems
- Low self-awareness
- Numb
- Self-anesthetizing habits
- Inertia
- Unmotivated
- Confused
- Low energy
- Other's agenda
- Indifferent
- Inessentials replace priorities

NEGATIVE INTERRUPTION
- Escapism
- Impact in physiology through food &/or substances
- Other unproductive or destructive behavior

When Nines are less aware or under stress, their attention gets hijacked/derailed by a strong desire to maintain an internal and external sense of peace, sometimes at any cost. In this state their focus of attention shifts more exclusively to things that can alter their sense of peace.

4. BRING AWARENESS TO THE SIX HUMAN NEEDS

According to Human Needs Psychology, we all have six basic human needs (Madanes, 2009): Certainty, Variety, Love/Connection, Significance, Growth, and Contribution. These needs are not merely desires, but true drivers mobilizing our behavior.

Exercise for Type Nine: The six human needs. Look at the Stuckness Zone and from the whole range of behaviors there described, pick the most frequent ones: "What human needs are you trying to fulfill by engaging in these behaviors?"

Please score each need from 0 to 10.

Certainty. Does engaging in these behaviors make you feel certain? Give you a sense of security? Apart from these behaviors: Do you also know how to obtain certainty in a more positive way?

Variety. Does engaging in these behaviors bring you a sense of variety? Apart from these behaviors: Do you also know how to obtain variety in a more positive way?

Love/connection. Does engaging in these behaviors make you feel connected to others? Experience a sense of love?
Apart from these behaviors: Do you also know how to obtain love/connection in a more positive way?

Significance. Does engaging in these behaviors make you feel important? Special? Apart from these behaviors: Do you also know how to obtain significance in a more positive way?

Growth. Does engaging in these behaviors give you a sense of development, make you feel that you're growing? Apart from these behaviors: Do you also know how to obtain growth in a more positive way?

Contribution. Does engaging in these behaviors give you a sense of going beyond your own needs, of giving to others? Apart from these behaviors: Do you also know how to obtain contribution in a more positive way?

Coaching case study. Take as an example Aileen, one of our coachees, a Type Nine. She came to coaching feeling abused in both her marriage and her job. During our sessions together she discovered she has strong needs for *Connection* and *Certainty*. The problem was that she was trying to satisfy these needs in a negative way. In order to maintain her sense of Connection, she avoids conflict, and most of the time says "yes" when she means "no." This, in turn, was interpreted by others as an invitation to request whatever they wanted from her. She kept adapting herself to the situation for years, with the hope that "problems will take care of themselves." The result today is her feeling abused. The breakthrough came when she discovered that taking a stance and asserting her needs contributes to the creation of healthy relationships based on mutual respect, and thus to a deeper sense of *Connection*. We worked on developing her assertiveness. Regarding her need for *Certainty*, she fulfilled it by adapting herself to other people's agendas, by not trusting her own criteria. In this case, the breakthrough came when she began listening to her own voice, to ask herself what *she* wants. We encouraged her to use her arrow to the higher side of Six: to be able to trust her own internal guide.

One important point to take into account: pay special attention to the needs of Growth and Contribution. Does the coachee meet these needs in healthy or in destructive ways? As we integrate our personality, the needs of Growth and Contribution begin receiving high scores while also being met in positive and healthy ways. The reason for this is that when we move out of our Stuckness Zone, we act from new, conscious, chosen responses. This allows us to overcome our old habits and grow. This integration, in turn, always will bring greater contribution to others. In contrast, if we continue acting without awareness, out of our old patterns of reaction, we disempower ourselves and let our egos manage our lives. This always causes suffering to ourselves and to others.

5. PRODUCE LEVERAGE

The next step is to gain leverage by bringing awareness to the costs and suffering that the unhelpful patterns of the type are causing for the client.

Exercise for Type Nine: Gaining awareness of the costs of patterns
- How much does it cost you, in terms of your relationships, to please others, to avoid conflict at all costs, and to be passive-aggressive?

- How much does it cost you, in terms of your health, to numb yourself with anesthetizing habits?
- How much does it cost you, in terms of your professional career, to automatically assume other people's agendas, to be unmotivated, and to replace important priorities with inessentials?
- How much does it cost you, in terms of your personal fulfillment and own sense of happiness, to live dissociated from your emotions, thoughts, and experiences, and to live by inertia?

6. PATTERN INTERRUPTION: BUILDING OUR ATTENTIONAL MUSCLES

TYPE NINE VISUALIZATION

Visualizations are a great tool for coaching in general and when doing personality-types coaching in particular. The following is a comprehensive visualization/meditation script for Type Nine. It encompasses working with the type's strengths and weaknesses, training attentional abilities through the Impartial Spectator, training conscious breathing, acceptance, and relaxation. In a single coaching session, you don't have to use them all. You can use these visualizations modularly, by selecting one or more of the sections that follow.

Script for Type Nine: Visualization/Meditation

Relaxation

Begin by finding a comfortable sitting position. Keep your spine straight in a natural way. Let your arms become loose. Lightly, with palms facing up or down, rest your hands on your lap. Take one deep breath, to begin relaxing your whole body. Inhale. . .Exhale. . . You can gently close your eyes and take another deep breath as a way to become centered and focused. Inhale. . .Exhale . . .

Training the Impartial Spectator

Let's begin by bringing awareness to the Impartial Spectator. Think of the Impartial Spectator as your friend who objectively watches your behavior from the outside. It helps you make wise decisions and allows you to regulate your automatic pilot.

The Impartial Spectator will do so by training your mind to be sensitive to the activity in your three centers of intelligence: the Body (our physical sensations), the Mind (thoughts, plans, future, past, images, ideas, imagination), and the Heart (feelings). Our breath, which symbolically represents our connection to our soul, will allow us to remain centered and to shift our attention from one center to the other. It will also help us to remain non-judgmental and to bring the qualities of gratitude, compassion, and acceptance to this exercise. Every time your mind wanders, you can use the moment to exercise those qualities of gratitude, compassion, and acceptance—for each one of those moments offers the opportunity to learn how to reorient our attention.

Begin by gently shifting your attention to your **Body** center of intelligence. Take a deep breath, and follow the path of the air in and out of the body. Do it slowly. Inhale again. . . and this time make the exhalation last a bit longer. Place your full attention on the path of the air getting in and out of your body, from beginning to end. Begin noticing your body sensations. Sense the contact points between your feet and the floor. What body sensations are in there right now? Move your attention to your back. Feel the support that the chair gives you. Stay with that sensation for a moment. Shift your attention to your hands. Focus on the contact point between the hands and your lap.

Place your hands over your chest, one over the other, and shift your attention to your **Heart** center of intelligence. What feelings do you have in this moment?

Now shift your attention to the **Head** center of intelligence. Is there a mental commentary about your feelings? Is there judgment or acceptance of your feelings? What is your mind saying about your feelings? What is it saying about this whole exercise? Serenely watch your mental discourse as it appears. Inhale. . .Exhale. . . Stay in the Head center, and now shift your attention to your memories. Imagine yourself watching an old black-and-white TV set on which your past history is being broadcast. You see yourself in the TV. Your life videotaped. Each stage of your life, on the screen, in slow motion. Nod when you actually see it. Inhale. . .Exhale. . . Still in the Head center, now move your attention to the future. Serenely reflect on each one of the following questions. Take a few moments as a pause between each question. What do you want your future to be like? How do you see yourself in the future? What plans do you have?

Visualization

Remain in the Head center, and you will now shift your attention to your imagination. Imagine yourself at the beach, at the sea shore, in slightly wet sand. Breath the air at the beach. Inhale. . .Exhale. . . Feel the wind. Listen to the waves in the sea. Feel the sand on your feet. Imagine yourself drawing an imaginary number eight, drawn horizontally, like the infinity symbol, in the slightly wet sand on the shore. Draw it slowwwly. Feel the contact point between your fingers and the sand.

Visualization of Stuckness Zone and costs

Now picture yourself putting all your problems and challenges *inside* that eight in the sand. One by one.

All my continuous attention to other people's points of view, ignoring mine. My inability to stand my ground. My fear of conflict, and doing anything to avoid it. My constant feeling that I don't count, that my opinion doesn't matter. My low energy and my feeling unmotivated to do anything, and my living by inertia. All the costs I've paid for ignoring my problems. All my repressed anger. All the suffering.

Feel the tension and anger. Feel it in your belly as you see all the issues inside the eight in the sand. Feel the tension in your whole body. Stay there for a moment.

This eight in the sand represents our Stuckness Zone. The place we get stuck with negative focus and negative feelings.

"It's human" section

Every human being has issues that make him or her precisely that, human. It's a personal, tailor-made set of challenges in life. Watch your own personal challenges without judgments. If your mind passes a commentary, it's OK. Don't worry and try to do this exercise "right." If there is a judgment, just watch the judgment. Listen to its script. Watch it as it occurs, outside of you.

It's human to have judgments about our experience. It's OK. Bring your attention to your heart. Now, grab the judgments you just heard in your head, the mental comments, and put them there, in your heart. Use the energy of your heart to soften them and feel how it fills your whole body with compassion. Take a deep breath, and feel the energy of your heart throughout your whole body. Feel the acceptance.

Why does life bring you challenges? Life brings you challenges so you can overcome them, and allow the next level of plenitude and vitality to become available to you. They are precious opportunities to grow. Precious opportunities to discover the strengths *you already have* that simply need to be reactivated. The strengths that will help you overcome your challenges, the strengths that will help you move from stuckness to growth.

Inside of you there is a part that doesn't want to give up. That wants to live life at its fullest. It's the voice of your soul. The voice that wants to stand up to the voices of the ego and the personality—and become the best possible you. You've been there before, and that's what brought you up to this moment. This moment in which you are here struggling to become the best person you can be, standing up and not giving up to your personality, to your automatic thoughts. It's the real you, it's the strength of your soul.

At this point your attention may automatically go to create thoughts about your thoughts. It's OK. Simply keep breathing consciously, following the path of the air in and out of your body, and let your Impartial Spectator witness the activity of your mind non-judgmentally.

Visualization of strengths, potential, and personal power

Now please move your attention to that part of yourself that doesn't want to give up. Look at the drawing on the sand: exactly in the center of the eight there is a point: the intersection between the right side and the left side of the eight. Let's call it the *point of courage*. From that point, imagine yourself drawing an arrow up. An exit from the eight. An exit from the stuckness.

This arrow points to what is available outside the eight. This arrow points to your strengths and to your potential. To the future that is available to you in any given moment.

Let's see what's outside the eight.

I want you to think of any moment in the past in which you really felt truly present. It can be any moment in which you felt fully engaged in your life. Bring it from any area of your life: you could have been by yourself, with a friend, with a group of friends, or with your family. In your personal or your professional life. Go to the past and bring back that moment. It could be a special moment or just a simple one. Feel it. Feel the relaxation of that moment in your whole body, especially in your neck and shoulders. Feel it also in your abdominal area.

Search your memories for that moment in which you were serene and dynamic at the same time. Tolerant while productive. Accepting but firm, knowing how to stand your ground. Feel the relaxation of that moment in which you let go of avoiding conflict. Everything flowed harmoniously and everything actually worked well and turned out well, without your trying to maintain a sense of peace. Take a deep breath and feel that moment.

Let's see what else is outside the eight.

I now want you to envision yourself in a new future. A future in which you are totally present in your life. A future in which you are constantly growing and encouraging others to grow. A future in which not only do you assert yourself, but you also lead others. In which you accept yourself as a human being, including some less positive aspects. In which you are in touch with your heart, and can forgive yourself and others for the mistakes human beings will naturally make.

Please put your hands one over the other, and over your heart. Feel your heartbeat. Feel your humanity. Since you are human, you are allowed to express your anger from time to time. To engage in conflict from time to time, instead of automatically avoiding it. Feel how much energy gets liberated from that, how much tension and anger gets dissolved. Since you are not afraid of conflict, you can healthily approach it and even help others to deal with it. This helps you fulfill one of your true dreams: growing as an effective mediator, a person who allows peace among people and brings harmony to the world.

Bring that moment from the future and feel it in your body, in the present moment. Feel it in your heart and in your mind. Feel the power of your mind, heart, and body working together and see what you can achieve, and most important: how all that is inside of you now and you *already* are the good person you always wanted to be.

Let's gently finish the meditation by slowly going back and watching the whole drawing in the sand. Watch the eight, together with the point of courage and all the potential that is available *within* you.

End of visualization

I acknowledge you for your courage, for being here and trying to grow as a person, for trying to overcome yourself, for the efforts you do, for not giving up. The mere fact of your doing this exercise is a testimony of your inner strength and of your not giving up. I also want you to acknowledge yourself for your courage, for not giving up. And I want you to thank life for the challenges it brings you, for the many opportunities it brings you every day, so through them you can become in touch with your strengths, to grow and also to contribute to the world, to give to the world around you the gifts of your real self.

7. RE-PATTERNING: EXERCISES FOR FILTER FLEXING AND INTEGRATION

Develop your assertiveness

If Nines spend too much time in the Stuckness Zone, they get used to conflict avoidance and become very unassertive. Their connections to Types Three, Eight, and One can help them become more assertive and develop their usually hidden leadership abilities.

Exercise for Type Nine: Developing assertiveness
- Use your connection to the high side of Type Three. Ask yourself: What are my goals? How can I persuade my interlocutor of my point? What do I need to *do* in order to achieve this? What's the fastest way to get there? Are we being efficient? Am I delivering my message with confidence? What are possible distractions or inessentials that can be an obstacle to my obtaining my goals? How can I lead others to achieve an important goal?
- A common complaint of Nines in the Stuckness Zone is to feel almost everybody "walks all over them." Use your Eight wing: Am I dealing well with my personal boundaries in this situation? Am I saying "Yes" when all I need is to deliver a plain "No"? Am I bottling things up and then being passive-aggressive instead of simply asserting my needs in a straightforward yet respectful manner, right when this needs to be done? Can I see the difference between a productive conflict and an unhealthy one? Do I allow for daily professional disagreements to happen, or prefer to automatically avoid them? What happens in my personal relationships: Do I allow room for some healthy conflict that can help exchange views and thoughts and help people grow together?

Or do I automatically enter into "conflict avoidance" mode?
- Use your One wing to learn how to actively *voice* your opinions and ideals. To defend your views. This wing will also help you in developing a sense of personal mission, a sense that your work "counts." It will help you to engage in all aspects of your life more passionately and to assert your needs and will.

Paying attention to the speaking style

Language is powerful: it's the vehicle that transports meaning. When we interpret reality through our filters, we put words to it. Therefore, if we are able to change the words that we attach to our experiences, we can indirectly impact our emotional states, since a big percentage of our emotions comes from our language. People are hypnotized by their own language patterns, creating blind spots that don't allow them to see reality accurately (Robbins and Madanes, 2005). By always using the same phrases and words to describe their experience, each personality type ends by not seeing what's in front of it. Literally, the description of reality becomes the *actual* reality. Those phrases and words are simply a manifestation of the underlying limiting beliefs that each type holds. Changing the speaking style can thus help us expand our frames of reference, allowing us to see the situations in our daily lives from many more angles.

It is important for coachees to develop the ability to catch themselves in the act when their personality mechanisms hijack their language. For Type Nines in the Stuckness Zone, this manifests in a discursive style that reflects passivity and their tendencies to follow others' agendas and avoid conflicts. Many times their language is vague and unclear.

It is common for Nines in the Stuckness Zone to have a sleepy facial language that reflects their internal sense of confusion. Using their connection to Three may help Nines to shift from a speaking style that is indefinite and unclear to one that is more congruent, clear, and effective. It also helps them be more eloquent and articulate, to get the other's attention, and to be fully engaged in their conversations. They begin paying attention to their word choice and *how* they deliver their words.

A very important distinction in working with Nines' language patterns is NLP's "being at cause" idea. When you are "at cause" you take responsibility for your life. When you are "at effect" you place the responsibility for your well-being on others.

Exercise for Type Nine: Flexing the discursive style
- Check the frequency of use of phrases indicating vagueness and confusion, such as the classic, foggy "I don't know." Pay special attention to your body language at that moment, especially to your eyes.
- Pay attention to the conversation topics and format. What percentage of the time have we been talking about *my* plans and wants in relation to other people's? Am I asking questions or only responding to other people's? It is very important in your conversations that you become the asker of questions instead of automatically being the responder. Am I waiting until the other person initiates a topic, or do I propose too? Am I making suggestions and recommendations? Am I showing my competencies? Am I following my own agenda?
- Become aware of the following: Is my language plagued with excuses? Do I tend to blame external factors? Practice the language of *choice* and *responsibility:* What do *I* think about this? What do *I* believe about this? What choices do *I* have? How can *I* take responsibility for this? What can *I* personally do to advance my agenda and make things happen?

Work with the Jungian preferences: Integrating our less-dominant qualities

When coaching a Type Nine, it is very important to pay attention to his or her Jungian preferences. If a coachee has done an MBTI profile, ask for his or her four-letter type and discuss how Jungian preferences may play together with the coachee's Enneatype. Also, when clients get stuck in the lower side of their Jungian preference, we can use the same pattern interruption techniques described all through this book to help them shift out and grow. For a description of the Jungian preferences, please refer to Part I of this book.

Some examples of the usage of the Jungian preferences in coaching a Type Nine:
- Although you'll find many Extraverted, gregarious Nines, there is a

high correlation between Nineness and Introversion. Take this into account, especially if you are an Extraverted coach. Slow your pace to match theirs. Nines tend to be quiet and soft. They are intimate and reflective, needing more space and time to think about what's being said in the sessions. With them the sessions will move slowly, so don't overwhelm them with too much or too fast talking. Match their pace by taking a deep breath from time to time, while deeply reflecting on what the Nine coachee is saying and feeling. But put special emphasis on maintaining a good structure in your coaching sessions to help the Nine remain on task.

- Some Nines in the Stuckness Zone may become deeply impractical and dreamy. They may benefit from adopting the Jungian lens of Sensing. Mention the importance of learning to perceive the world also from this angle: being realistic and concrete; developing the ability to be practical, to channel what they sense into practical applications; developing a need for clarity, considering good, practical ideas that may seem to them to have a potential of bringing conflict, instead of ruling them out automatically; being specific in their communication: asking specific questions, giving specific answers, communicating facts in a direct manner.
- Another dimension that is very useful for some development goals of Nines is Judging. Here too, mention the importance of learning to watch the world from this angle: developing the ability to plan and seek for closure; to finish a project until the very end before moving on to anything else (especially inessentials or any anesthetizing habit); developing the ability to be on time and respect other's time, the ability to plan and commit to a time frame to create and maintain structure, to be organized and unclutter the environment.

Between-Sessions Exercise for Type Nine: self-observation

During the week, actively engage in self-observing a particularly unhelpful pattern of your type. When you become aware of your patterns in real time, begin a spontaneous, one-cycle breath meditation. Follow the sequence described in Part II for observing the pattern and slowing it down. Share your insights with your coach in your next session.

Bibliography

Allen, J., & Brock, A. (2000). *Health care communication using personality type*. London: Routledge.

Ashcraft, L. (2005). *Recovery coaching*. Phoenix: Recovery Innovations.

Baron, R. (1998). *What type am I? Discover who you really are*. London: Penguin Books

Bandler, R. and Grinder, J. (1975). *Patterns of the hypnotic techniques of Milton Erickson, Vol.1* Cupertino, CA: Meta Publications.

Baron, R., & Wagele, E. (1994). *The Enneagram made easy: Discover the 9 types of people*. New York: HarperOne.

Bartlett, C. (2007). *The Enneagram field guide*. Portland, OR: Enneagram Consortium.

Bast, M., & Thomson, C. (2005).*Out of the Box: Coaching with the Enneagram*. Louisburg, KS: Ninestar Publishing.

Bayne, R. (1995). *The Myers-Briggs type indicator: a critical review and practical guide*. London: Chapman and Hall.

Beck, A.T., Freeman, A., and Davis, D.D. (2003) *Cognitive Therapy of Personality Disorders*. New York: The Guilford Press.

Bradberry, T. (2007). *Self-awareness*. New York: Putnam.

Compton, M.T. (2007). Recovery: Patients, families, communities. *Conference Report, Medscape Psychiatry & Mental Health*, October 11–14, 2007.

Condon, T. (1999). *Enneagram movie and video guide*. Portland, OR: Metamorphous Press.

Covey, S.R. (1999). *The 7 habits of highly effective families*. New York: St. Martin's Griffin.

Covey, S.R. (2004). *The 7 habits of highly effective people*. Washington, DC: Free Press.

Cullen, A. (2006). Interview with Professor Nava Ashraf, *Adam Smith, Behavioral Economist?* Retrieved from Harvard Business School website, http://hbswk.hbs.edu/cgi-bin/print/5168.html

Daniels, D., & Price, V. (2000). *The essential Enneagram.* San Francisco: HarperCollins Publishers.

Didonna, F. (2010). *Clinical handbook of mindfulness.* New York: Springer.

Falikowski, A. (2001). *Mastering human relations* (3rd ed.). London: Pearson.

Forsyth, J.P., & Eifert, G. (2008). *The mindfulness and acceptance workbook for anxiety: A guide to breaking free from anxiety, phobias, and worry using Acceptance and Commitment Therapy.* Oakland, CA: New Harbinger.

Frankl, V. (1992). *Man's Search for Meaning*, Boston: Beacon Press.

Freud, S. (1990). *Obras Completas.* Buenos Aires: El Ateneo.

Goldberg, M. (1999). *The nine ways of working.* Cambridge, MA: Da Capo Press.

Goldin, P. (2008). *Cognitive Neuroscience of Mindful Meditation.* [GoogleTechTalks video] Retrieved from http://www.youtube.com/watch?v=sf6Q0G1iHBI

Goleman, D. (1985). *Vital lies, simple truths: The psychology of self-deception.* New York: Simon and Schuster.

Goleman, D. (1996). *Emotional Intelligence:Why it can matter more than IQ.* New York: Bantam.

Grant, A. M., & Cavanagh, M. J. (2007). Coaching psychology: How did we get here and where are we going? *InPsych*, June, 6-9.

Gurdjieff, G.I. (1999). *La vida es real solo cuando yo soy.* Malaga: Editorial Sirio.

Howe-Murphy, R. (2007). *Deep Coaching: Using the Enneagram as a catalyst for profound change*, El Granada, CA: Enneagram Press.

Haley, J. (1967). *Advanced techniques of Hypnosis and Therapy*

-Selected Papers of Milton H. Erickson. New York: Grune & Stratton.

Jung, C. (1976). *Psychological types.* Princeton, NJ: Princeton University Press.

Kahneman, D. (2003). A perspective on judgment and choice: Mapping bounded rationality. *American Psychologist, 58*(9), 679-720.

Keirsey, D. (1998). *Please understand me II: Temperament, character, intelligence.* Del Mar, CA: Prometheus Nemesis Company.

Keyes, M. F. (1992). *Emotions and the Enneagram: Working through your shadow life script.* Muir Beach, CA: Molysdatur.

Kise, J. (2006). *Differentiated Coaching.* Thousand Oaks, CA: Corwin Press.

Lapid-Bogda, G. (2004). *Bringing out the best in yourself at work: How to use the Enneagram system for success.* New York: McGraw-Hill.

Lapid-Bogda, G. (2007). *What type of leader are you? Using the Enneagram system to identify and grow your leadership strengths and achieve maximum success.* New York: McGraw-Hill.

Lapid-Bogda, G. (2009). *Bringing out the best in everyone you coach: Use the Enneagram system for exceptional results.* New York: McGraw-Hill.

Lawrence, G. (2009). *People types and tiger stripes.* Gainesville, FL: Center for Applications of Psychological Type, Inc.

Lencioni, P. (2005). *Overcoming the five dysfunctions of a team. A Field Guide.* San Francisco: Jossey-Bass.

Levine, J. (1999). *The Enneagram intelligences: Understanding personality for effective teaching and learning.* Santa Barbara, CA: Praeger.

Levine, J. (2003). *Know your parenting personality: How to use the Enneagram to become the best parent you can be.* Hoboken, NJ: Wiley.

Lutz, A., Slagter, H. A., Dunne, J., & Davidson, R. J. (2008). Attention regulation and monitoring in meditation. *Trends in*

Cognitive Sciences 12 (4), 163-169.

Madanes, C. (1980). Protection, Paradox and Pretending. *Family Process,* 19:73-85.

Madanes, C. (1981). *Strategic Family Therapy.* San Francisco, CA: Jossey Bass.

Madanes, C. (1984). *Behind the one-way mirror.* Eugene, OR: Wipf & Stock Publishers

Madanes, C. (1994). *The Secret Meaning of Money.* San Francisco, CA: Jossey Bass.

Madanes, C. (1992) Stories of Psychotherapy, in J.K. Zeig (Ed.) *The Evolution of Psychotherapy : The Second Conference* (pp.39-50). New York : Brunner/Mazel, Inc.

Madanes, C., with Keim, J., & Smelser, D. (1995). *The violence of men*. San Francisco: Jossey-Bass.

Madanes, C. (2006). *The therapist as humanist, social activist and systemic thinker.* Phoenix: Zeig, Tucker & Theisen.

Madanes, C. (2009). *Relationship breakthrough: How to create outstanding relationships in every area of your life*. New York: Zeig and Tucker.

Madanes, C. (2011). Personal communication.

Madanes, Y., & Stelzer, Y. (2004). *Daber elai yafe*. Jerusalem: Idan Chadash.

Maslow, A. (1954). *Motivation and personality.* New York: HarperCollins Publishers.

McKay, M. (2007). *Thoughts & feelings: Taking control of your moods and your life.* Oakland, CA: New Harbinger.

McKenna, J., Kyllegard, K., & Lynder, R. (2003). Linking psychological type to financial decision-making. *Journal of Financial Counseling and Planning, 14*(1), 19-29.

Moncrieff, J. (2007). *The myth of the chemical cure.* Basingstoke, UK: Palgrave Macmillan.

Moore, C. (2003). *The mediation process*. San Francisco: Jossey-Bass.

Morris, J. & Stone, G. (2011) Children and Psychotropic Medication: A Cautionary Note, *Journal of Marital and Family Therapy*, 37(3), pp. 299-306.

Moynihan, R. & Cassels, A.(2005). *Selling sickness: How the world's biggest pharmaceutical companies are turning us all into patients*. New York: Nation Books.

Nemade, R., Staats Reiss, N., & Dombeck, M. *Cognitive behavioral therapy for major depression*. Retrieved May 2011 from http://www.turningspirit.com/Articles/CBTDepression.htm

O'Hanlon, W.H. (1987) *Taproots: Underlying principles of Milton Erickson's therapy and hypnosis*. New York: Norton.

Oppenheimer, R.D. (2005). *Veshinantam lebaneja*. Buenos Aires: Ajdut.

Palmer, H. (1988). *The Enneagram: Understanding yourself and the others in your life*. San Francisco: HarperCollins Publishers.

Palmer, H. (1995). *The Enneagram in love & work: Understanding your intimate & business relationships*. New York: HarperOne.

Palmer, H. (2009). *The inner observer. A guided meditation*. [Audio] www.Enneagramworldwide.com

Raphael, D. (2009). *The impartial spectator, Adam Smith's moral philosophy*. Oxford: Clarendon Press.

Riso, D.R. (1993). *Enneagram transformations: releases and affirmations for healing your personality type*. Boston: Mariner Books.

Riso, D.R., & Hudson, R. (1996). *Personality types: Using the Enneagram for self-discovery*. Boston: Mariner Books.

Riso, D.R., & Hudson, R. (1999). *The wisdom of the Enneagram: The complete guide to psychological and spiritual growth for the nine personality types*. New York: Bantam.

Robbins, A., & Madanes, C. (2004). *Breaking through—creating the life you deserve.* A film from the Robbins-Madanes Center for Strategic Interventions. La Jolla, CA.

Robbins, A., & Madanes, C. (2004). *Conquering overwhelming loss.* A film from the Robbins-Madanes Center for Strategic Interventions, La Jolla, CA.

Robbins, A., & Madanes, C. (2004). *Starting over: How to let go of the past and celebrate your life.* A film from the Robbins-Madanes Center for Strategic Interventions, La Jolla, CA.

Robbins, A., & Madanes, C. (2005). *Back from the edge.* A film from the Robbins-Madanes Center for Strategic Interventions, La Jolla, CA.

Robbins, A., Madanes, C., & Peysha, M. (2005). *Love & passion: The ultimate relationship program action book.* La Jolla, CA: The Robbins-Madanes Center for Strategic Interventions.

Rojas, E. (1994). *La conquista de la voluntad.* Barcelona: Planeta.

Rojas, E. (1997). *El amor inteligente.* Madrid: Planeta

Rojas, E. (2000). *El hombre light.* Barcelona: Planeta.

Sarlo, B. (1994). *Escenas de la vida posmoderna.* Buenos Aires: Ariel.

Satir, V. (1975). *Self esteem.* Berkeley, CA: Celestial Arts.

Seward Barry, A.M. (1997). *Visual intelligence: Perception, image, and manipulation in visual communication.* Albany: State University of New York Press.

Seligman, M. (1990). *Learned optimism.* New York: Alfred A.Knopf, Inc.

Sharfstein, S. (2005). Big Pharma and American Psychiatry: The Good, the Bad, and the Ugly *Psychiatric News, 40(16).*

Stoltzfus, T. (2008). *Coaching questions.* Virginia Beach, VA: Coach22.

Stone, D., Patton, B., & Heen, S. (2010). *Difficult conversations: How to discuss what matters most.* London: Penguin.

Tieger, P., & Barron-Tieger, B. (1998). *The art of speedreading people.* New York: Little, Brown and Company.

Wagele, E. (1997). The Enneagram of parenting: The 9 types of children and how to raise them successfully. New York: HarperOne.

Weiss, A. (2008). The wholesale sedation of America's youth. *Skeptical Inquirer, 32 (6),* 31-36.

Wile, D. (1995). *After the fight.* New York: Guilford Press.

Wyman, P. (2002). *Three keys to self-understanding: An innovative and effective combination of the Myers-Briggs Type Indicator assessment tool, the Enneagram, and inner-child healing.* Gainesville, FL: Center for Applications of Psychological Type.

Recommended Resources

Coaching

Online Certificate in Enneagram Coaching, The Madanes School of Enneagram Coaching, www.madanesschool.com (see ad in last page of this book)

Madanes, C. (2009). *Relationship breakthrough: How to create outstanding relationships in every area of your life.* New York: Zeig and Tucker.

Out of the Box Coaching, Mary Bast, PhD.
http://www.breakoutofthebox.com/

Enneagram Tests

Riso, D.R., & Hudson, R., The Enneagram Institute, RHETI test www.enneagraminstitute.com

Palmer, H., & Daniels, D., Enneagram Worldwide, Enneagram test www.enneagramworldwide.com

Katherine Chernick Fauvre and David W. Fauvre, MA, Enneagram Explorations & Fauvre Research www.enneagram.net

Introduction to the Enneagram

Riso, D.R., & Hudson, R. (1996). *Personality types: Using the Enneagram for self-discovery.* Boston: Mariner Books.

Riso, D.R., & Hudson, R. (1999). *The wisdom of the Enneagram: The complete guide to psychological and spiritual growth for the nine personality types.* New York: Bantam.

Daniels, D., & Price, V. (2000). *The essential Enneagram*. San Francisco: HarperCollins Publishers.

Palmer, H. (1988). *The Enneagram: Understanding yourself and the others in your life*. San Francisco: HarperCollins Publishers.

The Enneagram in Business

Goldberg, M. (1999). *The nine ways of working*. Cambridge, MA: Da Capo Press.

Lapid-Bogda, G. (2004). *Bringing out the best in yourself at work: How to use the Enneagram system for success*. New York: McGraw-Hill.

Lapid-Bogda, G. (2007). *What type of leader are you? Using the Enneagram system to identify and grow your leadership strengths and achieve maximum success*. New York: McGraw-Hill.

The Enneagram in Education

Levine, J. (1999). *The Enneagram intelligences: Understanding personality for effective teaching and learning*. Santa Barbara, CA: Praeger.

The Enneagram in Parenting

Levine, J. (2003). *Know your parenting personality: How to use the Enneagram to become the best parent you can be*. Hoboken, NJ: Wiley.

Wagele, E. (1997). *The Enneagram of parenting: The 9 types of children and how to raise them successfully*. New York: HarperOne.

The Enneagram and Mindfulness

Palmer, H. (2009). *The inner observer: A guided meditation*. [Audio] www.Enneagramworldwide.com

The Enneagram in Relationships

Palmer, H. (1995). *The Enneagram in love & work: Understanding your *intimate & business relationships.* New York: HarperOne.

Baron, R., & Wagele, E. (1995). *Are you my type, am I yours? Relationships made easy through the Enneagram.* New York: HarperOne.

The Jungian Preferences

Jung, C. (1976). *Psychological types.* Princeton, NJ.: Princeton University Press.

Keirsey, D. (1998). *Please understand me II: Temperament, character, intelligence.* Del Mar, CA: Prometheus Nemesis Company.

Berens, L. (1999). Dynamics of Personality Type: Understanding and Applying Jung's Cognitive Processes. Huntington Beach, CA: Telos Publications.

Berens, L. and Nardi, D. (1999). The 16 Personality Types: Descriptions for Self-Discovery. Huntington Beach, CA: Telos Publications.

Bayne, R. (1995). *The Myers-Briggs type indicator: a critical review and practical guide.* London: Chapman and Hall.

About the Authors

Ruth and Yechezkel Madanes, MA are certified professional life coaches who have been using the Enneagram as a key instrument in their practice for almost a decade. They have studied Strategic Interventions from Tony Robbins and Cloé Madanes at their Coach Training Program. Yechezkel and Ruth are President and Executive Director of the Madanes School of Enneagram Coaching, where they have developed a best-selling series of books and a widely acclaimed online certificate program and where they also consult, lecture, and conduct one-on-one coaching sessions. They have brought their innovative methodology to leading corporations and to thousands of school students, teachers, and parents in several countries.

Coaching Sessions via Skype with the authors of this book

The power of Enneagram Coaching in individual, 90-minutes, online sessions with Yechezkel and/or Ruth Madanes.

Life Coaching, Executive Coaching, Professional Supervision and Mentoring, help in setting up and mantaining a successful private practice.

To reserve your session please email coaching@madanesschool.com

To learn more about our coaching sessions and Enneagram programs, please visit www.madanesschool.com

Madanes
School of Enneagram Coaching

GET CERTIFIED IN ENNEAGRAM COACHING!
Online Campus

With today's technology you can earn this prestigious certificate no matter where you live or what hours you work. This highly respected, career-enhancing program will help you become one of the best prepared, most well rounded professionals in the field. The Madanes School of Enneagram Coaching is committed to give you a quality academic experience in this online course.

WORLD-CLASS FACULTY
The course is taught entirely by the authors of this book, Yechezkel and Ruth Madanes, who are highly respected professionals and are the pioneers in this widely acclaimed methodology.

STATE-OF-THE-ART TRAINING
This highly practical and empowering program will give you all the tools you need to carry a professional career as an Enneagram Coach.

CONVENIENT ONLINE FORMAT
With its superb flexibility, this program allows you to learn according to your schedule, minimizing the disruption of your professional and personal life. You can access your class from the convenience of your office or home, or in your travels, at any time that suits you.

FULLY SUPPORTED LEARNING ENVIRONMENT
The program is offered completely online, through multimedia video training modules. Faculty is available to videochat in realtime during the weekly online office hours or by personal appointment, to help you with any questions or challenges you may have. And for administrative issues, the friendly staff at the Madanes School is committed to help you from day one and is available to support you throughout the entire course.

Visit our website to enroll or to contact us via email or online chat. Our staff will be more than happy to help you with any questions.

WWW.MADANESSCHOOL.COM

Printed in Great Britain
by Amazon.co.uk, Ltd.,
Marston Gate.